# BRAVE
# DECISIONS

**Also by Harry J. Maihafer**

From the Hudson to the Yalu:
West Point '49 in the Korean War

# BRAVE DECISIONS

## MORAL COURAGE FROM THE REVOLUTIONARY WAR TO DESERT STORM

*Col. Harry J. Maihafer,*
*U.S. Army (Ret.)*

Brassey's

Washington . London

*Grateful acknowledgment is given to the following institutions for permission to reproduce art and photographs in their collections*:
National Archives—p. 1; United States Military Academy Library, Special Collections Division—pp. 20, 65, 80, 196, 226; U.S. Army Military History Institute—pp. 99, 115, 131, 148, 163, 179, 211; U.S. Army Military History Institute/Massachusetts Commandery, Military Order of the Loyal Legion—pp. 34, 47.

Library of Congress Cataloging-in-Publication Data

Maihafer, Harry J., 1924–
   Brave decisions: moral courage from the Revolutionary War to Desert Storm/Harry J. Maihafer.
      p. cm.
   Includes bibliographical references and index.
   ISBN 0-02-881108-9
   1. Leadership—moral courage. 2. Military art and science—Decision making. 3. United States—History, Military. I. Title.
U22.3.M31 1995
355'.00973—dc20                                                                94-38919
                                                                                    CIP

Maps by John W. Hopper

10 9 8 7 6 5 4 3 2 1

Printed in the United States of America

*To Jeanne—great wife, best friend,
and trusty proofreader*

# CONTENTS

# Illustrations

# Foreword

*F*ire! When taken in the context of military confrontation, this chilling and concise order evokes images of both bravery and terror. It conjures visions of clenched teeth and white-knuckled fingers squeezing an infantryman's weapon or the controls of a fighter plane. This command has been the prologue to actions brave and daring, a dictate pronouncing the commencement of what has been the final action of many American fighting men. This unambiguous directive has inspired heroic actions, actions that have secured victories to sustain our nation as the beacon of freedom for the world.

It is impossible to live in the United States and remain ignorant of the actions undertaken by warriors who have protected our way of life with their own blood. Throughout our nation, town squares boast statues of sword-wielding soldiers grasping the reins of rearing horses, charging forth into the jaws of battle. Simple obelisks mark locations where the fate of the nation was decided in a now obscure pasture or on the outskirts of a small town. Within our nation's capital, the very architecture of the city seems to have been inspired by an intent to accentuate memorials to U.S. war heroes. Memorials appear at every turn. They exist as striking and often moving reminders of the actions of individuals who put country above self and frequently paid the ultimate sacrifice. Again, it is impossible to remain unmoved or untouched by the contributions of those selfless Americans who have gone before us.

What is less understood and rarely memorialized are the unique actions of *moral bravery* that preceded the confrontations and battles wherein these heroes made their individual marks on history. Today, U.S. society wrestles with concerns over declining morals, diminished optimism for the future, and a disquieting sense of detachment from the patriotism embodied in servicemen and -women whose actions preserved this great nation. Therefore, it seems fitting to review the unsung heroic actions that transpired not in plain view on a battlefield, in the skies, or on the seas, but that occurred quietly in the hearts and minds of military decision makers.

*Brave Decisions* thoughtfully illustrates that the singular actions of uncommon valor in combat are themselves not solely responsible for the freedom we all enjoy today. Acts of heroism executed by individual combatants are, as the author points out, predictable precipitants. Battlefield valor has always been the necessary and probable result derived by placing average Americans in circumstances that have forced them to reach deep within themselves for the strength to overcome extraordinary adversity.

The decisions that have shaped the fates of these individuals have rarely been made without considerable forethought, soul-searching, and a heart-wrenching acceptance of calculated risk by military commanders. Long after flags are hoisted, the dead are buried, and medals of valor are awarded, our nation's battlefield leaders have had to live with the consequences their decisions have had on the lives of individuals, the fate of our nation, and often the fate of the world.

Harry Maihafer has provided a stirring and long overdue account of these heroic decisions, decisions that have gone largely unknown by the beneficiaries of superior moral courage. This work brings valuable insight into the often emotional battles that have raged within the minds of leaders faced with the decision to place their charges in harm's way. One cannot study his account without coming to the realization that the United States is great not only because of the actions of fighting men; Maihafer reminds us that the greatness embodied in American heroes can often be traced to a willingness to choose pain over comfort—to sacrifice for success.

This tribute also provides ample proof that acts of moral courage occur as frequently today as they have throughout our history. From the battles for independence from British oppression to the actions that have opposed and contained the aggressions of nations against nations in the 1990s, *Brave Decisions* chronicles the moral struggles experienced by American military leaders. This account provides compelling evidence to support the notion that although the world has changed dramatically, and with it the role of the United States, the fortitude of our military commanders has remained consistent.

Those who have lost their faith in the ability of the United States to persevere should study these pages carefully. From U.S. battlefields to struggles on distant shores to the cloistered National Security Council, *Brave Decisions* appropriately reminds us that American heroes are not a dying breed.

John S. McCain
United States Senator

# Introduction

O God, our Father, Thou Searcher of human hearts, help
us draw near to Thee in sincerity and truth. . . . Make us
to choose the harder right instead of the easier wrong,
and never to be content with a half truth when the whole
can be won. Endow us with courage that is born of loyalty to all that is noble and worthy, that scorns to compromise with vice and injustice and knows no fear when
truth and right are in jeopardy.

*—from the Cadet Prayer, U.S. Military Academy*

In this day of antiheroes, question-
able morality, and challenges to personal values, it helps to remind
ourselves how often American leaders have chosen "the harder
right."

Some years ago at West Point, I heard British general W. P. Oliver,
vice chief of the Imperial General Staff, as he told the U.S. Corps of
Cadets that too often we speak of bravery in a physical sense, so we
tend to give insufficient credit to the other, and rarer, virtue of moral
courage. Personally, he said, he had known men with physical bravery
who were morally weak, but he had never known one with moral

courage who did not also own the other, and lesser, attribute of physical bravery.

In a similar vein, American general Ed Rowny, accepting West
Point's Distinguished Graduate award in May 1993, began his
remarks by quoting a tactical officer he remembered from cadet days,
then-Major Omar Bradley, who said: "Physical courage is important,
but moral courage is ten times as hard and ten times as important!"

"And I've seen that through the years," Rowny went on,
"Eisenhower, making the tough, lone decision to hit the beaches
when it looked as though the weather might be bad. Again,
McAuliffe at Bastogne, when he was told to give up and you know
what he said. And again, MacArthur, when he was told by the Joint
Chiefs of Staff that Inchon would fail, saying 'Never take counsel of
your fears,' went through and made Inchon a great success. I could
go on and on about the real necessity of keeping moral courage
uppermost."

An army of sheep led by a lion, says an old military axiom, will
defeat an army of lions led by a sheep. Or, as the German strategist
Alfred von Schlieffen put it: "The first thing is character."

Down through the years, our country has been blessed with a series
of military figures who consistently put country and honor above self.
A few of their stories are told in this book, stories about conscious
decisions to choose "the harder right" even though a safe, honorable
alternative was available and even when it meant putting one's career
or one's life on the line. Not only can Americans be thankful for such
leaders—their countrymen of any age can be proud to read about
them and make their acquaintance.

*H.J.M.*

# BRAVE
# DECISIONS

CHAPTER 1

# Decision at Cowpens

Duct during the American Revolution, Washington's officers were forced to rely mostly on militiamen, citizen soldiers who took up arms only for limited periods and in limited geographical areas. The sad truth is that, after the initial heroics of Bunker Hill, these militia simply weren't very effective; time after time they broke and ran before the steady advance of British regulars.

It was with these men, nevertheless, that Washington knew he had to win in pitched battle—either that, or settle for prolonged and indecisive guerrilla warfare. The trick, of course, was to convince the American amateur he could stand up to European professionals. For six years, from 1775 to 1781, Yankee officers looked for the key.

Daniel Morgan, "Ranger of the Revolution," finally showed the way. While the Battle of Saratoga, fought and won in 1777 by Horatio Gates and Daniel Morgan, was deservedly called the turning point of the Revolution, it was only later, at the Battle of Cowpens, that Daniel Morgan, demonstrating both moral courage and military shrewdness, finally taught the militiaman what he could do. At the time, many had urged Morgan to disperse his forces, to let the men go home in safety, perhaps to continue the fight as guerrillas. He knew, however, that if he once let his men go home, it was doubtful that such a band could be reconstituted—ever.

The harder choice Morgan made, to stand and fight at the Cowpens, was one he believed to be right. Until that time, the colonists had engaged in six bloody years of formless war. Ten months later, standing in even ranks, these same men watched Cornwallis surrender at Yorktown.

Daniel Morgan rose in his stirrups, twisting as he did so to peer back along the trail. The morning fog still clung to the ground, obscuring the rear of the column. From what he could tell, however, the men were keeping the formation well closed up. These were regulars, of course (in 1780 one said "Continentals"), and Morgan had always been able to get regulars to march, at least when he himself was leading.

Morgan settled back into his saddle. Doing so, he was hit by another quick pain. He gritted his teeth, tried not to think about it. The pain was ironic. Morgan's strength was something of a legend. At six foot two, broad of shoulder and chest, he towered a full head above the average eighteenth-century male. Yet now, leading an independent command and truly needing to be fit, he was suffering from painful sciatica and a recurrence of malaria.

He hunched forward in his saddle, trying to ignore the torment by concentrating on the day's route. They had left Charlotte Town that morning, heading west toward the Catawba. His column included Maryland and Delaware Continentals, Virginia riflemen, and Colonel William Washington's regiment of light dragoons—600 men in all. It was hardly an imposing force, but on this day of December 20, 1780, it represented half of General Nathaniel Greene's Southern Department, hence half the men available to defend the Patriot cause in the South.

Some might wonder why he and Greene had separated their forces. Militarily, it seemed unwise, yet the answer was simple. They had split apart so they could eat. When the Army lingered in any one area, the countryside was soon picked bare. It was hardly the way to win support from local farmers. Moreover, while the Continentals stayed in Charlotte, the British roamed the rest of the Carolinas at will. In their wake, Tories were exacting bloody reprisals on families who had supported the Revolution. So Greene and Morgan had decided to separate, to find forage for their animals, food for their men, and also, in Greene's words, to "annoy the enemy" and "spirit up the people."

The forest roadway entered a swamp, where the ground's natural sogginess, plus three days of rain, had turned the trail into soft, clinging mud. In places the path disappeared entirely and men slogged miserably through a watery ooze.

Officers' voices urged them forward. "Keep moving! Stay on the trail!" In late afternoon they reached Biggon Ferry on the Catawba. The troops looked hopefully for signs of boats or rafts. There were none.

Morgan dismounted and, leading his horse, plowed into the chill December waters. Cheerfully he told his men to come ahead, saying the water was only hip deep. Soldiers looked at each other and grinned wryly. Morgan's "hip" came to most men's chests.

A half-hour after sunset, Morgan lifted his arm to signal the halt. He ordered a perimeter established, and he personally checked the pickets and outguards. Only when he was satisfied did he let the Continentals drop their gear and start campfires. Soon a score of blazes dotted the twilight.

Before his headquarters tent, Morgan peeled off his soggy buckskins and wrung them out. As he held his fringed shirt toward the fire to toast dry, the firelight revealed a network of scar tissue on his bare back. Lines of purple, white, and blue were interwoven on every square inch of flesh. By now he could speak lightly of that long-ago flogging, but Dan Morgan was not likely to forget his "present" from King George.

He had been nineteen, a restless, boisterous youngster who had left home and hired himself out as a British teamster. In 1755, during the French and Indian War, he had driven for the ill-fated Braddock expedition, when British and American troops under General Edward Braddock were attacked by a French and Indian force from Fort Duquesne and almost wiped out. Braddock himself had been mortally wounded. Not long after, there had been a wagonload of supplies to be hauled to Fort Chiswell on the Virginia frontier. One afternoon at the fort, he had argued with an English lieutenant. Angered by the impudence, the lieutenant had drawn his sword and used the flat of the blade to swat the youngster contemptuously.

Morgan responded instinctively with a hard right to the jaw. He grinned good-naturedly as the startled lieutenant crumpled from the single punch.

The boy was seized by rough hands, promptly given a drumhead court-martial, and just as promptly awarded five hundred lashes. Many a man had died from less.

Morgan was stripped to the waist and tied to an oak tree, his arms wrapped around the trunk, his face pressed against the bark. Then two soldiers, each wielding a cat-o'-nine-tails, began the whipping. Each stroke brought a flash of pain, and as his back became shredded, each stroke made it worse. At one point Morgan had fainted, been revived, then fainted again. Somehow he had kept from crying out—even toward the end, when pieces of flesh were hanging down like remnants of a frayed garment.

Finally it was done. The provost, finishing the count, called out: "Four hundred ninety-eight . . . four hundred ninety-nine . . . five hundred. . . . The sentence has been executed. Release the prisoner."

Morgan had also been counting. Although nearly unconscious, he had noticed when the provost had skipped a count, and took grim satisfaction in having been given only 499 lashes instead of five hundred. Ever after, he would claim King George "owed him one." As he was untied and started to slump to the ground, friendly hands caught him and dragged him off. Even the accusing lieutenant looked in horror at what he had caused.

The officer came forward. "I'm sorry," he said softly. Somehow Daniel had managed a nod and a weak smile of forgiveness. Even now, however, more than twenty years later, he had not forgotten.

They marched for three more days. In his report, Morgan mentioned the "very steep hills" they had crossed, referred to the march as "very unpleasant." With that, his men would have agreed quite readily.

Finally they stopped, camping at Grindall's Shoals on the banks of the twisting Pacolet. Despite bad weather and difficult terrain, they had come fifty-eight miles in four days. Now they waited for Andrew Pickens and his militia to join up.

They came marching in on Christmas Eve, solemn, rawboned Andrew Pickens and sixty South Carolina comrades. Andrew Pickens, a grave Presbyterian elder whose deliberateness made men charge him with "putting words between his fingers to examine before he utters them," was a welcome Christmas present, even if Morgan wasn't yet sure how he would be used.

On Christmas Day they rested, men at war remembering the Prince of Peace. Morgan, pondering his situation, had no illusions about the reinforcements. He agreed with Greene, who had written that "militia are always unsuspicious and therefore more easily surprised. Don't depend too much on them."

Usually Greene tried to be encouraging. This time, however, he had agonized: "If the State of North Carolina continues to bring out such useless militia as they have in the past season, it will be impossible to subsist."

Militia kept drifting in, and by this time Morgan's army was neither regular nor militia, but a disjointed combination of both. Up to this point, Morgan was known as a leader of fast, hard-hitting light infantry, a master of unconventional war. At Saratoga, his most noted battle, his Virginia rangers had used guerrilla tactics to outsmart Britain's finest. Now, however, the situation was different, and so were the men he led.

Two days after Christmas, while they were still camped at Grindall's Shoals, a Whig spy Morgan had recruited came galloping into camp.

The story came in bursts: "Raiders . . . two hundred and fifty Tories from Georgia . . . twenty miles to the south . . . torches shining in the night . . . homes burning . . . looting . . . men beaten . . . wives and daughters assaulted . . ."

In North Carolina, where tales of terror and atrocity had been told before, the American Revolution had become one of the cruelest and fiercest civil wars ever fought.

Despite his portly frame, William Washington, like his cousin the commander-in-chief, was an excellent horseman who could move fast when the occasion called for it. Within the hour, he and his dragoons, plus two hundred mounted militia, took out after the raiders. The invaders slipped away, but Washington's men rode hard, made forty miles in a single day, and caught up on December 30 at Hammond's Store.

The surprised Loyalists panicked and ran. This was not the sterile, formal contest painted in history books. Rather it was a battle of snorting horses, of saber striking bone, of screaming, bleeding, running men.

"Hold up, men, they've had enough!" The cry came from Washington and from militia major James McCall. However, there was no stopping the enraged colonists. When it was over, 150 Tories had been killed, another forty taken prisoner, and the remaining sixty put to flight, all without a single loss to Washington's horsemen.

Washington made one more thrust, toward a Loyalist base at Williamson's Plantation, but this time his opponents escaped. Then he rode back to the Pacolet, where Morgan was still gathering militia. The latest addition was a 120-man group from North Carolina.

The new recruits had had no military experience. Contrary to legend, the average colonist was an unskilled marksman and an indifferent woodsman. Training would be difficult, and no one knew it better than Morgan. His best hope, he supposed, was to instill some pride in unit, in state, in being one of "Morgan's men."

Morgan, however, realized that his brand of unconventional warfare was but an intermediate step, one which could punish the British and prolong the fighting but could never win a final victory. At some point Americans *had* to gather in force and defeat the enemy in pitched battle. Meanwhile, "we have to feed such a number of horses," Morgan wrote Greene, "that the most plentiful country must soon be exhausted."

It wasn't like Dan Morgan to vacillate, especially when told to use his own judgment. However, Greene was 140 miles away, and Morgan, without orders, wrote his commander again: "When I shall have collected my expected force, I shall be at a loss how to act. Could a diversion be made in my favor by the main army, I should wish to march into Georgia."

He would not go, however, if Greene felt he couldn't be spared. Neither was he going to retreat. To let Whig families see him withdraw, he said, would have the "most fatal consequences."

While Greene and Morgan debated their next step, the initiative was slipping away. Next move would be made by the enemy, in the person of Lieutenant Colonel Banastre Tarleton, leader of a British force at a town called Ninety-Six. Cornwallis, learning of the defeat at Hammond's Store, had sent Tarleton to retaliate.

At twenty-six, handsome Banastre Tarleton was already known as a winner. With wit and urbanity, he had shown to advantage in London town houses and at Oxford. His friends knew him as one who scorned the colonists as much for their lack of breeding as for their ingratitude to the Crown. After Lexington and Concord, when London society debated the legality of England's position, he had said scornfully: "To hell with the law! These miserable Americans must be taught their places!"

Soon Tarleton had acquired a major's commission in a cavalry regiment bound for America. Once in action, he had developed rapidly as a military leader. Along the way, however, he had also acquired a taste for brutality.

At the Waxhaws, when Colonel Abraham Buford's Continentals tried to flee, Tarleton's men had slaughtered without reason or mercy. Earlier, Tarleton had let his "green dragoons" saber fugitives from the Battle of Camden and cut up Thomas Sumter's unarmed men at Fishing Creek. Throughout the Carolinas, the phrase "Tarleton's quarter" had come to mean pitiless execution.

Now, at Ninety-Six, Tarleton was reading a letter from Cornwallis: "If Morgan is anywhere within your reach, I should wish you to push him to the utmost. . . . No time is to be lost."

Tarleton issued orders which would thrust his legion toward Morgan like a plunging sword. In addition to his Tory Legion, he would take with him the 7th Royal Fusilier Regiment, some light artillery, and the 1st Battalion of the 71st Highlanders. In all he would have more than eleven hundred men, surely enough to overwhelm any band of ragged colonials!

On January 6, Tarleton put his column in motion. The sun broke through the clouds, causing polished metal to gleam as husky cavalrymen moved out to the front and flanks. Companies in green, white, or red swung into line; bands and pipers struck up a tune. In high spirits, Tarleton wrote boastfully to Cornwallis: "I must either destroy Morgan's corps or push it before me over Broad River."

The question seemed to be whether Morgan, still encamped on the Pacolet, would hear of Tarleton's plans in time. Actually the news came in an unorthodox fashion. Dan Morgan's luck seemed to be holding—at least for the moment.

The news came from a Carolina Whig and his nine-year-old son. The nervous lad, according to legend, told his hero, Morgan: "Sir, I drove the old bull and some potatoes down there to Cornwallis's camp, and my daddy told me not to forget anything I heard."

"That's fine, son," Morgan said, "and you know, I might just have a guinea for a youngster who told me something worthwhile."

"I couldn't take the guinea, sir, but I'll tell you all the same. I was near the general's tent when that fellow in green come up; I heard someone call him 'Colonel.'"

"Tarleton . . ."

"Aye, that was his name. They talked a long time. Then the general fellow told the other one to take a thousand men and follow you up and fight you wherever you could be found. And they know where you are now!"

"My boy," said Morgan, "you've more than earned this gold piece. Will you take it now?"

"No thank ye, sir, but I'd be kindly obliged if you'd let me join up as a drummer."

"Done!" cried Morgan, and (at least, so the story goes) Morgan's army had gained another recruit.

Other sources confirmed the youngster's story: Tarleton was on his way. Morgan gave orders to strike camp. Where he himself was concerned, Daniel Morgan was among the bravest of men. Now, though, worrying about the safety of his troops, he was frightened. In his mind's eye, the "Old Wagoner" could picture Tarleton catching the colonials by surprise and ruthlessly slaughtering his victims as he'd done at the Waxhaws.

Leaving scouts to watch the crossings of the Pacolet, Morgan led his army northward toward Broad River. Half these men had joined him at the last encampment; this was his first chance to watch his entire force on the march.

For most of January 15, Morgan pushed the men hard. Then his column seemed to come apart. Militiamen were meandering at their own pace and by their own routes. Their officers seemed unable to cope, and frequently seemed unaware that any problem even existed.

Muttering to himself, Morgan decided he'd best learn to take these men as they were; these were the soldiers he had to work with, and apparently Ban Tarleton wasn't going to wait for them to improve.

That night they camped at Burr's Mills on Thicketty Creek. Morgan, discouraged, wrote Greene of the militia's "fatal mode of going to war," concluding ruefully: "It is beyond the art of man to keep the militia from straggling."

As Morgan withdrew, he heard Tarleton was already across the Tiger River and heading for the Pacolet. The "green dragoon" had sauntered into the American camp only hours after Morgan's departure.

"Tarleton's across the Pacolet!" At dawn on the sixteenth, riders came pounding into Morgan's bivouac shouting that Tarleton was not only across the river, he was now only five miles behind the Americans.

In his mule-skinner's voice, Morgan called for his men to get moving. Breakfast fires were stamped out, and after much clatter and shouting, wagons were loaded and an order of march was established.

McCall's dragoons pushed on ahead. Maryland and Delaware Continentals fell into ranks with the careless ease of regulars. Militiamen from Georgia and the Carolinas jostled and joked, stuffing crumbly cornmeal into their mouths as they took their places. At last they were under way, and somehow the column seemed less ragged than it had the day before. However, it was another wearying march and another test of Dan Morgan's leadership. The time for harsh decision had arrived, and in Greene's absence, it was a decision left entirely to Morgan. Greene, in fact, had he been on hand, would have urged caution. "Put nothing to the hazard," he would write Morgan. "A retreat may be disagreeable but not disgraceful. Regard not the opinion of the day. It is not our opinion to risk too much, our affairs are in too critical a condition."

Morgan rode silently by himself, pondering whether to release the militiamen and send them home. Most had neither uniforms nor training; they would have no trouble reassuming the role of neutral farmers. With the remainder, he could make a dash to rejoin Greene, using part of his force, perhaps the riders of William Washington, to slow Tarleton's pursuit. That would be unabashed retreat, of course, but a retreat by which he might live to fight another day. The alternative was to offer battle to an army generally the size of his own but which outnumbered him in regulars by three to one.

Afterward, Morgan was never sure exactly when he made his decision. Perhaps it was during the afternoon, when a message came from Andrew Pickens, saying he had assembled more volunteers. Where, he asked, should he meet up with Morgan?

Pickens had been busy, sending riders to nearby farmers to sound the alarm and to call for their services. The dour Presbyterian elder was "spreading the gospel" enthusiastically.

Morgan sent word to meet him at Hannah's Cowpens. Not only was it on his line of march, it was also a place the local farmers would know.

Daniel Morgan had decided to confront British regulars with American militia. If this new land were ever to win its freedom, it would have to use the type of carefree individualist he now had at hand. Morgan did many brave things in his life, but he never showed more courage than at that moment, when he sent word to assemble at the Cowpens.

Back with Tarleton, an air of confidence prevailed. The cocky young colonel knew he was closing in; now it was a mere question of time. He halted the main body near Thicketty Creek, again using a campsite Morgan had just left. A sense of well-being filled the English camp; men gathered around campfires, smoked, swapped stories, cleaned muddy equipment, agreed they would teach the rebels a proper lesson, after which they could return to warm winter quarters. British success they took for granted, although some of the veterans repeated stories they'd heard of Virginia riflemen and their uncanny marksmanship.

Five miles north, Daniel Morgan, camped in a pleasant wooded ravine with a stream running through it, learned Tarleton was still on his trail "like a bloodhound." Recalling what he'd told Greene, that "no attempt to surprise me will be left untried," he sent pickets well out from the main body.

That afternoon, while his men were still marching, Morgan and his staff had ridden ahead to study the Cowpens area. They found it rolling, grassy, and dotted with patches of oak and pine. Morgan noted two low but prominent ridges, one about eighty yards behind the other. Suddenly his staff began to realize that Morgan was considering this site as a possible battlefield. They began to protest: The ground was too open; their flanks would be fair game for Tarleton's cavalry; they should find a river or at least a swamp to anchor the line.

Morgan reasoned, however, that the proud Tarleton wouldn't deign to encircle, but rather would come at him head-on. He began describing a formation with three lines: a row of sharpshooters in front, then a line of militia, finally a row of Continentals. Behind the formation, in reserve, he'd hold Washington, McCall, and their horsemen.

As for having a swamp on his flank, that was exactly what he *didn't* want. At the first sound of a bullet, the militia would be heading for any such swamp and trying to hide. His reasoning had followed a logical sequence based on the tendency of militia to run in the face of a disciplined Redcoat advance. Very well, then, he'd *let* them run, even tell them to, but only in a direction that would let them reassemble and return to action. Having reached that decision, he moved to guide his men into their bivouac area.

It was a night to remember. Farmers in homespun clustered with Continentals in buckskin. All tried to ignore the chilling rain. They watched as supply wagons rumbled into camp, watched also as a few more of the local farmers arrived to throw in with them. Food was issued from the wagons just before dark.

Morgan moved from group to group. At each stop he described his plan of battle. The soldiers were impressed by this general who took the trouble to explain things in language they understood.

In the first rank, Morgan said, he would put the sharpshooters from Georgia and Carolina. They'd been telling him what good shots they were. Now was their chance to prove it. He also told them the same thing he'd told the lads at Saratoga: When the time comes, fire low, stay cool, and don't forget to aim at the officers, the men wearing the epaulets.

At another campfire, Morgan reminded the militiamen of atrocities committed by Tarleton's soldiers. Rather subtly, he also reminded them there was no point in running away; Tarleton was famous for cutting down stragglers, and in any case, Broad River, five miles to their rear, would block any runaway deserters.

Thomas Young, one of Washington's cavalrymen, wrote: "It was upon this occasion that I was more perfectly convinced of General Morgan's qualifications to command militia than I had ever before been."

Even after dark, volunteers continued to trickle in. Again and again Morgan went over his battle plan, sometimes sketching it out on the ground with a stick. To the fainthearted, Morgan said with grim simplicity: "On this ground, I will defeat the British or lay my bones."

Thomas Young wrote admiringly of Morgan's courage and vigor, adding, "I don't believe he slept a wink that night."

But Young saw only the exterior. Inwardly, Morgan was struggling with self-doubt. After most of his men were asleep, the Old Wagoner moved into the shadows. On an impulse, he seized an overhanging tree limb and swung himself into the lower branches. He climbed higher. Then, alone in the silence, he looked out beyond the stars. Later he said at that moment he had "poured out his soul in prayer for protection."

Earlier, Morgan had sent two scouts to monitor the enemy's movements. All night they had lain in the darkness, shivering in the

January mist, only a few yards from a British sentinel. Now they heard the sounds of a waking camp. By three A.M., there was no mistaking it: Tarleton was marching.

The scouts eased back to their tethered horses, mounted in the darkness, and raced northward to sound the alarm. Galloping into camp, they found Morgan and told him the British were under way. January 17, 1781, the most eventful day the Old Wagoner would ever know, had begun.

Morgan stretched his huge frame, planted his legs wide apart, and began to call out: "Get up, boys, Banny is coming!"

The unorthodox formation, which until now had existed only in Dan Morgan's head, began coming to life. Farthest south, and closest to the enemy, Morgan positioned as skirmishers his raw Carolina and Georgia militiamen. In the second rank, 150 yards to the rear, he placed other militiamen under the command of Andrew Pickens. In his final line, atop the first rise, he put General John Howard with the Maryland and Delaware Continentals. These were the regulars he was counting on to stand firm.

At the very rear, behind the second ridge, he placed the horsemen of Washington and McCall. Finally, just as the first rays of dawn appeared in the east, all were in place. The day broke clear and high, with a pale, gray-washed sky that slowly turned blue.

Morgan moved along the line of sharpshooters. "Relax, men, stretch, ease your joints," he said, telling them he expected no superhuman feats. He *would* insist, however, that everyone fire at least twice. After doing so, each man was free to join Pickens at the second position.

"Don't forget, now, fire low and stay cool." Again he reminded them to look for the "epaulet men." Riding along the line, he asked: "Who's it going to be, boys? Which will do better—the lads from Georgia or the ones from Carolina?"

He trotted back to Pickens's line, where he told the men they, too, could fall back after two shots. He showed them the route to follow, which let them wind to the left and behind the sheltering ridges. When they got there, he'd be on hand to tell them what to do next.

The morning light became stronger, and now men could see farther to their front. As if on schedule, there was stirring in a distant tree line. A squad of horsemen, dressed in green and wearing the brass helmets of the hated dragoons, broke clear for an instant. The riders darted back into the trees. Soon they reappeared, this time accompanied by men in scarlet. Next came the foot soldiers, at first a

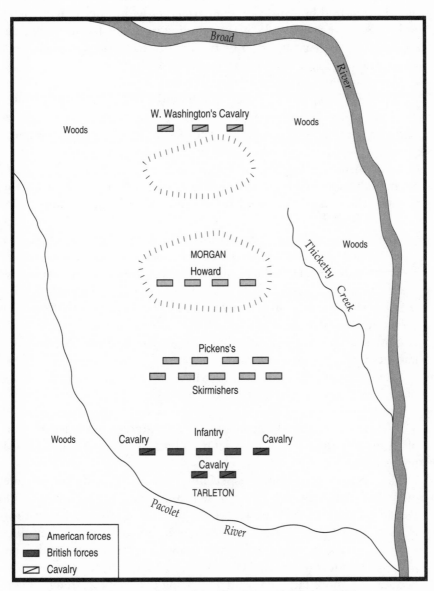

First Position, Battle of the Cowpens—17 January 1781

trickle, then a steady stream. Drums rolled, and their sound carried clearly in the morning air. Tarleton's Legion formed ranks as if on parade; the precision was impressive.

Morgan, like those he led, felt the hollowness gather in his stomach. He realized he was leading an armed crowd rather than an army. Still, they were a crowd he was beginning to understand. He decided to interrupt their admiration of the British drill. Riding to where all could see, he rose up in his stirrups and yelled:

"Are you ready to fight?"

"Yes!" they roared back, and somehow the tension seemed to ease.

Morgan noticed a group of riders—he suspected they included Tarleton himself—impudently trot forward to examine the American position.

Tarleton was feeling better by the moment. As he later wrote, he'd found a "proper place for action." He made a final check of his formation, then calmly signaled for the attack to begin. Drums rolled and fifes shrilled.

"Forward!" Redcoats greeted the command with cheering that could be heard all the way to the line of Continentals.

"They give us the British halloo, boys," Morgan said, "now give them the Indian whoop." Weird but enthusiastic noises came from the American ranks, and a few of the advancing British looked at each other in surprise.

Now the lines were a mere hundred yards apart and the shouting had stopped.

"Steady, men, hold your fire," officers were saying. Then the distance had closed to fifty yards and it was time.

"Fire!"

Sharpshooters and skirmishers shot deliberately, loaded with fumbling fingers, fired again, then scuttled back to Pickens's line according to plan.

The British were stung, especially since several of the "epaulet men" had fallen. Bravely, they closed ranks and pressed forward. On Pickens's order, another powerful volley crashed into the English formation. This time the Redcoats staggered, but once more they filled the gaps and kept moving. By now they were breathing hard. They had walked most of the night and now, as Morgan had foreseen, they became still more fatigued from advancing over a long stretch of continuously rising ground.

In the middle of Tarleton's formation, artillerymen set up the light cannon they called grasshoppers. At point-blank range they sent ugly

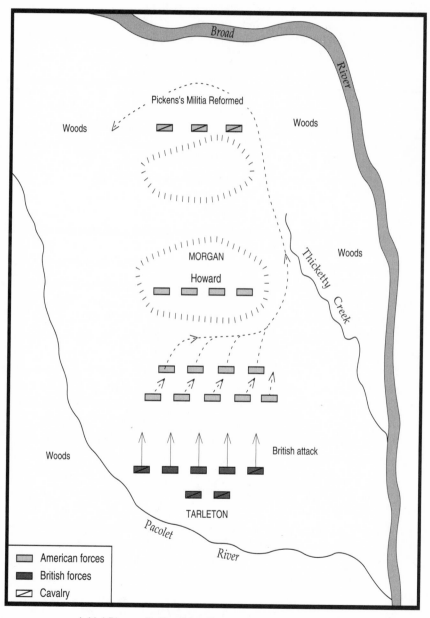

Initial Phase, Battle of the Cowpens—17 January 1781

hot cannonballs into the American ranks. Men were hit and went down screaming.

Pickens's line began a withdrawal, but a withdrawal different from the wild militia retreats the British had seen before. Men stayed together, loaded on the run, turned and fired into the massed scarlet formation, then resumed their dog-trot to the rear.

Tarleton saw Americans withdrawing and mistakenly assumed he'd once more caused green militia to panic. He waved his dragoons forward.

"Finish them off!" Tarleton called. Men of the Tory Legion drew sabers and rode out with gusto. As they overtook the scattering militia, they yipped, broke ranks, and swung their blades lustily. Before much damage was done, however, the dragoons heard a rumble of hoofs on their flank. Bearing down on them was stout William Washington, leading expert riders with sabers of their own.

Many of the surprised dragoons were unseated. Others tried to make a fight of it, but their broken ranks put them at a disadvantage. Tarleton, trembling in anger, watched his dragoons break off and head for the rear.

Despite this reversal, Tarleton decided that on the whole he was winning and that the militia's withdrawal was the start of a general retreat. Wisely he had kept in reserve one of his crack units, the battalion of Highlanders. Now, feeling the critical moment had come, he sent the Scotsmen forward. Bagpipes sounded their eerie notes, and men in kilts came on with a dash.

From atop the first rise, Howard and his Continentals were shooting as fast as they could load and aim. Both sides fired rapidly and continuously; smoke became so dense that men in opposing ranks could barely see each other. Lines became entangled, and men fought with bayonets, with clubbed muskets, even with fists. The British attacked bravely, but the colonists refused to give way.

While Howard's regulars were struggling with this frontal attack, Morgan was active to the flank and rear, waving his saber and urging the militia to regroup:

"Form, form, my brave fellows," he called. With the help of Pickens, he was able finally to shoo them into formation.

Howard, meanwhile, discovered the Highlanders turning his right flank. He ordered his right-hand company to block them, presumably by turning around and then executing a left wheel. In the confusion of battle, the company made its about-face but then headed straight to the rear, all the while maintaining good order. Seeing this, the

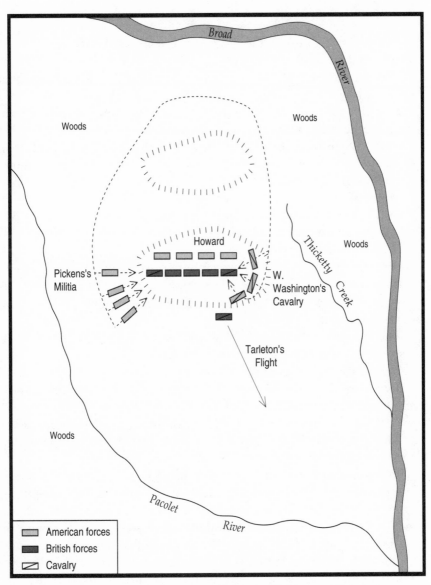

Final Phase, Battle of the Cowpens—17 January 1781

other companies thought a general retreat had been ordered and started to follow suit.

Morgan, riding up just then, watched in horror. He sensed the crisis, knew a mere whisper could turn orderly withdrawal into headlong flight.

"What's going on?" he asked Howard.

"I was trying to protect my right flank," Howard said.

"Are you beaten?"

"Do men march like that when they're beaten?" Howard replied rather testily.

"Right," Morgan said. "I'll pick you out another spot. When you get there, turn around and give them another volley."

Morgan galloped ahead. Just then William Washington, back from chasing off Tarleton's dragoons, sent word that he and his horsemen would be willing to try a charge when Morgan gave the word.

Howard's troops had reached the position chosen by Morgan. The British, meanwhile, encouraged by the seeming retreat, had broken formation and were crowding in.

"Fire!" yelled Howard. His Continentals turned; muskets blazed and the British reeled. Just then, with perfect timing, Pickens and his re-formed militia (who had made a complete circuit of the battlefield) appeared on the British left. Simultaneously Washington was driving in on their right.

The Redcoats, stunned by this double envelopment, fell back in disorder. Howard realized the enemy's confusion.

"Fix bayonets and charge!" he ordered.

Swiftly the tide had turned. The British threw down their weapons and either ran for safety or raised their hands in surrender.

"Give them Tarleton's quarter!" a Continental yelled, but that was as far as it went. Morgan and Howard shouted to stop the killing, and men who wanted to give up were allowed to do so.

Tarleton assembled the remaining dragoons and tried to mount another charge. Washington drove him off in disorder. Few things about a battle are humorous, but afterward men chuckled at the memory of portly William Washington and his personal duel with the dashing Tarleton. There had been a brief cavalry clash, marked more by curses than by casualties, and at some point in the mêlée Tarleton and Washington came face to face. Tarleton thrust with his saber and Washington parried easily. Then Tarleton fired his pistol at Washington, but succeeded only in grazing Washington's horse. With that, Tarleton understandably galloped away. It had not been his day.

Back with the main force, Britishers were surrendering en masse. A few of them escaped, making it to the wagon road where, in the words of Thomas Young, they "did the prettiest sort of running."

When casualties were counted, the one-sidedness of the American victory was staggering. Morgan had lost but twelve killed and sixty wounded. On the other side, there were a hundred dead and 830 prisoners, 230 of the latter also being wounded. As additional booty, Morgan captured eight hundred muskets, thirty-five baggage wagons, a hundred horses, considerable ammunition, both the Britishers' light cannon, and "all their music."

Tarleton had escaped with only a handful of men. It had been a punishing loss, and one from which the forces of Lord Cornwallis would never completely recover.

Although Cornwallis later assured Tarleton that "you have forfeited no part of my esteem as an officer by the unfortunate event of the 17th," one wonders if he would have been so generous had he foreseen the future. His own surrender to Washington was now only ten months away.

On the American side, Cowpens caused widespread celebration. Greene wrote George Washington: "The event is glorious. . . . The brilliancy and success with which it was fought does the highest honor to the American arms."

Perhaps the most significant result of Cowpens was psychological. American militiamen now knew they could stand up to British regulars. Equally important, the British knew it as well.

Daniel Morgan had chosen "the harder right" and risen to the occasion. Greene put it all very neatly: "After this, nothing will appear difficult."

CHAPTER 2

# Decision in Panama

U nlike many Civil War leaders, Ulysses S. Grant worried very little about personal "image." His brother officer George Meade, in fact, once wrote almost in awe: "Grant thinks, as long as a man is sustained by his own conscience, his superiors, and the government, it is not worth his while to trouble himself about the newspapers." This self-effacement permitted others to try defining him, and may explain historian Bruce Catton's saying that Ulysses Grant "was somehow destined to go down in history as an odd combination of things that he was not."

Among other things, Grant was notable for his fervent hatred of war. "Let us have peace" were the words he spoke when accepting the presidential nomination. "Let us have peace" was also the phrase a grateful nation would put over his tomb on Riverside Drive in New York City.

In later life, this abhorrence of war made him hesitant to tell of his own experiences, a reluctance that often frustrated those who would have liked to hear of his military exploits.

"The truth is, I am more of a farmer than a soldier," he once told a startled German crown prince. His reticence continued right up until his final days, when financial needs prompted the writing of his remarkable and unforgettable *Memoirs*.

Even before that, however, there was one story he *would* relate. Sometimes, when with friends, perhaps in the evening, with a glass in one hand, a cigar in the other, he would tell of one special experience. It took place, oddly enough, not on a battlefield but in the steaming jungles of Panama, and those who heard it would never again think of Grant as being insensitive to human life.

He was lonely, angry, and very frustrated. On this June day in 1852, thirty-year-old Ulysses S. Grant—his friends called him Sam—was on Governors Island in New York Harbor, having just returned from Castle Garden on the southern tip of Manhattan. For the past week, he'd gone each day to the city to meet with the army quartermaster and make arrangements for the coming voyage.

He'd had little interest, however, in the sights and sounds of New York; his thoughts were back in Ohio with Julia and little Fred. Ever since they'd said good-bye—for who knew how long—he'd been blaming himself, feeling guilty, even wondering if he should resign his commission. Still, soldiering was what he knew best and, with a growing family to support, he needed the Army's security, at least for now. Nevertheless, here he was, about to sail for the West Coast while his wife and little son were left to fend for themselves. To make matters worse, he had once again failed to settle a problem of some missing funds, and that gave Julia still more cause to worry. What kind of husband was he?

While Grant, the "quiet man," normally kept things to himself, at the moment he had a reliable friend and confidant in the person of Major John Gore. Gore, more than anyone, could understand Grant's loneliness. Back in Madison Barracks, that cold, bleak post near Lake Ontario, and before that in Detroit, the Gore and Grant families had been inseparable. Now, as their regiment headed for

California, Gore's wife would be coming along while Julia Grant, seven months pregnant, would be forced to stay behind.

While their wives had formed close ties on those rather isolated army posts, John Gore's and Sam Grant's friendship had been sealed even earlier, and in battle. Five years earlier, in 1847, Grant and Gore had been in the same unit as part of Winfield Scott's army advancing on Mexico City.

As soon as the guardian fortress of Chapultepec fell, Grant and Gore's brigade had the mission of attacking down a broad causeway road leading to the San Cosmé *garita*, or gate. On either side of the causeway was a deep, wide ditch filled with water. Up ahead, commanding the San Cosmé approaches, were cannons supported by infantry.

Lieutenants Grant, Gore, and two other officers, together with a handful of men, had dashed forward, darting in and out of masonry arches that supported an overhead water sluice. Then, near the fringes of Mexico City itself, as the road took a right-angle turn, they were confronted by a barricaded cannon and Mexican riflemen firing from housetops.

The consensus, evidently, was to hold in place and wait for reinforcements to come up. In all likelihood, Grant was as afraid as anyone else. Nevertheless, he told the others he would go on alone to see if there was a way to outflank the enemy position.

He probably couldn't have explained his actions even to himself. Once, commenting on people who fought duels, he said he wasn't sure that risking death that way was a question of bravery; maybe it was just that neither duelist had the moral courage to back off. Was it possible he was moving forward only because he didn't have the nerve to stay put?

Whatever Grant's motivation, at the moment he didn't have time to ponder such things. He stole along the left side of the causeway, working his way forward under cover of a wall, past a silent house and a clump of trees. A few minutes later, still undetected by either riflemen or cannoneers, he found himself in the very rear of the barricade.

After noting the Mexican position, he slipped back to Gore and the others. If a dozen or so men would volunteer to come with him, he could get behind the enemy, rush them from the rear, and allow the main body to charge frontally.

A dozen volunteers stepped forward. Grant told them to follow him and, as he later wrote: "I watched our opportunity and got them across the road and under cover of the wall beyond, before the enemy had a shot at us. . . . When we reached a safe position I instructed my little command . . . not to fire at the enemy until they were ordered, and to move very cautiously following me until the San Cosme road was reached; we would then be on the flank of the men serving the gun on the road."

Unexpectedly, Grant came upon a second group of Americans who were pushing forward along a shallow ditch. The captain in charge, setting aside the question of rank, said that since Grant knew the situation, he'd let him take the lead. He and his men would follow along.

Grant and his force, once behind the barricades, made their move with gusto. As they attacked from the rear, firing and yelling, Gore and the others charged from the front. It became a race between the two parties. "The moment was a very exciting one," Gore later wrote, adding that he couldn't tell who had been first to reach the barricades. In any case, by this time the outflanked and encircled Mexicans had abandoned the position and fled in disorder.

Now, five years later, Grant's difficulties were of a far different order, with problems as much financial as military. Gore was sympathetic to Grant's financial predicament, and appropriately so, since he himself had even had a role in bringing it about.

As their regiment prepared to head home at the end of the war with Mexico, Grant, acting as regimental paymaster, had worried about the more than $1,000 entrusted to his care. The lock of his trunk being broken, he'd taken the money to Gore. They had locked the money in Gore's trunk, reasoning, as Grant later reported, that it was "safer to have public money in the room of some officer who did not disburse public funds" and whom thieves would thus consider less likely to have a large sum in his possession. Nevertheless, a few nights later, while Gore and his tentmate, John DeRussy, were asleep, Gore's trunk had been stolen.

Sam Grant, with a sinking feeling in his stomach, had known he'd be held accountable. Testimonials had been prepared, and no blame was attached to Grant. Still, files in Washington showed him responsible for the missing funds and, by law, only an act of Congress could clear his name. Grant's Ohio congressman had even submitted a petition on his behalf, but in typical bureaucratic fashion, nothing had come of it.

Now Grant told Gore that Colonel Benjamin Bonneville, their crusty new commander, after first refusing, had finally given him leave to go to Washington and settle the thing. However, Bonneville had allowed Grant only three days—had grumbled about even that much—and three days hadn't been nearly enough time to cut through the Washington red tape.

Gore asked if Grant had sought help from his representative. He had, Grant explained, but unfortunately Congressman Barrere had been out of town and not expected back for ten days; Grant, pressed for time, hadn't been able to wait. Then, to make matters worse, someone had told him that the whole Military Affairs Committee of Congress would have to act on it, and they weren't even in session! It was very disappointing; if he was ever made to pay back all that money . . .

Grant grew silent, and Gore could sense the frustration. For some reason Bonneville had taken a dislike to Grant and from the first had made it clear he would have preferred another man as regimental quartermaster. To allow so little time off, and begrudgingly at that, was especially ironic: After first saying he didn't want Grant as his quartermaster, now Bonneville was acting as though Grant were so valuable he couldn't be spared.

Just then the two were joined by Charles Tripler, the 4th Infantry's regimental surgeon. He, like Grant and Gore, had already had problems with their new colonel. Unlike the other two, however, the doctor was fairly outspoken in his negative remarks about Bonneville.

Neither Grant nor Gore wanted to comment, but it was common knowledge that Bonneville, a vain publicity seeker, had gained his position through political favoritism. His ability was also questioned, and while Army wives, like their husbands, generally watched what they said, Eunice Tripler once told her husband she was sorry he had to serve under Bonneville, such a "stupid man mentally."

Now, in addition to dealing with a prima donna colonel, Quartermaster Grant was given a new problem. A blundering War Department had booked passage for their regiment on the side-wheeler *Ohio* at the last moment, after all the ship's first-class cabins and most of its steerage berths had already been filled. It had become Grant's job to find room for all the latecomers and their baggage.

Grant got busy, making carpenters out of soldiers and having them build tiers of berths on deck for the men. His irritation showed, however, when he began realizing that no matter what he did, conditions on board would be, to say the least, far from pleasant.

As soon as the regiment was up to strength, it would be on its way. The plan was to send two companies to California "around the

Horn." The rest of the regiment, including Grant, would debark in Panama, cross the Isthmus, then board a waiting second ship for the remainder of the voyage. They were due to board the *Ohio* very shortly, with 700 soldiers and a hundred of their dependents.

Captain Grant kept busy right up until sailing. (Although he was still a lieutenant, Army practice was to use a man's brevet rank. Grant's Mexican War service had won him an honorary brevet promotion, but to the paymaster, unfortunately, he was still a lieutenant.)

Finally, on July 5, the *Ohio* cast off, heading south toward Panama. As feared, Bonneville's "testy temper" (to quote one of the wives) and the general crowding caused almost constant friction. Grant did his best to smooth things over, and the ship's captain, Navy lieutenant Finley Schenck, noted that the "disagreements" caused by the colonel's "hasty and uncertain" actions were referred to Grant as arbitrator, whose rulings were "distinguished by particular good sense."

Surgeon Tripler, responsible for the regiment's health, also had his concerns. Word had it that a cholera epidemic was raging in Panama; before they sailed, Tripler had told the Army Surgeon General it would be murder to try crossing the Isthmus with the epidemic in full swing. He'd merely been told not to worry, that the regiment would be crossing too rapidly for the epidemic to have any effect. Personally, he had his doubts.

The voyage continued; every evening saw Grant pacing the deck restlessly, silent and solitary, puffing on a clay pipe, head bent in deep thought. Several times he was joined by ship's captain Schenck. Often they smoked in silence, but sometimes they talked. Schenck later said he found Grant "a man of an uncommon order of intelligence" with a "good education, and what his mind took hold of it grasped strongly and thoroughly digested."

Missing his own family as he did, Grant often visited with the civilians on board. Once, mistaking a small woman named Mrs. Sheffield for one of the children, he called to her to come see the whales who were following the ship. Discovering that she was married, he chided her for traveling the world, saying one her size should still be at home with her mother. Occasionally he chatted with a small group of Catholic nuns. They were Sisters of Charity, bravely heading for California, where godless new towns in the roaring gold fields could doubtless use both their teaching and their good example.

The *Ohio* continued south. Days became warmer and drowsier. In the evening air, men imagined they could detect the lush scent of the tropics. Many of the officers (including Grant, who had been seasick much of the voyage) looked forward to being on land for a few days. Charles Tripler, meanwhile, continued to warn of tropical diseases, cautioning the officers to keep the men away from local fruits and liquors. They nodded sympathetically, but behind his back many scoffed at his fears. Grant, however, while in Mexico had seen six men die from disease for every one killed by gunfire; he understood and shared the surgeon's concern.

Finally, on July 16, twelve days out of New York, the *Ohio* arrived off Manzanilla Island, near present-day Colón. In 1852 the place was called Aspinwall, for a Yankee financier who was trying to build a trans-Isthmus railroad. The civilians on board looked at Aspinwall hopefully; they were a step closer to the California gold fields. At the same time, many of them, particularly the women, were offended by the crowd of yelling dockhands, drifters, and prostitutes lining the shore. Equally offensive was the all-pervading odor of slime and corruption drifting their way.

The soldiers, on the other hand, noted approvingly that Aspinwall's main industry seemed to be the dispensing of rum. Even from a distance, practiced eyes could discern groggeries in what only a charitable man could have called the town's business section.

Grant came ashore in a small boat and headed for the local steamship office to check on transportation. Soon he was walking gingerly along planks stretched above the sidewalks. The walks themselves, he noted, were some eight to ten inches underwater.

In the so-called town square, he saw workers from Ireland, Jamaica, England, even from India and China. Everyone, even the half-naked Indian children, seemed to be smoking a cigar. A sudden downpour erupted; just as suddenly it stopped, leaving the air humid and oppressive. Grant later wrote in his *Memoirs* that "these alternate changes from rain to sunshine were continuous in the afternoons. I wondered how any person could live many months in Aspinwall, and wondered still more why anyone tried."

Very few, in fact, lived there by choice. The town on Manzanilla Island had been in existence for barely two years, and only recently had it even acquired a name. The ambitious Aspinwall had imported laborers, mainly Irish, to work on his railroad, which now stretched for twenty miles of the Isthmus's fifty-mile width. His labor recruiters never mentioned the malaria and fever that prevailed. It didn't take the workers long to find out, however; soon they were muttering grimly that they had "buried an Irishman for every tie." As for Grant, he would probably have agreed with the nineteenth-century traveler who wrote:

> It would be hard to find in any other part of the tropics so many wretched hovels as can be found in Aspinwall. . . . All sorts of buildings have been erected, huddled together without regard to ventilation; inhabited by . . . people living more like pigs than human beings. . . . Leaving the back street, a few steps would carry you into swamp knee deep.

Grant, determined to get the regiment on its way as quickly as possible, hastened to the company offices, where he learned that the daily train had already left that morning. However, there were baggage cars on hand, and he was free to have them loaded in preparation for the next day's move.

The trek across Panama would be in three phases. The first part would be easiest: twenty miles by rail, as far as Barbacoas. Next would come travel by water, up the Chagres River to Cruces. From there, the company would provide mules for the final leg, twenty miles overland to their goal, the town of Panama City on the Pacific shore.

Grant, returning to the pier and welcoming the chance to be busy, began supervising the baggage unloading. At the water's edge, he met a tight-lipped Dr. Tripler. Despite Tripler's advice, many of the men had been turned loose in town. According to the doctor, "numbers of them sought the first tavern they could find, to indulge their fatal craving for liquor." Undaunted by his warnings, the soldiers celebrated being on land. That night, according to Tripler's report, "many were brought back on board intoxicated and drenched with rain."

By next morning, the last of the *Ohio*'s passengers had been ferried ashore. All was ready for the rail trip. The regiment was loaded, the civilian passengers were aboard, a signal was given to start, and the train whistle blew.

Nothing happened.

After a time, the engineer admitted that his locomotive wasn't powerful enough to pull the heavily loaded train. Accordingly, the group was moved in two trains an hour apart.

Peremptorily, Bonneville told Grant to stay behind and bring up the baggage by a later train. Under the treaty governing their passage across Panama, U.S. soldiers were forbidden to carry firearms, so the baggage included not only tents, band instruments, and other impedimenta, but all the regiment's rifles and ammunition chests as well.

At Barbacoas, the end of the rail line, amid much shouting and confusion, the group reassembled and began transferring to flat-bottomed dugouts the locals called bungos. Each boat carried thirty to forty passengers and a crew of six. The native crewmen, clad only in loincloths, were equipped with long poles which they used in a remarkable fashion. Alongside each boat was a wooden plank running from stem to stern. A crewman would start at the bow, plant his pole firmly, then walk rapidly to the rear. In this manner the boats proceeded up the Chagres.

For the moment, Sam Grant—riding with some of the dependents and a portion of the regimental baggage—forgot his problems. Ever since boyhood, he had wanted to see new places. Now, as they glided along, he gazed in fascination at thick jungle vegetation lining the banks, its lush green occasionally accented by the vivid plumage of a darting macaw. Chattering monkeys and humming insects provided a background to a chorus of shrill bird whistles.

But Grant kept thinking of Julia. How was she doing? Had the baby come yet? If only she and little Fred could have been along to see the jungle and share the experience, but without sharing the hazards, of course. Someday he'd have to tell them about it.

Suddenly a fight between crews erupted as one boat tried to pass another. Crewmen pulled knives, dived into the water, and made for each other. It looked as though blood would flow, but Army officers on the scene drew their swords and restored order.

A few hours later, word came back that a bungo of wives and children had capsized up ahead and that all were drowned. Grant once again thanked the Lord that Julia was safely back in Ohio. Quickly he and a company of men rushed to the scene, only to find it had been a false alarm.

That night the bungos tied up along the banks. The boatmen disappeared into a nearby village, where they partied and could be heard, according to one of the wives, "howling like drunken barbarians." While soldiers stood guard, the women and children huddled in the boats, shivering fearfully.

Next day the party reached the village of Gorgona. Ever since their arrival on the Isthmus, the *Ohio*'s passengers had been aware of their exposure to cholera. They had seen evidence of it in Aspinwall, but at Gorgona the epidemic was raging violently and the situation was far more frightening.

Colonel Bonneville made a decision. To minimize the time of exposure to cholera, he would march the troops overland from

Gorgona to Panama City. The imperious colonel then summoned Grant and abruptly ordered him to stay behind. With neither apology nor special guidance, Bonneville merely told Grant he was giving him a company of men and making him responsible for bringing forward the sick, the women, and the regimental baggage.

This much responsibility was a tall order for a junior oficer. It would involve continuing by boat up the Chagres, then traveling overland on muddy trails the rest of the way. Grant knew Bonneville resented him; maybe the colonel hoped his young quartermaster would make a mess of things, or maybe he felt that if some officer had to be exposed to cholera for a longer period, it might as well be Grant.

Grant told Surgeon Tripler, who was also staying behind, that supposedly the steamship company had made arrangements to provide baggage mules, plus additional mules (or porters with hammocks) to transport the passengers.

Bonneville marched off with most of the regiment, leaving Grant with about seventy men, the baggage, and an understandably anxious group of civilians. The young captain, trying to sound confident, gathered his group together. "We're on our own," he explained; "the troops are marching on ahead, but we'll keep going by boat as far as we can."

The little flotilla proceeded, arriving at Cruces, the head of navigation, on Sunday morning the eighteenth of July. They found to their horror that there, too, the cholera epidemic had reached crisis proportions.

Immediately Grant contacted the steamship company representative, a whining North American in a wrinkled linen suit. Quickly Grant asked about the mules and bearers that had been promised for the trek to Panama City.

"Sorry, Captain, none are available." The agent claimed that all the mules had been taken by civilians, and that even if they were available, the rains, the cholera, and other factors beyond his control had caused the price of renting a mule to more than double.

It was a maddening situation. Cholera was striking down a new victim almost hourly; frantic civilians traveling individually, willing to pay almost any price to escape, were proceeding forward with little delay. Meanwhile, Grant and his charges, limited to payment at government rates, were forced to wait, camped by the river alongside their piles of regimental baggage.

By Tuesday, July 20, the situation was critical. Surgeon Tripler was called to examine a soldier suffering from violent cramps.

"It's cholera," Tripler said. Six hours later the man was dead.

Grant ordered the healthy to march on to Panama City. He and the surgeon would remain behind with the sick and the baggage until the contracted-for mules appeared. Fortunately a few sturdy hammock-bearers were available to carry those unable to walk. In a company shack outside town, Grant discovered the Sisters of Charity he had met on the *Ohio*; one of them was suffering from cholera. As soon as the stricken sister had recovered enough to travel, he found Indian porters for each of the nuns. The grateful sisters, promising to remember "Captain Sam" in their prayers, were soon on their way to Panama City, being carried down the trail in swaying hammocks.

The company agent continued to insist he could find no mules. Nevertheless, hundreds of civilians along with their baggage were being sent on their way, carried on mules hired at outrageous prices. Grant and Tripler discussed the situation. Each hour saw more people coming down with cholera, and by this time four more soldiers had died. Tripler remarked that perhaps Grant should try hiring mules at *any* price. That was easy for Tripler to say. Grant, however, knowing how the Army worked and remembering his disastrous experience with the lost payroll, realized the possible repercussions. True, no one blamed him for that misadventure in Mexico, but the black mark still remained, and another financial blunder might keep him and his family in virtual slavery, reimbursing the government, for the rest of their days.

Each day the palavering contractor agreed to have the mules "mañana." Each day there was another excuse. By Wednesday the twenty-first, more and more soldiers and civilians were being stricken. Grant was feeling the loneliness of command. As a junior officer, he had no authority to exceed established terms, and mules that normally rented for $16 were now costing as much as $40.

Again, Grant conferred with Tripler; then he made his decision. He marched into town, and before nightfall had signed a contract for transportation—giving his personal guarantee for payment at whatever it took. One can only imagine the moral courage it took to give such assurances. He was putting at risk not only his own financial future, but Julia's as well. And what of Julia? What was happening back in Ohio?

Next day, July 22, things looked a bit brighter. The mules he'd bargained for at high prices, both saddle and cargo, began to appear. On the advice of Surgeon Tripler, everyone was told to ride rather than to try walking. Those too sick to ride a mule would be carried in hammocks. It was done, as Tripler later reported, "lest the fatigue of marching over so desperate a road should excite the disease in men predisposed to it."

As mules became available, either for passengers or cargo, they were sent on their way. By midday, nearly half the people and half the cargo had been dispatched. Then the rains arrived and everything had to be suspended.

That very morning, back in Bethel, Ohio, Julia had gone into labor, and before the day was over had given birth to a boy she named Ulysses after his father. She and the baby were doing fine, but the joy of bringing a new life into the world was tempered by the knowledge that many weeks must pass before her husband could learn of his new son.

Next day, back in Panama, the nightmarish process continued as more mules were dispatched with the remainder of Grant's party and their baggage. It was impossible to maintain any semblance of order. As Tripler described it: "The moment a rider or cargo is placed upon a mule's back, that moment he must set out, or the muleteer strips his mule and carries him off. Our movement was, therefore, of necessity a straggling one."

The travelers floundered along. By this time the constant rain had turned the trail into a sea of mud. At times the jungle path disappeared entirely, forcing people to slosh through filthy, snake-infested brown water. Almost hourly, cholera claimed another victim. Stubbornly, Grant kept the column moving, ignoring the mud that sucked at his boots and made every step an effort.

Three more soldiers died en route. With each death, people turned to Grant. What should they do? "We'll bury them," he answered firmly, "and then we'll press on." And so the men were interred in shallow jungle graves; hasty prayers were said; and "press on" they did.

The rains continued. Mud became so deep that when Charles Tripler doubled back to treat a soldier who had collapsed from the cholera, he found that the man had disappeared in the mire.

Finally Grant reached Panama City on the Pacific with his groaning, vomiting, muddy band of civilians and soldiers. There they learned that in Panama City cholera had already claimed the lives of six of the cabin passengers they'd known on the *Ohio*.

Most of the troops were already aboard the San Francisco ship *Golden Gate*, and now families who'd been with Grant's party were happily reunited with their sponsors. None was happier than John

Gore's tiny wife, who had been deeply worried about her husband. The major, in ill health before leaving the States, had been advised by Grant and other friends to delay his departure, but had feared the testy Bonneville might interpret this as malingering.

An old hulk nearby was leased as a hospital ship; Grant brought the ill from the *Golden Gate*, as well as those from his own party, on board to be nursed. The horror was not yet over. One of the military wives reported seeing strong men walk the deck of the *Golden Gate*, then writhe with sudden cramps and carried away to die. On board the hospital ship, enlisted men assigned as orderlies became frightened, neglected their duties, and when they saw their chance slipped over the side and swam ashore.

Charles Tripler, himself nearing exhaustion, asked for officer volunteers to come aboard the hulk and stand watch with him. First to step forward was Sam Grant, who voluntarily continued to serve on the "death ship" for more than two weeks, returning only intermittently to the *Golden Gate* to rest, relax, and gather supplies.

One officer said later that Grant was a tender hand at nursing, that he took "a personal interest in each sick man" and was "a man of iron, so far as endurance went, seldom sleeping, and then only two or three hours at a time." Yet, said the officer, Grant's "work was always done, and his supplies always ample and at hand. . . . He was like a ministering angel to us all." (Let anyone who has read of a later Grant, at the Wilderness or Cold Harbor, and heard him described as cold-blooded and insensitive, read *those* words and ponder.)

On August 1, back on the *Golden Gate*, Grant, Gore, and another officer were playing cards when Gore, who'd been feeling ill for several hours, felt a sudden cramp. He dropped his hand, turned pale, and gasped: "My God, I've got the cholera!"

Grant, hoping to calm his friend, said: "No, Major. I'm sure it's just something you ate that doesn't agree with you." But Gore was right. His wife was summoned, and a few hours later, Major John Gore, beloved husband, faithful friend, and gallant soldier, was dead.

Grant wrote his wife of Gore's death, saying that Mrs. Gore, who by this time had already started home, had taken it very hard. He went on to tell Julia how his heart went out to the grief-stricken widow, who now had to undergo crossing the Isthmus for a second time. His only consolation was that his darling Julia had been spared a similar experience. "My dearest," he wrote, "you never could have crossed the Isthmus at this season, for the first time, let alone the second. The horrors of the road, in the rainy season, are beyond description."

Men continued to die; Grant, as quartermaster, furnished canvas to wrap the dead and cannonballs to weight the bodies for burial at sea. By this time more than a hundred men of the Fourth Infantry lay moldering in graves or turning lazily with the tides on the bottom of Panama Bay.

On August 3, the captain of the *Golden Gate* announced his intention to put to sea the next day, adding that he would refuse to take on board a single sick man. The Army was forced to give in to his demands, and next day the *Golden Gate* sailed, carrying the surviving civilians and 450 well men of the 4th Infantry, including Grant. Most of the sick were by now recovering; they, along with Surgeon Tripler, were able to secure passage four days later on the steamer *Northerner*.

So finally the crisis was over and Grant went on—on to Oregon and California, where loneliness made him resign his commission and where some said he was too fond of whisky; on to Missouri and Illinois, where his neighbors said he was a good man, and wasn't it a pity he had never amounted to much. Then, after 1861, Sam Grant went on to other places: Fort Donelson and Shiloh, Vicksburg and Appomattox, finally Washington and the White House.

Grant never forgot Panama, though, nor the mule contract by which he had risked his family's future and that eventually passed unchallenged into musty Army files. In Panama, moreover, he had learned the important lesson that disease, not bullets, is the soldier's greatest hazard. More important, perhaps, he had learned something about his own inner strength. It was a strength for which the Union one day would be deeply thankful.

CHAPTER 3

# Decision at Arlington

In May 1787, delegates met in Philadelphia and, after struggling for five months, finally managed to draft a Constitution. Ratification, however, was still very much in doubt. Much depended on Virginia, whose population was one-fifth that of the entire Union, and whose territory, including the districts of Kentucky and West Virginia, actually reached the Mississippi. If the powerful Old Dominion refused to ratify, other wavering states might well follow her lead.

Feelings ran strong on both sides of the issue as men met in Richmond to consider the proposed Constitution. At Mount Vernon, George Washington waited anxiously for Virginia's decision. Not surprisingly, one of the strongest voices for ratification was that of Washington's friend, war hero Henry "Light Horse Harry" Lee. After heated debate, Lee, along with James Madison and others, managed to overcome a strong anti-Federalist bloc led by Patrick Henry and secure approval for the new Constitution.

Light Horse Harry was many things: a patriot, a gifted soldier, a charming conversationalist, an author of stirring phrases (as when, on Washington's death, he spoke the memorable tribute: "First in war, first in peace, and first in the hearts of his countrymen").

Unfortunately, Harry Lee was also an irresponsible, self-indulgent dilettante, one whose postwar life was marked by steady decline. Although at various periods he held public office, both as governor and congressman, he also spent time in debtors' prison after squandering the fortunes of two wives. When his son Robert was born, Harry was leading a literally fugitive existence, hiding from a swarm of creditors. Above all else, however, Harry Lee was a great soldier and a great patriot. It was not surprising that his son Robert grew up with a love of country and that he also chose the profession of arms.

Robert E. Lee had graduated from West Point in 1829, second in his class and the first man in history to finish the course without a single demerit. He had been assigned to the U.S. Corps of Engineers, and during the next seventeen years, had married, raised a family, and served with distinction in the peacetime army. It was not until 1846, however, during the Mexican War, that he first saw action.

Well, he had wanted to gain field experience, but he'd never expected something like this! Thirty-nine-year-old Captain Robert E. Lee, holding his breath, remained perfectly still. From his hiding place under a fallen log, he could hear the voices of nearby Mexican soldiers.

In a way, he supposed, the chain of events putting him here had begun two years earlier, when he'd first met General Winfield Scott. Lee had been one of the officers sent to observe final examinations at West Point, which duty for a time had placed him in daily contact with the army's imposing general-in-chief. Scott, impressed by the young engineer, had made a mental note to keep him in mind.

In August 1846, three months after the start of the Mexican War, Lee had received his orders for field duty. He had left his wife, Mary, and the children behind at Arlington, had proceeded to Texas, and there had reported to General John Wool. In the campaign that followed, Lee had accompanied Wool, whose force, together with a main body under Zachary Taylor, had advanced almost unopposed well south into Mexico. Meanwhile, Winfield Scott was assembling a second force to launch an amphibious end run, a landing at Veracruz to be followed by a cross-country move toward Mexico City. At this point, Scott had written Taylor, specifically requesting the services of junior engineer Lee.

In March 1847, following a three-day bombardment, Veracruz had surrendered, and Scott's men, in sweltering heat, had begun the next phase, marching steadily but uncomfortably along sandy roads and scratching their way through clouds of mosquitoes. Thirty miles inland, as they left the coastal lowlands and began to climb, the weather had grown better and the men's spirits had improved. Then, on April 11, their advance had come to a sudden halt. Up ahead, near Cerro Gordo, lay a series of mountain ridges whose crests were lined with fortifications backed by lines of Mexican artillery under General Santa Anna.

The impulse of American general David Twiggs, in the lead, was to attack the position straightaway. Caution prevailed, however, particularly when an initial scouting suggested that it might be possible to outflank Santa Anna's position. It was decided to await the arrival of Winfield Scott, the overall expedition commander.

Scott arrived on the fourteenth and next morning sent his hand-picked junior engineer, Captain Lee, to check out the terrain. For hours, Lee climbed up and down hazardous canyon walls, pushing his way through matted brush that tore at his clothing, all the while working his way around the Mexican position. At last he reached a point from which he could see the entire left flank as well as the valley beyond. He began to envision a plan of attack. Wanting to gain the fullest information, he kept on going, not knowing that up ahead was a spring used by Mexican soldiers. Pushing aside a thicket, he saw the Mexicans before they saw him. Softly, he slid to the ground and crawled under a log.

So there he was, the normally dignified young captain, in a most undignified predicament—afraid to move, almost afraid to breathe.

Lee could hear the soldiers, chattering and laughing. They seemed in no hurry to leave. An hour passed; he squirmed uncomfortably, trying to shift his position without making a sound, trying to ignore the crawling, biting insects. Then he heard footsteps, and a pair of voices coming closer. To his horror, two of the soldiers sat above him on his very own log, carrying on an unhurried conversation.

Time passed—it seemed an eternity. Finally the soldiers left, allowing Lee to make a cautious withdrawal, back to the American lines, where he reported on the topography, the best route for an encirclement, and the plan's likely strategic effect. It was a masterful performance, one that won him high praise from Scott, who described Lee as "indefatigable" and called his reconnaissance not only "daring" but "of the utmost value."

So thoroughly did Scott trust Lee's judgment, that two days later, he had Lee guide forward the entire division of General Twiggs. They moved out at first light, and by eleven o'clock had gotten within 700 yards of the enemy without being discovered. As American artillery shelled the startled enemy, Twiggs's men assaulted the slopes of Cerro Gordo. The entire left and center of the Mexican army collapsed, the right wing surrendered, and Santa Anna himself barely escaped with a handful of troops.

Further adventure awaited Lee as the army drew near to its goal of Mexico City. This time it involved the Pedregal, a vast, grotesquely patterned lava bed that looked to one observer like a storm at sea turned to stone.

It was either find a way across the Pedregal or move head-on against a prepared Mexican position and its massed artillery. Once again Scott called on Lee, who'd become his reconnaissance expert. The tireless Lee, at one point spending thirty-six straight hours in the saddle, at last found a path that engineers could turn into a passage for troops and artillery.

When Mexican general Gabriel Valencia heard that American guns were coming through the Pedregal, he roared with laughter: "No! No! You're dreaming, man. The birds couldn't cross the Pedregal!"

As American divisions moved into position and prepared for action, Winfield Scott waited for word of the battle plans. In the darkness, and amid a violent tropical thunderstorm, engineers from Scott went out seven different times; not a one managed to make it across the Pedregal. Meanwhile, Captain Lee, with the advance party, volunteered to get word back to Scott. In a fierce driving rain, he set out alone and on foot, over trackless wastes, guided only by his sense of direction and an occasional flash of lightning. Climbing, stumbling, at times crawling over the jagged lava, he made his way back to the Zacatepec rock pile where he'd last seen Scott, only to find that the general had returned to his headquarters at San Agustin. Lee

pressed on, drenched and exhausted, finally reaching Scott and deliv-
ering his report around eleven P.M. He then recrossed the Pedregal
and rejoined the troops so as to be on hand for the next day's action.

Scott, impressed, would call Lee's effort "the greatest feat of physical and moral courage performed by any individual, to my knowledge." A fellow officer, Erasmus Keyes said Scott's feeling for Lee
was "almost idolatrous." The old general, said Keyes, estimated Lee's
military ability "far beyond that of any other officer of the army." Lee
was not only a hero; in Scott's army he had become almost a legend.

After Mexico, Lee spent four years on an engineering assignment
in Baltimore. This was followed by three years at West Point, as
superintendent. Then it was off to the West for duty with troops.
Leaving the family was never pleasant; as Lee wrote his wife's cousin
Martha "Markie" Williams: "My happiness can never be advanced by
any separation from my wife, children and friends." Nevertheless,
duty came first. In an earlier separation, when a sickly Mary had
urged him to come home, Lee sent what was for him a very strong
answer: "Why do you urge my *immediate* return, and tempt me in
the *strongest* manner, to endeavor to get excused from the performance of a duty imposed on me by my profession, for the pure grati-
fication of my private feelings?"

In Texas, Lee became second-in-command, under Albert Sidney
Johnston, of the newly created 2nd Cavalry Regiment. Many, including Scott, thought it should have been the other way around.
However, the final decision had been made by Johnston's close friend
and admirer Secretary of War Jefferson Davis.

As things worked out, however, Johnston was recalled to
Washington in August 1857, and Lee was given command of the regiment. It was the best possible assignment for a career officer, the sort
of thing he'd always wanted. Suddenly, though, he had to decide
between career and family obligation.

Word came from Arlington that Mary's father, George Washington
Custis, had died; Lee was appointed executor of the estate.
Unfortunately the gentle, impractical Custis had left Arlington in bad
shape. Not only had the plantation declined physically but also
Custis's will included certain generous bequests which the estate,
through insufficient funds, was in no position to honor. It was up to
Lee to put things in order.

Gritting his teeth, Lee returned to Arlington, put in for a leave of
absence, and went about restoring the plantation to the physical and

financial health that would enable it to honor Custis's wishes. For the soldier turned involuntary plantation manager, this "unpleasant legacy," as he called it, was hard, dreary, depressing work. Never once, however, did he shirk what he saw as a duty. Still, to his son Custis, he confided: "I have no enjoyment in my life now but what I derive from my children."

Lee was also uncomfortable about having to use slave labor to carry out the terms of his father-in-law's will. Robert owned no slaves himself, nor did he approve of slavery. From Texas, he'd written his wife that "in this enlightened age, there are few I believe, but what will acknowledge, that slavery as an institution, is a moral and political evil in any country. It is useless to expiate on its disadvantages. I think it however a greater evil to the white than to the black race."

At Arlington, meanwhile, and in nearby Alexandria, everyone was talking about the possibility of secession. Lee hated such talk, and when time came to return to his regiment, the pain of leaving his family was eased by the thought that an army post might at least let him avoid such conversation. To him, secession meant rebellion; personally, he wished he didn't have to think about it. After all, he loved the Union, and how could he not? Wasn't his father, the friend of Washington, and whose memory he revered, one of those who'd fought to establish this new Union? And hadn't he himself sworn an oath to defend it?

Even in Texas, however, as he tried to concentrate on military matters, he couldn't avoid such discussions. When with friends, he affirmed his loyalty to his native Virginia, but insisted that did nothing to weaken his love for the Union. Lest the family have any doubt of his feelings, he wrote Custis: "As an American citizen, I prize the Union very highly and know of no personal sacrifice I would not make to preserve it, save that of honor."

Custis understood the implication of that reference to honor. Robert E. Lee was first of all a Virginian. In this, he was echoing the sentiments of his own father, Light Horse Harry, who although a proven American patriot and staunch defender of the Constitution, had said: "Virginia is my country; her I will obey!" It was only logical that his son Robert should feel the same way. The son's hope, of course, was that serving Virginia would also mean serving the Union.

For perhaps the first time in his life, Lee felt deeply depressed— depressed about the state of the country, about the separation from his family, about the apparent stagnation in his personal career. At age fifty-three, and after thirty-one years of commissioned service, he was still only a lieutenant colonel; some twenty-two senior officers stood between him and possible general officer rank. His classmate Joe Johnston, meanwhile, through the influence of his cousin, new secretary of war John Floyd, had been nominated to become a brigadier general. Lee, who'd never been willing to use political maneuvers himself, merely said of Johnston: "His plan is good, he is working for promotion. I hope he will succeed."

Predictably, when Johnston's promotion came through, Lee penned a gracious, sincere note of congratulations. Personally, though, he began to wonder—was it time to admit his own life was a failure?

With the election of Abraham Lincoln in the fall of 1860, secession talk intensified. "It is difficult to see what will be the result," Lee wrote to Custis, "but I hope all will end well. . . . My little personal troubles sink into insignificance when I contemplate the condition of the country, and I feel as if I could easily lay down my life for its safety. But I also feel that would bring but little good."

Recently he'd been reading a life of George Washington, and he wrote, almost with a groan: "How his spirit would be grieved could he see the wreck of his mighty labors."

Then came a surprising dispatch: orders relieving Colonel Robert E. Lee of his regimental duties and directing him to return to Washington, and to report in person to the general-in-chief no later than April 1. Lee read the orders more than once. What did they mean? Was this a preliminary to that long-sought promotion? Or was it merely a new assignment? In any case, it probably had something to do with the national crisis.

Well, at least a return to Arlington would help him look after his family. He'd been concerned about them during this time of trouble—had written Markie Williams to say how much he wanted "to be near those who claim my protection, and who may need my assistance."

Lee began getting his baggage together and, before he left Texas, had a heart-to-heart talk with his friend Charles Anderson, a Northerner who wondered about Lee's intentions.

"If Virginia stands by the old Union," he told Anderson, "so will I. But if she secedes, though I do not believe in secession as a constitutional right, nor that there is sufficient cause for revolution, then I will follow my native state with my sword, and if need be with my life."

Anderson shook his head sadly, started to say something himself, but before he could, Lee added: "I know you think and feel very differently, but I can't help it. These are my principles and I must follow them."

Leaving Texas, as it turned out, was not without difficulty. In San Antonio, as he pulled up in front of the Read House, he saw that an armed mob had gathered and seemed to have taken over the city.

On the sidewalk, he saw Mrs. Caroline Darrow, the wife of a Unionist friend. "Who are these people?" he asked.

"They are McCulloch's," she said, referring to Ben McCulloch, a well-known leader of the Texas Rangers. "General Twiggs surrendered everything to the State this morning, and we are all prisoners of war."

Lee, shocked and stunned, felt the tears gather in his eyes. "Has it come so soon as this?" he murmured.

At his hotel, he found the rumors were true. Twiggs, a Southerner, had indeed surrendered Federal properties to a Texas show of force. Soldiers loyal to the Union were already on their way out of Texas. Lee, despite his own leanings, knew had he been in Twiggs's place, he would have acted far differently. As long as he was wearing the Federal uniform, he would have felt honor bound to defend government property, at gunpoint if need be.

Lee strode across the San Antonio plaza to his former headquarters office, only to find it occupied by three civilians.

"Texas is out of the Union," they told him rudely, "and you must declare yourself for the Confederacy. Otherwise you will not be allowed transportation for your belongings."

For one of the few times in his life, Robert E. Lee lost his temper. With all he was going through, all the pent-up sadness and frustration, he was hardly in a mood to be bullied. His dark eyes flashed, and in a cold, chilling voice, he said: "I am an officer of the United States Army! Also, I am a Virginian, *not* a Texan!" With that, he did an about-face and stormed out of the room, leaving three brash Texans properly chastised.

Lee told his friend Anderson of the confrontation and of his outrage. Nothing had been said about detaining Lee personally, and Anderson said he'd take care of forwarding any baggage, so next day Lee was on his way.

In late March 1861, Robert E. Lee, soldier, husband, and father, was once more riding up the long hill to Arlington and seeing the familiar white columns fronting that wide portico. He dismounted, squared his shoulders, and put a smile on his face as he went to greet his wife and daughters.

For several years, Mary's health had been in steady decline; now, with a shock, Lee saw it had worsened. She was in a wheelchair; her arthritic right arm dangled uselessly at her side. As for Mary, much as she'd wanted her husband home, she'd dreaded the homecoming and having him see her condition. However, for this one moment at least, her beloved Robert's return brought a bit of cheer and put the light back in her eyes.

Next day, following his orders, Lee rode across the Potomac and reported to General Scott's headquarters. He was ushered into Scott's office by an old comrade: the general's military secretary, Lieutenant Colonel Erasmus Keyes. Keyes watched as the old general greeted Lee with warm affection. As Keyes waited at his desk, curious about what would be said, the door closed. And it remained closed—for three full hours. Neither man ever revealed what was spoken during those hours; however, one can speculate.

Scott, we can expect, once again assured the younger man of his esteem and respect. If he'd had his way back in '55, it would have been Lee, rather than Sidney Johnston, who was given command of that newly formed Second Cavalry. More recently, he'd have liked to see that quartermaster general's star go to Lee rather than to Joe Johnston. Regardless of the past, he may have hinted, he was now in a position to make amends.

What did he say next? That he and Lee were *both* Virginians? That the Old Dominion had always been at the very heart of the Union, with sons who helped write both the Declaration of Independence and the Constitution? That of the fifteen presidents before Lincoln, seven had been Virginians? That Lee's own father had been one of the Founding Fathers and one of Washington's closest friends?

Winfield Scott, at age seventy-five and carrying more than 300 pounds on his huge frame, was clearly in no position to take the field in person. His mind was still clear, however; he could develop strategy, but he needed a younger man to implement it.

Moreover, Scott may have argued, if hostilities were to break out, would it not be better to form a mighty army at the very outset, one which would clearly show the folly of armed resistance? And might Scott not have discussed what later became known as his anaconda plan—the strangling blockade that could bring surrender without requiring armed invasion?

Wisely, it seems, Scott did not make a specific, direct offer to Lee, nor did he ask for an immediate choice between country and state. For the moment, Scott merely wanted Lee to consider his options most carefully. Lee, we can be sure, listened courteously and attentively. At this point—perhaps naively, or perhaps just hoping against hope—he may have told Scott there was a good chance Virginia would remain in the Union. For even as they spoke, a convention was meeting in Richmond, and it was said the delegates were two to one against secession.

With nothing settled, except perhaps their mutual respect, Scott and Lee agreed to await developments. As a tormented Lee rode slowly back to Arlington, he was feeling, more than ever, a deep affection for his old commander. Eventually, he and Scott might differ about the proper course, but nothing would mar their feeling for each other.

Scott felt that as long as Lee retained his commission persuasion might still be possible. On April 28, a tempting carrot was dangled. Lee received papers that promoted him to full colonel and appointed him commander of the 1st U.S. Cavalry Regiment. As he looked at the new commission, he saw it had been signed personally by Abraham Lincoln.

Probably about this time, a letter also arrived at Arlington from L. P. Walker, the Confederate secretary of war, offering Colonel Lee a direct commission as brigadier general, the highest rank then authorized in the Southern army. It was ironic—after all these years of professional stagnation, potential honors were now coming from all directions. First, the colonel's eagles from the Federal army; now, a star from the Confederacy. Lee, however, considering himself a citizen of Virginia, chose to ignore the Southern offer. While his native state remained in the Union, he had two loyalties—to the Union and to Virginia—and he wasn't about to let any third government make a claim on him.

As April began, all eyes were on Charleston harbor. It still seemed possible that Fort Sumter would be evacuated and a clash could be avoided. However, when the North forced the issue by attempting to resupply the Sumter garrison, Charleston batteries, under the command of Lee's Mexican War comrade P.G.T. Beauregard, took the fort under fire. Sumter surrendered on April 14, and the long-dreaded conflict had begun.

By April 17, Lee heard the Richmond Convention had gone into secret session, undoubtedly to consider secession. That same day, from across the river in Washington, he received a letter and a message. The letter, from Winfield Scott, asked Lee to call at his office on the eighteenth. The message, transmitted in a note from his cousin

John Lee, was a puzzler. It asked Lee to come next morning to the home of Francis P. Blair, Sr.

What Lee didn't know was that secret, closed-door meetings had been taking place, and strenuous efforts, involving the President himself, had been launched in an effort to retain his services for the Union.

Lee knew little of Washington's inner workings, although he'd met Blair, knew he was the father of Lincoln's postmaster general, and probably knew as well that Blair was head of the country's most powerful political family. He was unaware, though, that the elder Blair's son-in-law, Samuel Phillips Lee, Robert E. Lee's cousin, had told his father-in-law that Colonel Lee might still be a loyal Union man. In any case, those in high places had felt Blair might be a good person to take a sounding.

On the morning of the eighteenth, Lee left his home at Arlington and rode to the Washington seat of the Blair family—Blair House, just opposite the Executive Mansion. Francis Blair greeted Lee, ushered him into the parlor, and bade him be seated. (Interestingly, Blair House had once been rented by Ohio senator Thomas Ewing. In 1850, William Tecumseh Sherman, Ewing's stepson, had been married in that very parlor.)

After the normal pleasantries, Blair said with a smile: "I am told, Colonel Lee, that Napoleon once said every soldier in his army carried a marshal's baton in his knapsack."

Lee nodded politely.

"I am sure you need no explanation of that quote, Colonel. You have been a soldier all your life. You have worked hard, and brilliantly, to rise in your profession, all for the chance of someday holding a major command. Well, sir, it can be yours, a major generalcy, command of all the Federal forces, head of an army ten times greater than that which General Scott led in Mexico."

Blair made it clear that he was speaking on behalf of both President Lincoln and Secretary of War Simon Cameron. It was a stunning offer—to lead an army more powerful than any known to Caesar, Frederick, or Napoleon—to be placed at the very summit of his profession—to serve the flag he loved. For an instant, Lee might have been tempted, but if so, it was for *only* an instant.

"You hesitate, Colonel Lee. Is it because of the slavery question?"

"Sir, if I owned every one of the country's four million slaves, and I had it in my power, I would gladly free them in order to prevent a war and to save the Union."

"Then will you accept?"

In later years, a Southern orator, speaking at Lee's grave, was almost idolatrous as he compared Lee's situation to the three temptations of Christ. "Since the Son of Man stood on the Mount, and saw all the kingdoms of the world and the glory of them stretched before him, and turned away, to the Cross of Calvary beyond, no follower of the Savior can have undergone a more trying ordeal."

Lee simply told Blair he could never draw his sword against his native state. Leaving Blair house, he then went directly to Scott's office, where he gave the same answer to Scott.

The old general, who had been Lee's friend, admirer, and greatest supporter, told him, "You have made the greatest mistake of your life, but I feared it would be so."

Scott, who also knew something about honor, raised a point Lee himself might not have confronted. As long as Lee retained his commission, he was subject to orders, and it was less than honorable to wear the uniform when one wasn't fully prepared to carry out those orders, however distasteful they might be.

"There are times," Scott said, "when every officer in the United States service should fully determine what course he will pursue and frankly declare it. No one should continue in government employ without being actively employed."

Then Scott, setting aside his personal feelings toward Lee, summed it up rather bluntly: "If you propose to resign, it is proper you should do so at once; your present attitude is equivocal." That hurt, but Lee knew Scott was right.

Equivocating or not, however, Lee postponed his decision. Obviously he was still hoping for good news from the Richmond Convention. Next day, he rode into town, bought a copy of the *Alexandria Gazette*, and read the fateful news: Virginia had seceded. The convention had voted two to one to leave the Union, and the Old Dominion was now part of the Confederacy.

Before leaving town, Lee went into a pharmacy to pay a bill. Noting that most townspeople were cheering the news, he remarked sadly to the druggist: "I must say, that I am one of those dull creatures that cannot see the good of secession."

That night, Mary Lee heard her husband pacing the floor, agonizing over his dilemma. He was a soldier and a man of honor; acceptance of orders, and loyalty to one's oath, were at the very core of his being. The most despised word in his vocabulary was "traitor."

And wasn't it possible that others, equally honorable, and even in his own family, might see it differently? "Tell Custis," he later wrote, "he must consult his own judgment, reason and conscience as to the course he may take. I do not wish him to be guided by my wishes or example. If I have done wrong, let him do better. The present is a momentous question which every man must settle for himself and upon principle."

So here he was, married to the granddaughter of George Washington, Father of his Country, and faced with the prospect of abandoning that country. Still, as was written in the Declaration of Independence, governments derived their just powers from the consent of the governed. And had not Washington himself led a revolutionary army in support of that belief?

Late that night, an agonized Lee, true to his sense of honor, penned a note to Secretary of War Cameron: "Sir, I have the honor to tender the resignation of my commission as Colonel of the First Regiment of Cavalry. Very respectfully, Your Obedient Servant."

In a second letter, to Winfield Scott, he spoke movingly of "the struggle it has cost me to separate myself from the service." Then, speaking from the heart, and knowing his old commander was disappointed in him, he wrote: "I shall carry with me to the grave, the most grateful recollection of your kind consideration, and your name and fame will always be dear to me."

Mary Lee understood the cost, in terms of family fortune and personal career, all as sacrifice to a war she and her beloved husband both believed unnecessary. Yet she understood. To a friend, she wrote: "My husband has wept tears of blood over this terrible war, but as a man of honor and as a Virginian, he must follow the destiny of his State."

# CHAPTER 4

# Decision on the Mississippi

Chief Justice John Marshall once referred to America's rivers as national arteries, ones which carried the movement, the growth, and the commerce of a young nation. In 1861, these arteries were just as vital for waging a war, and soon after the fall of Fort Sumter, Northern leaders recognized that war in the west would be fought for control of those very same rivers. For the foreseeable future, however, the Union navy had to devote its attention to matters on salt water. As a result, the Army

War Department, through necessity, established its own river force of sorts by purchasing steamboats and converting them into odd-looking, clumsy river gunboats.

On the evening of November 6, 1861, two such gunboats, the *Tyler* and the *Lexington*, together with four transports hauling some 3,100 blue-clad soldiers, left the docks of Cairo, Illinois, and headed down the Mississippi. Ranking naval officer for the expedition was fifty-four-year-old Captain Henry Walke of the *Tyler*, a Virginia-born Ohioan and a pugnacious saltwater veteran.

Henry Walke, his craggy, almost handsome face framed by a luxuriant growth of seagoing whiskers, listened to the comforting, steady chug of the *Tyler*'s engines and the splash of her sidewheel. Peering into the darkness, he wondered what the next twenty-four hours would bring. Off abeam, he could see the *Lexington*; astern, trailing in the gunboats' wake, were the army transports that were now his responsibility. Although he'd agreed to go along as their guardian, he still thought the mission seemed a bit too vague.

Fortunately Walke had confidence in his army counterpart, a newly created brigadier general named Ulysses Grant. Grant, of course, was young—still only thirty-nine and not yet tested in this war, but it was said that down in Mexico he'd been a cool man under fire. Well, Walke thought, the next day or two should tell more about Grant, and at the same time, maybe tell more about the caliber of his *own* crewmen. Heaven knew they were a strange conglomeration.

Of the seamen from the East, there were Maine lumbermen, New Bedford whalers, Philadelphia sea lawyers, and hard-boiled New Yorkers. There were also foreigners, mostly Irish, but with a few Englishmen, Scots, Frenchmen, and Scandinavians mixed in. Some had experience on the Atlantic, some on the Great Lakes or on rivers, some none at all. How well they'd work together remained to be seen. For that matter, who could say how effective his and Grant's partnership would prove to be?

All Walke knew, from what Grant had relayed, was that they were heading downriver to "demonstrate" against the Confederate fortress at Columbus, Kentucky, where General Leonidas Polk, the erstwhile bishop, had assembled some 10,000 men and nearly 150 cannon on a high bluff dominating the river.

The situation, in a way, was the fault of M. Jeff Thompson, the irrepressible Confederate irregular. Thompson was strictly an amateur, and his men didn't look much like soldiers, but he somehow had a knack for stirring things up. At the beginning of November, the irregulars were reported in the vicinity of Greenville, Missouri. Grant had been told to send someone to "help drive Thompson into Arkansas." In compliance, he dispatched Colonel Richard Oglesby with four Illinois regiments. A second order then instructed Grant to conduct a demonstration to the south, presumably to keep Polk occupied and make the Confederates think twice before sending any more troops westward.

Accordingly, Grant had now loaded his men on transports, arranged with Walke for a gunboat escort, and started downriver. Aboard the transports were five regiments of infantry, a battery of artillery, and two companies of cavalry, making Walke suspect the Army had something more in mind than a mere demonstration.

Nine miles south of Cairo, they dropped anchor for the night and waited for daylight. Well before that—at two A.M.—they received a message saying Confederates from Columbus were streaming across the river into Missouri, apparently moving to intercept Oglesby's column. It was a logical move for the Southerners, and increased Grant's desire to hold Polk's main body at Columbus. Since his force was inadequate for assaulting Columbus itself, he chose as his objective Belmont, the steamboat landing on the opposite shore, where the enemy column was said to be assembling.

Early next morning, the gunboats and transports got under way. Three miles short of Belmont, the transports stopped and the troops were unloaded. Walke, with his gunboat covering force, kept going, stopped below Polk's fortress postion on the bluff, and took the fort under fire.

Within minutes, Confederate gunners sprang into action, taking aim at the gunboats and loosing a shower of deadly cannonballs. As gunners tried to find the range, shots began plunging into the river, each miss sending a geyser of water high into the air. The volume of fire increased, and Walke's frail wooden side-wheelers were plainly outclassed. Prudently, they withdrew out of range.

On shore, the infantry found themselves among dense timber and marshland, broken here and there by farm clearings. In high spirits, they began to move forward. For the Federal troops, it was the first taste of action, which may account for their enthusiasm. Skirmishers were sent out, there were some cheers (even a few speeches by politicking officers), and men in blue began to advance and to drive in the Confederate pickets. Minutes later they started receiving rifle fire, followed by a headlong Rebel charge. There was spirited fighting, a temporary pulling back, but then Grant's Iowa and Illinois regiments mounted a charge of their own, drove everything before them, and soon overran the Confederate camp.

Leonidas Polk, watching the action from an observation post on the bluffs at Columbus, hurried troops across the river as reinforcements. Out on the river, Walke's gunboats returned to action, steaming back to the danger zone below the bluff, and offered supporting fire to Union troops on the ground. To confuse Polk's gunners, Walke kept his boats circling in constant motion. Eventually, however, the *Tyler* and *Lexington* again were forced to pull back.

At Belmont, Confederate resistance had ceased, and the green, exhilarated Union troops, led by equally green officers, began scampering through the Rebel camp, laughing, cheering, picking up odds and ends of abandoned property, and getting completely out of hand. Grant, the veteran, knew the battle was far from over, and dashed from place to place trying to restore order.

Confederate reinforcements continued to arrive, and suddenly the tide had turned. Men who moments before had been dancing with joy and collecting souvenirs now found they were being pushed back. To make matters worse, one Confederate force was landing behind them, threatening to cut them off from the transports. Quickly, elation changed to panic; some officers immediately began talking of surrender.

On the river, Walke bravely returned to the fight, risking the shells of Southern gunners who by this time had found the range. With a roar, followed by an ugly crunching sound, one cannonball crashed obliquely into the *Tyler*, passing through the side and deck, killing one man and wounding several others. With that, having done far more than just demonstrate, Walke pulled back out of range, but to a point where he could still guard the transports.

On the ground, Grant, keeping cool, said they had fought their way in, and they could just as easily fight their way out. Casualties mounted on both sides, but after the hardest fighting of the day, the Union troops managed to force their way back to the transports.

As troops began climbing aboard, a large number of men in gray, hot on the Federals' heels, were seen streaming into a nearby cornfield, from which point they began directing rifle and artillery fire against the transports. However, as Walke later wrote: "A well-directed fire from the gunboats made the enemy fly in the greatest confusion."

Moments later, Ulysses Grant shouted to a boat captain on one of the transports: "Chop your lines and back out!" The lines were cut, the boat backed off a few feet, and sailors laid a plank from the deck to shore. With a neat bit of horsemanship, Grant slid his horse down the bank, looked around, then calmly rode aboard the unsteady plank. He was the last Union soldier to leave Belmont.

On the whole, with losses about equal, Belmont was an inconclusive draw, one that both sides later claimed as a victory. Polk could say with justification that his men held the field at the end of the day, surely anyone's definition of a win. Grant, on the other hand, had made his demonstration and interfered with Southern movements, so he, too, felt satisfied with the outcome.

Henry Walke could also feel satisfaction. He had bombarded Polk's forces at Columbus and, after being driven back had twice returned to the fight. Also, his guns had provided covering fire as the Union troops withdrew (some said escaped) to their boats. Moreover, he had protected the transports and, equally important, had preserved his vulnerable wooden gunboats. Had they been destroyed, it almost surely would have meant the loss of the Army's depot at Cairo, the most important one in the west.

Back in August, some three months before Belmont, Secretary of the Navy Gideon Welles had commissioned contractor James B. Eads to build seven ironclad gunboats for use in the West. Before many weeks had passed, shipyards at Carondelet, near St. Louis, and at Mound City, just up the Ohio River from Cairo, began building these brand-new warships. They were squat, ugly, and heavily armed craft, and men called them turtles.

In September, with construction under way, Flag Officer Andrew Hull Foote arrived in St. Louis to take charge of naval operations on the Western rivers, under the command of General John Frémont and the War Department. His first task, of course, was to hasten the building of the gunboats and mortar boats.

"Spare no effort to accomplish the object in view with the least possible delay," Frémont told him. Tough, crusty Andrew Foote needed little urging. The pugnacious Foote, now fifty-five, had entered the U.S. Navy as a seventeen-year-old midshipman, had commanded his own brig, and had demonstrated his skill in battle all the way from the North African coast to the waters off Canton, China.

Henry Walke, for one, was glad to see Foote arrive to take command. The two had become acquainted years earlier, in 1827, as fellow midshipmen on the *Natchez* of the West India squadron; even then Foote was known as a bright, promising officer. After that, they didn't meet again for thirty-four years, until February 1861 at the Brooklyn Navy Yard, where Foote was the executive officer. Despite the hiatus, Walke well knew Foote's reputation as a devout Christian who often preached to his crew on Sundays and as an ardent foe of alcohol. Indeed, at one point a few years earlier, while commanding three vessels on the China station, Foote had somehow convinced every officer and man on each of his ships to sign the temperance pledge. (Eventually he managed to attain a lifelong goal: that of having the navy's rum ration permanently abolished. He thereby won undying but dubious fame among future generations of U.S. sailors.)

By January 1862, four ironclads had been completed and brought down to Cairo. One such "turtle," proudly named *Carondelet* by its builders, was placed under the command of Captain Henry Walke.

By this time, the new departmental commander in St. Louis, replacing Frémont, was bug-eyed Henry Wager Halleck, a man the army called Old Brains. Halleck, a fine administrator, somehow seemed more interested in rearranging lines of authority than in taking the initiative. Grant and Foote, meanwhile, were pondering the strategic advantages to be gained from controlling the major rivers. Specifically, they had been eyeing two vital waterways to the east, and the Confederate forts that guarded them: Fort Henry on the Tennessee River and Fort Donelson on the Cumberland.

On January 24, in separate messages, Grant and Foote both wired Halleck for permission to move against Fort Henry. Somewhat cautiously, Halleck gave his consent. Foote and Grant were quick to seize the opportunity.

Promptly, on February 2, the ironclads, plus transports carrying 17,000 of Grant's men, left Cairo and headed down the Tennessee. Heavy rains had been falling, causing the river to rise rapidly to an unusual height. On the night of the fifth as the fleet anchored a few miles north of Fort Henry, the current became so swift that Walke's *Carondelet*, despite having dropped both anchors, had to keep her engines going full force to avoid being swept downstream.

Next morning, with the weather clearing, the boats got under way. Three miles short of the fort, the soldiers disembarked and began to move overland. An hour later, the gunboats, having steamed within range, began exchanging shots with Fort Henry.

For a time, the firing was intense. The gunboats sent deadly shells tearing into the earthen ramparts of Fort Henry, tossing great heaps of dirt over Southern guns. As Navy marksmen found the range, Henry's largest gun, a 128-pounder, was torn from its mount and filled with earth as an incoming shell exploded near its muzzle. Nearby, a rifled gun was hit; as it burst, the mangled bodies of two of its gunners were hurled into the water.

During the action, Walke's boss, Commodore Foote, was aboard his flagship, the *Cincinnati*, which was hit thirty times, with one man killed and several wounded. Oddly enough, Walke's *Carondelet*, while also struck some thirty times by heavy shot and shell, suffered not a single casualty.

Finally, with every one of its guns disabled, Fort Henry raised a white flag, well before Grant's soldiers, who had just begun to deploy, could even begin their assault. Confederate general Lloyd Tilghman, along with two or three of his staff, put out in a small boat, which was rowed to the *Cincinnati*. There he surrendered his sword to Commodore Foote.

Foote, wanting to share the moment, sent for Henry Walke. He introduced him to Tilghman, then asked Walke to take command of Fort Henry and hold it until the arrival of General Grant.

Rather stiffly, Tilghman told a reporter who'd come along on the expedition: "Sir, I do not desire to have my name appear in this matter in any newspaper connection whatsoever. If General Grant sees fit to use it in his official dispatches, I have no objection; but, Sir, I do not wish to appear at all in this matter in any newspaper report." The reporter nodded sympathetically, then made sure to get the correct spelling of "Tilghman" so he could print both the general's name and his naïve remarks in full.

*New York Herald* headlines shouted: "Important Naval Victory— Surrender of Fort Henry to the Union gunboats—The Union Troops Not in the Fight." The *Chicago Tribune*, not to be outdone, reported rather breathlessly, "The taking of Fort Henry by Com. Foote, though insignificant in the number of killed and captured, is undoubtedly the most important achievement of the war."

"It was magnificent," said the *Tribune* in a report written from one of the gunboats:

> The whistling shot . . . and the cheering of our men as our shots took evident effect. . . . At precisely 1:40, the enemy struck his flag, and such cheering, such wild excitement as seized the throats and arms and caps of the 400 or 500 sailors of the gunboats. Well, imagine it. . . . The land force under command of General Grant did not arrive at the fort till after the rebels had surrendered, and their army escaped.

Fortunately, despite the rather disparaging reference to Grant, neither he nor Foote worried about who got the credit as long as the end
result was satisfactory. Foote, Walke, and Grant were happy to be
partners and, in Foote's words, the Army and Navy, working together
on the Western rivers, were like blades of shears, "united, invincible;
separated, almost useless."

A week later, on February 13, Henry Walke was on a different
river, the Cumberland, and again peering through the morning mist,
wondering what the day would bring. Would Fort Donelson fall as
easily as had Fort Henry? Henry, he had to admit, hadn't been much
of a triumph. Although Tilghman and his men had put up a good
fight, the fort, poorly constructed and situated too close to the
swollen Tennessee River, had been nearly indefensible. Donelson,
however, might be a different story.

The engines throbbed steadily, reassuringly, and Walke began to
count his blessings. He had a brave crew and a fine new boat with
armored sides—a great improvement over the wooden *Tyler* he'd
commanded at Belmont. As he looked out, squinting at the shoreline
and searching for the outlines of Fort Donelson, he also felt appreciation for General Grant, the army commander on this expedition.
Over the past few weeks, Henry Walke and Ulysses Grant had developed a strong mutual respect.

Today's plan was rather simple: Grant would begin a siege, encir-
cling Donelson from the land side; then Union gunboats would
pound the fort into submission.

Walke, in the *Carondelet*'s pilothouse, heard a call from a lookout.
Fort Donelson had come into view. For the moment, the *Carondelet*
was by herself. Foote and the others were still en route from Cairo.
Taking the initiative, Walke decided to test the situation. He shouted
a command to his two bow guns: "Commence firing!"

The guns barked; the shells whistled across the river; and, as they
exploded, they seemed to have found the mark. Strangely, there was
no response. Had the place been abandoned? Hills and woods, lightly
covered with snow, obscured part of the fort, but Walke could still
make out black rows of heavy guns. He shuddered; they made him
think of the rows of dismal-looking sepulchers he'd seen years ago in
the hills overlooking Jerusalem.

The *Carondelet* pulled back, dropped anchor, and waited. The
next move was up to Grant, whose troops, anxious this time not to
let the Navy get ahead of them, had marched the twelve cold, muddy

miles from Fort Henry, across what locals called the Land Between the Rivers, and were now forming a rough semicircle around the fort.

Early next morning, Grant sent word of his arrival and asked if Walke could open a bombardment. If so, said Grant, "we will be ready to take advantage of every diversion in our favor."

Walke was happy to comply, and by nine A.M. he had moved into position and opened fire. Moments later, Fort Donelson's heavy guns replied with authority; it was clear the place was far from empty. The duel continued, and around eleven-thirty the *Carondelet* took a massive solid shot through her side, sending enough splinters flying to put twelve seamen out of action. Walke backed off, evacuated his wounded, then returned to the fight. The bombardment continued most of the afternoon, with no significant effect, and by this time it was obvious that what had toppled Fort Henry would never be enough to take Donelson.

Around midnight, Commodore Foote arrived with five more gunboats, three of them ironclads. Next day, with all naval units on hand, the four ironclads—the *Louisville*, the *Pittsburgh*, the *Carondelet*, and Foote's flagship, the *St. Louis*—advanced abreast to resume the bombardment.

Within minutes, the air was filled with flying metal. Walke later wrote:

> We heard the deafening crack of the bursting shells, the crash of the solid shot, and the whizzing of fragments of shell and wood as they sped through the vessel. Soon a 128-pounder struck our anchor, smashed it into flying bolts, and bounded over the vessel, taking away a part of our smokestack; then another cut away the iron boat davits as if they were pipe-stems.

The shells kept coming. One struck the pilothouse, spraying fragments of iron and splinters and killing one of the pilots. "Still they came," wrote Walke, "harder and faster, taking flag-staffs and smokestacks, and tearing off the side armor as lightning tears the bark from a tree."

Meanwhile, fifty-seven shots had hit the *St. Louis*; one of them killed the pilot and wounded Commodore Foote. The *Pittsburgh*, the *Louisville*, and the *St. Louis* all fell back, limping and wobbling out of control because of damaged engines and rudders.

The *Carondelet* was alone, and now all the fort's guns could concentrate on her. Two 32-pound shells skipped off the water and
struck near her bow; she began to leak badly. Despite the mounting
casualties, the ship's crew bravely continued to operate the guns and
to fire into the fort.

Finally the *Carondelet* pulled back. First to enter the fight, she now
became last to leave, having by this time been struck fifty-four times
and taken more casualties than all the other gunboats put together.
By this time, however, Grant's forces had completed the investment.
The entrapped Southerners attempted to break out, but after heavy
fighting, all but a handful were driven back into the Fort.
Confederate general Simon Bolivar Buckner asked for terms, whereupon Grant penned his famous note demanding "unconditional surrender." Buckner, although complaining about the lack of "chivalry"
from a man who had been a comrade in the old Army, was forced to
accept. Soon Fort Donelson was in Union hands.

By mid-March, the gunboats had shifted their attention to the
Mississippi, and to Island No. 10, a two-and-a-half-mile-long muddy
strip rimmed with strong ramparts and heavy guns. Today, No. 10 (so
named because it was the tenth Mississippi island below the mouth of
the Ohio) no longer even exists, thanks to the ever-meandering
course of the Big Muddy. In the spring of 1862, however, and especially after the abandonment of the Confederate strongpoint at
Columbus, Kentucky, its blocking position on the river was crucial.

At the time, the Mississippi turned sharply west just below the
Tennessee-Mississippi line, then doubled back in a twisting lazy S,
first moving north, then again west, until finally heading south
toward Memphis and the Gulf. Island No. 10 sat at the bottom of
the first loop. At the top of the next loop, on the Missouri side, was
the town of New Madrid, which was now in the hands of Union
general John Pope. Opposing him, fifteen miles farther downstream
on the Tennessee side, were strong Confederate gun positions near
Tiptonville.

Pope wanted to cross the river and overrun the Tiptonville batteries. Once he had done so, he would have cut the only land approach
to Island No. 10. The island's surrender would then be but a question
of time, and the Mississippi would be in Union hands all the way to
Memphis.

Through Yankee ingenuity, Pope's men had built a six-mile-long
canal that allowed shallow transport boats, though not the heavier

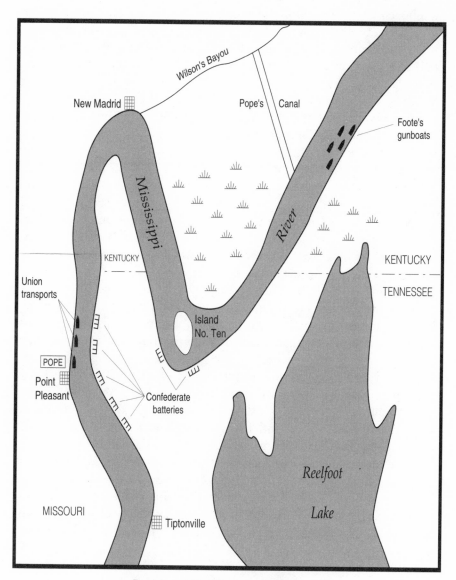

Decision on the Mississippi—March 1862

gunboats, to bypass Island No. 10. Hence Pope had the means of fer-
rying his 20,000 troops across the Mississippi. The river, however,
was a mile wide at that point, ruling out artillery support of the crossing, and the Confederates had positioned heavy guns near every feasible landing. If Pope tried to cross without gunboat support,
Southern guns would blow his transports out of the water.

Understandably, Pope urged the Navy to bring gunboats into position and silence the Tiptonville shore batteries. The Navy in this case
was represented by Andrew Foote, whose flotilla of seven ironclads
and eleven mortar barges was now anchored safely upriver.

At Forts Henry and Donelson, the Navy had led the way, with the
Army content to follow. Now the situation was reversed. Foote, still
suffering from his Donelson wounds and stumping around on crutches, was uncharacteristiclly reluctant to help. He told Pope he couldn't
take the risk; his boats, even the ironclads, had shown how vulnerable they were to shore batteries. They would never get past Island
No. 10, and it would be a needless sacrifice of boats and their crews.

Foote was being consistent. In the overall picture, he sincerely
believed his boats were every bit as important as Pope's divisions.
Earlier, when his well-meaning brother, a prominent Cleveland judge,
told him the people wanted "dash and close fighting—something
sharp and decisive," Foote had responded angrily, "Don't you know
that my boats are the only protection you have upon your river
against the rebel gunboats—that without my flotilla everything on
your rivers, your cities and towns would be at the mercy of the
enemy? My first duty is to care for my boats if I am to protect you!"

As an alternative, Foote tried the tactic that had worked so well at
Fort Henry. Perhaps sheer firepower could force the enemy to abandon his strongpoint. The mortar barges, having been towed into position, began a long-range bombardment. Three weeks of constant
shelling, however, produced little result. By this time impatient Union
officers were starting to mock the Navy.

"What are they doing?" one would ask.

"Oh, they're still bombarding Tennessee at long range," the other
would sneer.

Pope continued to pester Foote for gunboat support, saying he felt
it quite possible that one of the ironclads could slip past Island No.
10 under cover of darkness.

On March 20, Foote's delegate, Commander Stembel, asked each
of the boat commanders what he thought of the idea. For the

moment, Foote himself stayed out of the discussion, perhaps wanting to make sure his captains spoke frankly.

With the exception of Henry Walke, who said it might be worth a try, each said basically the same thing: Any boat foolishly attempting to run past those batteries would most certainly be destroyed. It would be suicide. The commanders also pointed out that river conditions here were different from those at Fort Donelson. At Donelson, on the Cumberland, the Union boats had been headed upriver, against the current. Hence, when Confederate gunners had disabled their steering mechanisms, the powerless boats had drifted back downstream to safety. Now, however, they would be moving *with* the current. Even if a ship weren't sunk when it tried to run the gauntlet, it was almost sure to be disabled, in which case it would float hopelessly downstream into the hands of the enemy.

For the next week, John Pope continued to fret, at one point hinting almost insultingly that the Army might be willing to furnish gunboat crews if the Navy wasn't. Had Pope known Foote better, he'd have realized that when principle was involved, this was not a man to be swayed either by pleas or by sarcasm.

No, Andrew Hull Foote—devout Christian, fervent foe of alcohol and slavery, sometimes called "the Union's Stonewall Jackson"—knew the importance of his gunboats and was rock firm in his convictions. Just recently, substituting for an ill Cairo minister, he had taken as his Sunday sermon text "Let not your heart be troubled: ye believe in God, believe also in me." (A little girl in the congregation told her father Foote really meant, "Ye believe in God, believe also in the *gunboats!*")

On March 29, as pressure from Pope continued, a still-reluctant Foote called his commanders to the *St. Louis* for a council of war. As the boat captains gathered, it was obvious that Foote's Donelson wounds were causing considerable pain. Nevertheless, his voice was firm as he began the meeting and outlined the situation. There were fifty enemy guns on Island No. 10 and the nearby shore batteries. However, General Pope felt that a single gunboat, under cover of darkness, might be able to run the gauntlet and join him at New Madrid. Personally, he, Foote, didn't think it possible, and he was unwilling to order anyone to make the attempt. He would, however, appreciate it if each of them gave his professional opinion.

Foote, looking tired, leaned his crutches against the wall and eased himself into a chair. No one could question Andrew Foote's personal courage, either moral or physical, but plainly he didn't want to end his days by ordering gallant crews to almost certain death.

There was an awkward silence. Men shifted uncomfortably in their chairs, looked around, waited to see who would speak first. Then one of the senior captains spoke up. Reluctantly, he said, he had to agree fully with Foote's convictions about the failure of any such undertaking. He could understand General Pope's position, but unfortunately Pope was mistaken. The gun crews on Island No. 10 would certainly detect and smash any ironclad foolhardy enough to try running past them.

A second captain nodded his agreement. It was no use; they'd never get past the batteries.

"Suicidal!" muttered a third.

Now other voices joined in. It seemed unanimous: Running the gauntlet past Island No. 10 would cost not only a boat, but many lives as well. Only Walke had yet to speak, and now all eyes swung in his direction.

Henry Walke felt his face growing flushed; the hollowness gathered in his stomach. How could he dispute his superior officer, whom he'd known for years, and whom he admired and respected? Moreover, after Foote had stood up to the Army, risking his own reputation in the process, how would he view a challenge to his professional judgment?

Foote, of course, was normally amiable, even mild, but Walke also had seen the face of an angry Foote, one described by shipbuilder James Eads "as being most savage and demoniacal." Why not, thought Walke, take the easier way, and simply go along with the others? Why not indeed? Hadn't the men of the *Carondelet* already done more than their share?

Foote then asked Walke for his opinion. Walke, feeling self-conscious, said in a low voice that, with all respect, he *favored* the undertaking. In other words, he recommended going along with Pope's request.

Foote, startled, raised his head. In a solemn voice, he put it to Walke directly. Was Walke, then, ready to make the attempt with the *Carondelet*?

Walke said that he was. The cabin grew still. Henry Walke, holding his breath, waited for Foote's reaction. After a momentary hesitation, Foote seemed to relax, even to offer a grim smile. Rather than being annoyed, he was obviously grateful. He thanked Walke with evident sincerity, even as he was reiterating his own opinion that such an expedition had little chance of success. Frankly, he said, his conscience would not permit him to order someone onto such a perilous undertaking. By volunteering, he said, Walke had relieved him from what had been a heavy responsibility.

Walke's was a brave offer in more ways than one. Not only had his *Carondelet* already taken more than her share of casualties and Confederate gunfire, but a recent freak accident had caused still more problems, both for the boat and for crew morale. They'd been moored along the riverbank, holding a position that allowed them to protect the mortar boats, when suddenly two huge cottonwood trees had given way, crashing onto the deck, killing one man, wounding another, and causing extensive damage. Even now, crewmen were working around the clock to make repairs.

Walke was brave, but he wasn't foolhardy. All things considered, he decided his best chance, once his boat was in shape, was to make the run in silence and by the dark of the moon. There would be a new moon, early down, on April 4, which gave him five days to get ready.

On March 30, work crews began reinforcing and padding the *Carondelet*. Planks from a wrecked barge were stacked on deck to give protection from plunging shot. Surplus chains were coiled around the pilothouse, right up to the windows. A coal barge, piled high with hay and coal, was lashed to that part of the port side which lacked plating.

"I wouldn't recognize it as a warship," someone said with a laugh. "Looks to me like a farmer's wagon heading for market!"

Farmer's wagon or no, Walke was taking every precaution. Engineers attached pipes leading escape steam into the wheelhouse to avoid the puffing sound normally heard from the smokestacks. Cordwood was piled to form a barrier protecting the boilers. Physically, the *Carondelet* was ready.

But what if she were to be disabled and the Confederates tried to seize her? Walke was determined this would not be. If the worst happened, he would sink her himself rather than let her be captured. First, however, he would put up one hell of a fight.

Crewmen were armed with cutlasses and pistols, and hot-water hoses were attached to the boilers so as to scald any would-be boarders. Then Army captain Hottenstein of the 42nd Illinois, along with twenty-three sharpshooters, volunteered to come along.

Walke welcomed them aboard, saying he was delighted to have them as shipmates. While ideally he might have preferred U.S. Marines, he was more than happy to have Army substitutes.

By ten P.M. on April 4, the moon had gone down and dark clouds from a gathering thunderstorm were hiding the stars.

"Cast off!" Walke commanded.

The *Carondelet*, her muffled engines throbbing quietly, eased away from her moorings and began moving downstream. Ahead lay ten batteries of heavy guns: five on Island No. 10, five on the opposite Tennessee shore.

Both sides knew what was at stake. In effect, the Confederates were blocked in by the swamps that lay between Reelfoot Lake and the river. The road to Tiptonville was their only means of obtaining supplies, and for that matter their only possible escape route. If John Pope ever put troops across the Mississippi and cut that road, the Confederates would be in a hopeless situation.

The *Carondelet* continued to move, slowly and silently, out into the channel and past the line of mortar rafts. Just then the storm broke in full fury. Rain came down in torrents, thunder crashed and rumbled, and lightning bolts, following each other in rapid succession, flashed across the sky.

In the darkness, the pilot, steering mostly by instinct, was using the lightning flashes to correct his course. Still undetected, they passed the first low point of land. The storm intensified; the thunderclaps grew still louder, the lightning even more brilliant.

"Almost every second," wrote a correspondent, "every brace, post, and outline could be seen with startling distinctness, enshrouded by a bluish white glare of light, and then . . . [the *Carondelet*'s] form for the next minute would become merged in the intense darkness."

Rerouting the escape steam, which normally would have been keeping the stacks moist, suddenly turned out to have been a mistake. The dry soot in the chimneys caught fire; a sheet of flame roared out of the smokestack, soaring into the sky and fully illuminating the *Carondelet* for every Confederate lookout.

Crewmen worked frantically, and after a few tense minutes, the fire was extinguished. Everyone on board now realized, however, that there was no longer the slightest hope of slipping past undetected. On shore, sentries began to shout, the alarm was sounded, and soon the roar of thunder was accompanied by the crash of gunfire. In a moment of darkness, the *Carondelet* swerved to the right, almost brushing the shore.

"Hard a-port!" screamed the pilot.

By this time more and more gunners had sprung into action, but most were firing wildly. Fire in the chimneys broke out once again, with flames soaring six feet into the sky, but again it was extinguished. From the shore, they heard the cry of "Elevate! Elevate!" Several guns had been depressed to keep out the torrents of rain, and now their crews were working hastily to elevate, aim, and load.

The *Carondelet* held her course as shots plunged into the water on either side of her. It seemed an eternity, especially since the coal barge alongside kept her from moving at normal speed. Finally, and miraculously, they were clear of the island.

Up ahead, however, lay a powerful floating battery, a dreaded Confederate "war elephant" designed to block the river permanently. Men on the floating battery, well alerted by this time, took the *Carondelet* under fire and managed to get off six or eight rounds as she passed by. None was effective (although later a shot was found lodged in the coal barge, another in a bale of hay).

The little ironclad, now out of danger, steamed onward as all aboard began to realize what they had accomplished. Around midnight, they pulled up to the New Madrid landing.

"Ahoy the shore!" Henry Walke, using a speaking trumpet, proudly announced their arrival, and on the shore, soldiers in blue threw their caps in the air and cheered lustily. No longer would anyone question the Navy's audacity!

As men on board the *Carondelet* once more began to breathe easily, Paymaster Nixon approached Commander Walke with a suggestion.

In a loud, clear voice, audible to all on the bridge, the paymaster said he thought it might be appropriate, in honor of the occasion, to overlook the Navy's temperance regulations just this once. Smiling in agreement, Henry Walke gave the time-honored signal to break out the grog: "Splice the main brace for all hands!" This time, even the teetotaling Foote would have to look the other way.

Two nights later, during another storm, the *Carondelet*'s sister gunboat the *Pittsburgh*, having been shown the way, also ran the gauntlet.

Pope was quick to take advantage of the gunboat support. A day later, the *Carondelet* was in action, shelling—and silencing—the Confederate batteries near the proposed landing sites. Calmly, but with understandable pride, Commander Henry Walke of the Navy announced to General John Pope of the Army that Navy gunboats had cleared the opposite shore of the enemy and stood ready to cover the crossing of the river and the landing of the Army.

Pope crossed the river unopposed. It took but an hour to cut the Tiptonville road, and before another day had passed, he was accepting the surrender of some 7,000 Confederates and huge quantities of equipment, all without the loss of a single man.

Henry Walke said a prayer of thanksgiving on behalf of his brave crew and the Army sharpshooters who had accompanied them. Now that the trial was over, men were able to admit how frightened they had been. As for himself, Henry Walke wasn't sure. In many ways, he had been too busy during the run to think about fear. His bravest moment, he thought to himself, probably came when he set his own professional judgment against that of his commander and his fellow captains. Or perhaps it came when he "spliced the main brace" in spite of Commodore Foote's well-known teetotaling convictions.

CHAPTER 5

# Decision at Chancellorsville

Even to his friends, Thomas Jonathan Jackson was a complex, contradictory figure. They knew him primarily as a man of noble character, a pious Christian whose religious fervor was all-consuming. Conversely, they also knew him as a demanding, unforgiving disciplinarian, both as a general and as a VMI professor. In peacetime, this shy, taciturn, awkward soldier was fair game for taunting students, many of whom heartily disliked him. In wartime, however, those same students would be included among the thousands who followed him, believed in him, and came to love him.

Today, Stonewall Jackson is a legendary, almost mythical figure, not only for Southerners, but for all Americans. In 1851, however, at age twenty-seven, Brevet Major Tom Jackson was an odd-looking, unpromising ex-soldier who'd just resigned his commission to accept a faculty position at the Virginia Military Institute in Lexington.

During the Mexican War, as an ambitious lieutenant of artillery, Jackson had distinguished himself in both his tactical ability and his courage. At Chapultepec, under heavy fire, he'd managed to wrestle one gun across obstacles and into an exposed firing position. Men and horses were falling fast, but Jackson, while his men cowered in a ditch, had serviced the piece himself with the aid of a single sergeant. Ignoring the enemy cannon fire and musketry, he had held his ground, exchanging shot for shot, even when told to fall back. Finally the enemy guns were silenced and the infantry was able to advance. Later he was asked if he'd been scared. "No," he said, "the only anxiety of which I was conscious during the engagements was a fear lest I should not meet danger enough to make my conduct conspicuous."

Now, however, on August 14, 1851, his second day in Lexington, he did not want to be conspicuous. He'd arrived during the period of summer training, and during the temporary absence of Major William Gilham had been asked to serve as acting commandant. However, although the Corps of Cadets had been told of his appointment, he had not yet officially taken over.

With himself, as with others, Jackson was scrupulously honest, and he was understandably concerned about his qualifications for this new role. He had left the Army—the life he knew best and for which he'd been trained—and although VMI's atmosphere was reassuringly military, it was nevertheless part of a new, rather foreign, civilian world. Moreover, he would now be called "Professor," and as such would be expected to teach demanding scholarly subjects. Shrugging and setting aside his doubts, he decided it was time to get started.

Throughout the summer, he knew, the cadets customarily held a morning parade, and each day a fair-sized crowd would gather to watch the drill. Jackson put on his recently acquired and ill-fitting VMI instructor's uniform, donned a huge pair of oversized, worn, but well-polished boots, and walked from the barracks over to the drill field. For the moment, he wanted merely to mingle with the crowd and watch the cadets unobtrusively.

If anyone chuckled at this unfamiliar new officer, who in his loose-fitting uniform and enormous boots looked like a ragamuffin, Jackson appeared not to notice. Then, from the ranks, a young cadet voice called out: "Hey, come out of them boots, they're not allowed in this camp!"

The cadet adjutant, Tom Munford, looked to see where the remark was directed, and to his horror, recognized the new faculty member, Major Jackson. Munford rushed to Jackson and apologized for not recognizing him and for not having passed the guard in review.

Jackson ignored the murmuring buzz that seemed to be coming from the cadet formation. Quietly, he thanked Munford for the apology, then said he was just looking on, seeing how things were done. To Munford's relief, he went on to say he was happy things had happened as they did. Jackson may have been glad, but Munford was decidedly shaken.

Jackson then told Munford: "Adjutant, I am here amid new men, strange faces, other minds, companionless. I shall have to rely upon you for much assistance until I can familiarize myself with the routine duties, and the facilities for executing them." Munford never forgot those words, and from that moment forward, Tom Munford was a lifelong Jackson admirer.

In the days and months that followed, the new physics teacher, grandly titled "Professor of Natural and Experimental Philosophy," was often hard put to stay a chapter ahead of his students. Jackson, only a mediocre scholar himself, was nevertheless a persistent one. When the material was unfamiliar, he forced himself to memorize long passages, which he would then repeat to his class mechanically, much to the amusement of the brighter cadets, who delighted in asking questions to stump or embarrass him.

Not only was Jackson an uninspiring teacher but in matters of discipline he was firm and unbending; many a cadet wrote home to complain about "Old Jack." Some, however, such as Tom Munford, were learning to appreciate the honorable Jackson. Munford later wrote: "I flatter myself to have had extraordinary advantages to learn to honor & to respect and to love . . . this grand, gloomy, & peculiarly *good* man."

Whatever his feelings, everyone appreciated Jackson's complete honesty and his lack of pretense. When he didn't know something, he was quick to say so. "I have no genius for *seeming*" was the way Jackson himself put it.

No doubt about it, though, this *was* an odd character, albeit an admirable one who worked constantly at improving himself. As a cadet at West Point, he had kept a book in which he wrote maxims such as "Through life let your principal object be the discharge of duty. . . . Sacrifice your life rather than your word. . . . Resolve to perform what you ought; perform without fail what you resolve."

Part of Jackson's peculiarity stemmed from his constant health problems, which caused him to adopt a variety of odd practices, either those recommended by contemporary quack doctors or deduced on his own. When sitting, for example, Jackson stayed perfectly erect, legs straight and uncrossed, his body forming two ninety-degree angles; this, he explained, was "to keep his alimentary canal straight." Again, when his friend Dabney Maury asked why he kept raising one arm in the air with disturbing regularity, Jackson explained that "one of his legs was bigger than the other, and that one of his arms was likewise unduly heavy." He raised the arm "so that . . . the blood would run back into his body and lighten it." Jackson, Maury concluded, was truly "the most remarkable character" he had ever known.

Above all else, Jackson was a man of passionate faith. He became a Presbyterian deacon, and throughout his life he lived, breathed, and slept religion, zealously striving to learn what Christ expected of him and to act accordingly. ("Slept" is probably an apt term, since, despite his fervor, he had the embarrassing habit of falling asleep during long-winded sermons.)

The Reverend Dr. George Junkins, his future father-in-law, once asked Jackson to explain what he thought St. Paul meant by "instant in prayer." He hoped, Jackson answered, it wouldn't be thought vain if he used his own habits as an example. "I have so fixed the habit in my own mind, that I never raise a glass of water to my lips without a moment's asking of God's blessing. I never seal a letter without putting a word of prayer under the seal. I never take a letter from the post without a brief sending of my thoughts heavenward. I never change classes in the section room without a minute's petition on the cadets who go out and those who come in." Asked if he sometimes forgot to do this, he answered: "I cannot say that I do; the habit has become as fixed almost as breathing."

By 1855, Professor Jackson had become an accepted member of Lexington society. He was courteous, thoughtful, and somehow, despite his unusual personality, people found him interesting and liked having him around. At this point, however, he risked his newfound popularity on a matter of moral conviction. Despite the raised eyebrows, he ignored Virginia laws against mixed racial assemblies and started a Sunday school for Lexington blacks, slaves as well as freemen.

It was as difficult a thing as he had ever done, and it wasn't just a question of public disapproval. A major problem, at least initially, was having to conduct the classes himself. Like most shy people, Jackson found it painful to speak in public, and he was really very poor at it. Moreover, he was utterly unmusical.

Well, Jackson may have thought, it was the Lord's work, and he trusted God would give him the means, as well as the skill, to carry it off. The following Sunday afternoon, the lanky professor, looking ill at ease, even a bit comical, stood in front of his little congregation and began the lesson by leading off with a hymn. After a few painful notes of "Amazing Grace," the group joined in, mercifully drowning him out. Soon all were singing out, clapping their hands rhythmically, and praising the Lord with a joyful noise.

Each Sunday thereafter, the group continued to meet. Ever the disciplinarian, Jackson set hard rules about conduct and attendance. Before long, people who'd laughed about "Tom Fool" Jackson's missionary zeal began to admire him for it. Eventually, others began helping, until finally, with Jackson having pointed the way, the Lexington Presbytery adopted the project as its own.

As 1860 began, Jackson, like others, sensed that war clouds were gathering. In January of that year, he wrote his nephew Tom: "People who are anxious to bring on war don't know what they are bargaining for; they don't see all the horrors that must accompany such an event. For myself, I have never as yet been induced to believe that Virginia will even have to leave the Union." That same month, he wrote his aunt: "I think we have great reason for alarm, but my trust is in God; and I cannot think that He will permit the madness of men to interfere so materially with the Christian labors of this country at home and abroad."

Jackson's hopes were ill-founded. Fifteen months later, in April of 1861, as that "madness of men" plunged the nation into a war of brother against brother, Jackson was called upon to serve his native Virginia.

After bringing a group of cadets to Richmond, where they were in great demand as drill instructors, Jackson was temporarily unoccupied. At this point someone recommended him to Virginia governor John Letcher. "And who is this Major Jackson?" asked Letcher.

"He is one," Letcher was told, "who, if you order him to hold a post, will never leave it alive to be occupied by the enemy."

Convinced, Letcher commissioned Jackson to take command of Virginia's forces at Harper's Ferry. There Jackson inherited an assortment of Virginians, including several well-to-do gentlemen who were strangers to physical labor. Ignoring the social niceties, Jackson began whipping the raw, undisciplined units into shape, and soon even the sons of Virginia's "best" families were undergoing rigid drills and doing their share of menial camp chores. Even so, they, like others, were coming to appreciate their new commander. This was a man who demanded all-out effort, but who meanwhile took care of his soldiers. When Richmond failed to come through with proper supplies, or even enough food, Jackson authorized his quartermaster to go into neighboring counties and take what was needed. "Impressment," using credit to obtain supplies even over the protests of farmers and merchants, was frowned on by the Richmond authorities. Jackson, assuming personal responsibility, did whatever seemed right. Colonel Jackson was a hard man, thought Quartermaster John Harman, meanwhile noting that while Jackson unhesitatingly took whatever was needed for the war effort—food, horses, or wagons—nothing was ever impressed for the colonel's personal use.

By mid-July, men of the brigade were starting to act like soldiers. It was well they were, for Bull Run, the war's first major battle, was only days away. At Manassas Junction, Confederate general Beauregard was assembling forces and waiting to confront a Union army under Irvin McDowell.

Jackson, who'd just been promoted to brigadier general, was one of those whose troops were summoned to Manassas. Part of the journey was by train; it was the first time in history a railroad had been used to move troops to battle. Men who had never "seen the elephant" were in high spirits. They laughed, cheered, and found it all very exciting. "We had a regular picnic," remembered one soldier, "plenty to eat, lemonade to drink, and beautiful young ladies to chat with."

Once battle was joined, however, the mood changed rapidly. On July 21, 1861, McDowell and Beauregard had similar plans, each wanting to assault the other's left flank. McDowell struck first, and Southerners outposted on the left were soon driven back. A small force under General N. G. Evans held out for a time, delaying the Union advance. Beauregard, sensing trouble, sent help in the person of Barnard E. Bee, whose raw brigade did what it could to stem the tide. Before too long, however, Bee's men broke and began retreating toward Henry House Hill, named for a small frame dwelling occupied by widow Judith Henry.

Jackson, nearby, despite having received no orders, began moving his brigade in the direction of the firing. Once on Henry House Hill, he hesitated. His military instincts served him well; it would do no good to keep going into the confusion. What the South needed at this point was a solid, disciplined line. He put his brigade along the hill's military crest and told the men to get ready.

Barnard Bee came galloping up, shouting to Jackson that the enemy would soon be upon them. What would they do in that case? "Then sir," said Jackson, "we will give them the bayonet!"

Bee, trying to encourage his disorganized troops, called out, in words which soon became immortal: "Look! There stands Jackson like a stone wall! Rally behind the Virginians!"

Firing became heavy, and men in battle for the first time were feeling a dryness in their throats. Typical was Lieutenant John Lyle, who remembered: "I was scared. I said all the prayers I knew, even to 'Now I lay me down to sleep,' and threw in some shorter catechism and scripture for good measure!"

Meanwhile, said Lyle, Jackson was walking his horse slowly up and down in front of the brigade, seemingly unmindful of the bullets, saying: "All's well, all's well," and using, according to Lyle, "tones as soothing as those of a mother to a frightened child."

Jackson, ever the artilleryman, positioned his own guns, then gathered other pieces, until he had considerable firepower, enough to stem the Union advance. Beauregard, seeing what was happening, added reinforcements and ordered a general charge. Jackson's brigade fixed bayonets and joined in. The tide had turned and, on this day at least, the South was victorious.

The brigadier would no longer be Tom Jackson. From that point forward, thanks to a newspaperman who reported Bee's words, this singular man would be known forever as Stonewall. Bee, who had been killed during the fighting, had helped establish a legend.

Next day, Jackson, pleased with the results and with his own performance, wrote his wife, Anna: "Whilst great credit is due to other parts of our gallant army, God made my brigade more instrumental than any other in repulsing the main attack. This is for your information only—say nothing about it. Let others praise, not myself."

\* \* \*

Jackson was promoted to major general and given command of the Shenandoah Valley District. "The choice of the Government has fallen on you," wrote Secretary of War Judah Benjamin. "The people of that District with one voice have made constant and urgent appeals that to you, in whom they have confidence, should their defense be assigned."

Jackson set to work vigorously, launching a series of attacks that sent the enemy reeling. By late fall he controlled most of the northern district. Then, as winter set in and campaigning slowed, units were outposted in various Shenandoah towns. At this point a minor crisis arose. Men under General William Loring stationed at Romney (now in West Virginia, which was then still part of Virginia) felt that Jackson had left them in too exposed a position. Ignoring all military rules, or even proper courtesy, they petitioned the government directly to have their units withdrawn, in the process bypassing both Jackson and *his* superior, General Joe Johnston.

Jackson received a telegram from Secretary of War Benjamin. With a shock, he read: "Our news indicates that a movement is being made to cut off General Loring's command. Order him back to Winchester immediately."

To Jackson, such interference implied that he, the man on the scene, did not know what he was doing. As a good soldier, however, he first did as he was ordered and had Loring pull back. Understandably, Stonewall was outraged by this affront to both his military judgment and his honor. He wrote Governor Letcher, "The order was given without consulting me, and is abandoning to the enemy what has cost much preparation, expense, and exposure to secure, and is in direct conflict with my military plans."

If the government had so little confidence in him, there was only one decent thing to do: He submitted his resignation. While he did so unhesitatingly, the decision wasn't easy. After all, the last few months had seen him rise from obscurity to a position of high acclaim; his wife was justly proud of him, as were his Lexington friends and neighbors. Nevertheless, his code of honor left him no choice.

General Johnston, Stonewall's military boss, knew he could ill afford to lose a man such as Jackson. Johnston penned a friendly note, asking Jackson to reconsider. It wasn't that he didn't understand. "Under ordinary circumstances," Johnston wrote, "a due sense of one's own dignity, as well as care for professional character and official rights, would demand a course such as yours." But, said

Johnston, there were bigger things to consider. Remember, he too had been bypassed; hadn't Loring's men offended him just as much as they had Jackson? Johnston held up the resignation papers, hoping Stonewall would change his mind.

As word spread, dozens of letters arrived, pleading with Stonewall Jackson, the newfound hero, to reconsider. Many of the letters were from clergymen, who were especially fearful of losing a true soldier of the Lord. The clincher came in a message from Governor Letcher, who said not only that Jackson was sorely needed, but that his departure would have a depressing effect on the country.

It was difficult, even embarrassing, but Jackson knew what was right, not for himself but for Virginia. Swallowing his pride, he withdrew the resignation. The Richmond authorities then helped the situation a bit by transferring the offending Loring out of Jackson's district.

During the next few months, Stonewall Jackson put together a series of unorthodox, ingenious maneuvers. Displaying outstanding leadership, tactics, and a feel for topography, he proceeded to confound a series of Federal generals. Historians consider that, taken together, his brilliant Shenandoah Valley actions during the first half of 1862 make up one of the classic campaigns in all military history. His actions at Kernstown, Cross Keys, Port Republic, and elsewhere have long been studied as tactical masterpieces.

Consistently, he was outnumbered. Yet he proved that daring use of a small force could bring far better results than careful use of a larger one. Jackson's "foot cavalry," in long forced marches, somehow managed time and again to appear where no one expected. "Old Jack," sucking on a lemon, his mangy-looking kepi pulled low over his eyes, urged them to "Press on; press on!"

Then they would strike, against Federal forces which, though far superior in overall numbers, somehow found that Jackson had concentrated his men so as to gain a local advantage. Along the way, he seized so many Federal supplies that men gave one Union general the nickname "Commissary" Banks.

Jackson's fame continued to grow throughout the South. Jackson himself, however, was remarkably unimpressed. His young staff officer Henry Kyd Douglas later wrote: "I cannot believe that any other great man ever went down to his grave knowing so little of his fame throughout the world, or of the love his people had for him."

Jackson deliberately avoided all stories about himself. "The reason, I am sure," said Douglas, "why he gave up reading the papers was that he was so modest that their broad compliments embarrassed and annoyed him." He conducted himself, Douglas went on, only "in accordance with his own ideas of right and wrong; he acknowledged accountability to no one but God and his superior officers."

Among those recognizing Jackson's worth was Robert E. Lee. In June 1862, he wrote Stonewall: "Your recent successes have been the cause of the liveliest joy in the army as well as in the country. The admiration excited by your skill and boldness has been constantly mingled with solicitude for your situation." Later that month, at Lee's request, Jackson left the Shenandoah Valley for Richmond. There he joined Lee's Army of Northern Virginia as it faced off against George McClellan.

McClellan was finally turned back in what became known as the Seven Days. Then, in the months that followed, Union commanders— McClellan, Burnside, and others—despite their superior resources continued to be frustrated by the embattled Confederates. The world heard much of Lee and Jackson, Jackson and Lee. Always their names were linked, and together they fought valiantly, and brilliantly, at Second Manassas, Antietam, Fredericksburg, and elsewhere. Always they seemed to understand each other, to be marvelously coordinated, to be joined in an almost mystical partnership.

In a ten-month period, they fought thirteen battles, large and small. Only at South Mountain, where they were outnumbered ten to one, did they fail to hold their position at the end of the fighting, and only at one other, Antietam, where they were outnumbered three to one, did they fail to dominate the field when the guns grew silent. Meanwhile, they had captured 75,000 small arms while losing less than a tenth as many. Similarly, they had taken some 155 cannons while losing only eight.

Without exception, Jackson credited every success to the Almighty. After a September victory, for example, he wrote Lee: "Through God's blessing, Harper's Ferry and its garrison are to be surrendered."

On that occasion, numbers of curious blue-clad Union prisoners lined the road to catch a glimpse of the famous Stonewall. As he rode by, one of them was heard to say: "Boys, he's not much for looks, but if we'd had him we wouldn't have been caught in this trap." Several voices were raised in agreement.

For many months, there had been little rest for Stonewall Jackson, now a lieutenant general and a corps commander. In the spring of 1863, however, with fighting at a temporary lull, he found a few weeks of peace and happiness. Thanks in large part to Jackson's example, religious interest remained high throughout the camps. Each day at headquarters began with morning prayers, with Jackson himself often leading the devotions. "Time thus spent," he wrote to Anna, "is genuine enjoyment."

In April, three months past his thirty-ninth birthday, Jackson found accommodations in a spacious house near Fredericksburg. Joyfully, he suggested that Anna visit and bring along the baby daughter he'd not yet seen. On April 20, Anna stepped off the train at Guiney's Station. She was met by her loving husband, who, after hugging her enthusiastically, began gazing in wonder at five-month-old Julia. Nearby, soldiers broke into cheers.

For Stonewall, the next few days, sharing confidences with Anna and playing with little Julia, were sheer delight. Then, on April 29, the spell was shattered. A message from Jubal Early: Union troops under General Joe Hooker were on the move; Stonewall must start seeing to business.

Jackson arranged for Anna's safe passage to Richmond, then rode to the front. Reports were coming in: Union engineers were pushing pontoon bridges across the Rappahannock; Federal forces were massed along the river, preparing to cross. Jackson scribbled a brief note, commending Anna and little Julia to Providence, apologizing for being unable to see them off, and urging them to be on their way home.

A young captain, sent by Jackson, awoke Robert E. Lee just before daylight to say that Hooker was on the move. Lee, in good humor, said: "Captain, what do you young men mean by waking a man out of his sleep?" With a gentle smile, he went on: "Well, I thought I heard firing, and I was beginning to think it was time some of you young fellows were coming to tell me what it was all about. You want me to send a message to your good general, Captain? Tell him that I am sure he knows what to do. I will meet him at the front very soon."

Fighting Joe Hooker's forces *were* indeed on the move. The Union general now commanded more than 160,000 men, outnumbering Lee by nearly three to one. For weeks he'd been plotting ways to force Lee out of his entrenchments and into the open, where the weight of numbers could be decisive. His idea, a good one, was to fix Lee in place by threatening him from the front, then to move upriver and get behind him. "My plans are perfect," Hooker told his people, "and when I start to carry them out, may God have mercy on Bobby Lee; for I shall have none!"

Lee joined Jackson near Fredericksburg, where by this time five bridges spanned the Rappahannock and where thousands of Federals were seen preparing to cross. The aggressive Jackson was all for attacking while the enemy was still astride the river. After studying the situation, however, he realized how costly an attack would be. Lee, in turn, when the Federals to his front made no effort to advance, wisely (and correctly) concluded that Hooker's main effort would come upriver, against the Confederate left.

Swiftly, Lee and Jackson moved to counter. A skeleton force was left overlooking Fredericksburg; Jackson and the others moved northwest, in the general direction of an obscure settlement called Chancellorsville.

For Hooker, things had gone extremely well. Almost uncontested, the bulk of five Union corps had crossed the Rappahannock and were now threatening Lee's rear. "The enemy is in my power and God Almighty cannot deprive me of them!" Hooker boasted.

In contrast to Hooker's semi-blasphemy, Stonewall, on his way forward, was sounding nearly reverent as he sent cavalryman Jeb Stuart a message that was more a prayer: "I trust that God will grant us a great victory."

Up to this point, men in blue had advanced against only scattered opposition. When they encountered Confederate entrenchments, however, Hooker seemed to lose his nerve even though commanders on the scene wanted to keep going. Maybe it was the mystique of Lee and Jackson that made him hesitate. In any case, he ordered his advance force to pull back and dig in.

At twilight, Lee and Jackson met near a crossroads to discuss their next day's plans. Shots from a Union sniper, high in a tree a few hundred yards ahead, began making things uncomfortable. Not hurrying, but not wasting any time either, they withdrew to a more sheltered position, found a fallen log, and sat down side by side.

A bit later, a high-spirited Jeb Stuart, spurs jingling, plumed hat at a jaunty angle, came riding up with interesting intelligence. It seemed that his lieutenant, the dashing Fitzhugh Lee, Robert E.'s nephew, had reported the Union right flank to be "in the air"—that is, not protected by any natural or artificial barrier. If that were the case, might it be possible to take advantage of the situation?

Engineers were sent to examine the roads, also to find local guides familiar with the area. Later, a cartographer, using a hastily drawn map, traced for Jackson a possible route by which he might make a wide sweep across the Union front, ending up near that exposed right flank. Together, Lee and Jackson examined the map.

"General Jackson, what do you propose to do?" asked Lee.

"Go around here," said Stonewall, pointing to the map.

"What do you propose to make the movement with?"

The moment had come. Obviously the prudent, normal course would be to send a division or two, meanwhile holding the bulk of the army to defend against Hooker's overwhelming front line. If Jackson were to take a sizable force around the flank, he'd be leaving his commander, the beloved, gray-haired Robert E. Lee, exposed and vulnerable.

What would happen to Lee if next morning Hooker decided to resume the attack? And what if Jackson's column was detected while he was on his approach march, strung out and defenseless? Most men would have taken the more conservative approach, just as most men would have left the decision, and the responsibility, to Lee. Stonewall Jackson, however, was not most men; he was willing to assume both the risk and the responsibility—to choose the harder right. What would he take with him?

"My whole corps," he told Lee.

Lee may have been startled. However, he merely asked: "What will you leave me?"

"The divisions of [generals Richard] Anderson and [Lafayette] McLaws," said Jackson. This meant, in effect, that some 28,000 would be going with Jackson. Lee would be left with only 14,000 to face five times that many Federals. Lee, as well as Jackson, needed to summon all the moral courage at his disposal.

"Well, go on, then," said Lee.

By eight the next morning, Jackson's corps was on the march; their route, more or less covered, took them on a twisting circuit all across Hooker's front. Stonewall kept urging men to keep the column closed up and moving. "Press on . . . press on . . ."

Old Blue Light, they sometimes called him, and men seeing him this day, blue eyes flashing with the spark of battle, could well understand the term. At one point, Union observers saw the column as it passed an opening in a distant tree line. The movement was reported, but not considered significant. If anything, thought the Federal high command, such a movement must indicate that the rebels were withdrawing; perhaps it was the start of a full-scale retreat.

In mid-afternoon, Jackson, astride his favorite mount, Little Sorrel, was guided by Fitzhugh Lee to a point where he could observe that dangling Union flank. Men in blue were lounging about; rifles were stacked; cooks were at work preparing supper. As

Jackson took in the scene, Fitz Lee saw what he called "a brilliant glow" lighting Stonewall's face.

Jackson galloped back to the column and began issuing orders. Soon he came upon a familiar figure—Tom Munford, the former cadet adjutant who'd greeted him that first day at Lexington. Munford, now a colonel commanding the 2nd Virginia Cavalry, was told to take his men and secure the column's left flank. As he prepared to move out, Stonewall shouted encouragement: "The Virginia Military Institute will be heard from today!"

By five P.M., Jackson's men were in position. For the Federals, the first sign of anything unusual came when deer, rabbits, and other animals, startled by the Confederate skirmish line, came crashing out of the woods. Moments later Union pickets heard the roar of cannons, the rippling, harsh sound of musketry, and worst of all, the high-pitched, spine-tingling Rebel yell.

Stonewall Jackson was in their rear! Men in blue, surprised and frightened, began falling back. Several, abandoning their weapons, began running as fast as they could, turning retreat into panic. Within minutes, Hooker's right flank more or less melted away. Federal officers tried in vain to restore order as jumbled units lost all identity. The Confederate charge kept going, farther and farther, running over everything and everyone in its path. Screams, gunfire, shouting—all became intermingled in a chaotic triumph, the greatest victory the Confederacy had ever known.

Only as daylight faded did the attack grind to a halt. Panting men needed to rest; dazed prisoners needed to be evacuated; units needed to regroup. It was near dark when A. P. Hill told Jackson his reserve force was up and in position. Should they continue the attack? Yes—press on; press on! Cut the enemy off from the ford; make the victory complete!

Despite the hour, and the darkness, Jackson gave no thought to stopping or consolidating. This was the man who had written in his student copybook: "Resolve to perform what you ought; perform without fail what you resolve."

A guide familiar with the area said a mountain road led toward the ford. Perhaps it was a way to cut off the entire Union army. Jackson, accompanied by the guide and a few staff officers, rode forward to see for himself. Almost unnoticed, they passed beyond newly established Confederate lines. Forward they rode, halting only when they came within sound of Union soldiers chopping trees and digging in. Jackson now knew the enemy's location; in the darkness, he and his group headed back.

Along a Confederate picket line, nervous men from a North Carolina unit heard the sound of hoofbeats. Horsemen were approaching—they must be Union cavalry. Fire! Give it to them!

There was a flash of gunpowder and a roar of musketry; a deadly fusillade tore into Jackson's party. Jackson was hit three times; one bullet, entering just below his left shoulder, fractured the bone and severed the main artery. Nearby, other men and horses had fallen. Jackson, in terrible pain, was so weak he could not remove his feet from the stirrups. Willing hands disengaged him and lowered him to the ground. On this, his greatest day, Stonewall Jackson had been mortally wounded by his own men.

There was emergency treatment by a field surgeon, then transport, first on a litter, then in a jolting, horse-drawn ambulance. Through the haze of pain, Jackson heard a doctor's voice: "I hope you are not badly hurt, General."

Jackson answered truthfully; he knew no other way. "I am badly injured, Doctor. I fear I am dying."

A field hospital had been established at Wilderness Old Tavern. Surgery was performed; a ball was removed from Stonewall's right hand; his left arm was amputated just below the shoulder.

Next day a gracious note arrived from Robert E. Lee: "Could I have directed events, I should have chosen for the good of the country to be disabled in your stead. . . . I congratulate you upon the victory, which is due to your skill and energy."

Jackson nodded his appreciation, but as always he took no credit for himself. "General Lee," he said, "is very kind, but he should give the praise to God."

As Jackson lingered, Hooker managed to slip back across the Rappahannock with the bulk of his army. In Stonewall's absence, the victory, although significant, had been less than total.

The minutes, hours, and days that followed were marked by confusion, sorrow, hope, then despair. For a time, the patient seemed to improve. Anna arrived to be with him; Jackson tried to comfort her—God's will be done. Then pneumonia set in; it worsened, and the end drew near.

In his final moments, Jackson murmured: "Let us cross over the river, and rest under the shade of the trees." Whether he meant the Shenandoah, or the river Jordan, no one would ever know. Then, Thomas "Stonewall" Jackson, good soldier and good Christian, went peacefully, and no doubt joyfully, to meet his Maker.

CHAPTER 6

# Decision at Round Top

On July 2, 1863, the name of Little Round Top became indelibly etched in American history. Until that day, it had been just another hill, an obscure piece of Pennsylvania real estate near a town called Gettysburg.

In the 1990s, the 1975 Pulitzer Prize–winning novel, Michael Shaara's *The Killer Angels*, brought twentieth-century recognition to Colonel Joshua L. Chamberlain, whose 20th Maine Regiment so valiantly defended the southern slopes of Little Round Top. Today, many know about the heroic deeds of Chamberlain and his regiment on that bloody July day. Few, however, are familiar with the 140th New York Volunteers, who also defended Little Round Top, or know of their remarkable leader, the brilliant Irishman Patrick Henry "Paddy" O'Rorke. This is unfortunate, for O'Rorke is surely someone worth knowing.

Paddy O'Rorke was generally a lad of composure. Some said it was a question of years; nearing twenty-five, he was the second-oldest cadet in his class. Most people felt, however, that his poise had a far wider base than mere age. Perhaps it came from the seemingly effortless way he excelled at academics, or even from the way other men paid attention when he spoke. No doubt it also had something to do with that elusive art called leadership. In any case, Paddy O'Rorke, though modest and unassuming, was also a man of self-confidence.

Tonight, however, glancing around the Cadet Chapel and seeing his classmates' worried faces, O'Rorke felt far from composed. He shifted in his seat, watched the impeccable staff officers move to the front of the chapel, heard the adjutant say, "Please rise, gentlemen."

O'Rorke and his classmates came to attention. There was a quick clatter of benches, then a stillness. The cadets thought the chapel a strange place for military ceremony. On the other hand, the superintendent probably knew what he was doing. The setting was solemn, but so was the occasion. Someone began to cough, then stifled it as the adjutant made an announcement: each cadet would now be asked to take an oath of allegiance to the Union.

Normally, this would have been a mere formality—West Point cadets expressing their loyalty. This was April 1861, however, and a few days earlier there had been firing in Charleston harbor. The cadets knew the happenings at Fort Sumter would change their lives. For many, tonight's decision would be far from routine. Those who lived south of the Potomac would have to choose between country and state. Most would choose state.

Three months earlier, in January, one Southerner had gone to the superintendent himself to ask advice. Should a Southerner stay at the academy or should he resign? The "supe," Major P.G.T. Beauregard of Louisiana, had said: "Watch me, lad. When I jump, you jump. What's the use of leaving too soon?" At the end of January, Beauregard had "jumped." Then, in February and March, many of the cadets had followed him south.

Rumor had it that the commandant himself was about to resign, that he would be leaving before the week was out. The popular "com," rollicking Lieutenant Fitzhugh Lee, had decided, as had his illustrious uncle, that his loyalty lay to Virginia.

The cadets were seated, then as his name was called, each man rose to take the oath: Julius W. Adams . . . Joseph C. Audenreid . . . Lawrence S. Babbitt . . . Thomas C. Bradford . . . but these were all Northerners. Then William H. Browne, O'Rorke's friend Will Browne of Virginia. The young man, standing rigidly, eyes straight ahead, said he was unable to comply. He'd be leaving the Corps of Cadets and heading south, presumably to offer his services to the Confederacy.

On an impulse, someone stamped his feet in approval. A few others started to join in, but were shouted down by an angry hiss from the Northerners.

"Gentlemen! Remember you are still at attention!" The adjutant's bark restored order; the ceremony proceeded: Eugene Carter . . . Alonzo H. Cushing . . . George A. Custer.

Yellow-haired "Autie" Custer from Michigan, smiling through a mass of reddish freckles, repeated the oath cheerfully. John R. Edie . . . Leroy S. Elbert . . . Paul F. Faison.

But Paul Faison of North Carolina could take no such oath. He too would be leaving the corps.

The list continued—Farley . . . Farquar . . . Flagler . . . Fuller . . . Hains . . . Then two in a row, Jones and Logan, both Virginians, said they were resigning. Soon it would be O'Rorke's turn to declare.

For him the choice was clear. He owed much to this land, and he welcomed the chance to start repaying. In a way, that was ironic: O'Rorke, who felt so strongly about the Union, was the only cadet present who was not native born.

As his friends would have testified, O'Rorke's story was unique, and he was indeed a most improbable young man. His parents had left Ireland in 1837, when Paddy was but a year old. Tragically, both his mother and father died during the voyage to the New World. When the ship docked, the child was taken to an orphanage in upstate New York's Monroe County.

Despite his grim start, Patrick showed a talent for landing on his feet. For one thing, he was an outstanding student. By the time he was twelve, he had distinguished himself in the Rochester, New York, public school system and been encouraged to continue his education. In a day when most Irish immigrants signed their name with an "X," this was no small thing. After secondary school, there was also a chance for a scholarship, but Paddy lacked even the minimal funds it would have taken to accept such an offer. Reluctantly, he had gone to work as a laborer. Three years later, however, there was a pleasant surprise.

The local congressman had not been fortunate in his selections for the military academy. One appointee after another, each carefully chosen from the ranks of the prominent, had failed to make the grade. Frustrated, the congressman determined to find someone who *could* graduate from West Point. He offered the appointment to O'Rorke, the lad who had performed so brilliantly in the Rochester public schools, and who was just finishing his apprenticeship as a marble cutter. This time Patrick seized the opportunity with both hands. Even then, however, there was a certain apprehension.

Once he told a classmate about his concern. Sure, he had a certain flair for academics, but what of the social niceties? Could he measure up when he lacked the influence and training of a normal home life? Paddy had stayed in the background, had merely grinned when they kidded him about his Irish brogue, and had studied the way others behaved, particularly those from the more favored homes.

Apparently he was successful. He had been at the academy a year when Morris Schaff of the class of '62 described him as "spare, medium in size, with raven black hair, his face inclined to freckles, mild as a May morning, his manner and voice those of a quiet, refined gentleman." It was hardly the description of a typical stone-cutter.

Truly, there was a rare charm in this soft-spoken Irishman. Steadily he had risen to the top of the lists, yet never did he seem to be what the cadets called a grind. After two years he stood number four in the class. The next year he tied for first, and it was decided that he and his rival would draw straws to determine who was placed number one in order of academic merit. "No," said Pat, "since he was ahead of me last year, that breaks the tie in his favor." The academic board had insisted on the drawing, however, and Paddy drew the long straw, according to his clasmate Joe Farley, "amid the rejoicings of the entire Corps of Cadets."

"For reasons such as these," a classmate wrote forty years later, "Pat O'Rorke was beloved not only by members of his own class, but by all others at the Institution. . . . We had him marked as the future commander of the Army of the United States."

Now, in 1861, the roll call continued. William F. Niemeyer (another Virginian, who announced his intent to resign) . . . Henry E. Noyes . . . Patrick H. O'Rorke . . .

Paddy repeated the oath of allegiance: "I, Patrick Henry O'Rorke, do solemnly swear that I will bear true faith and allegiance to the United States of America, and that I will serve them honestly and faithfully, against all their enemies or opposers whatsoever; and that I will observe and obey the orders of the President of the United States and the orders of the officers appointed over me, according to the Rules and Articles of War."

Finally all had taken, or refused to take, the oath of allegiance. Now it was a question of waiting for graduation, for initial assignment orders, for that eagerly anticipated graduation leave. This class had an odd history, one marked by crisis and uncertainty. They had entered West Point in July of 1857, presumably for five years. In 1858 the course had been tailored to four years, in 1859 relengthened to five. With the coming of war, it was again shortened. The senior class had left after being cadets for four years and ten months. O'Rorke's class, or what remained of it after the wave of Southern resignations, had also wanted an early graduation, and had so petitioned the secretary of war. The motion was acted on promptly and the cadets were examined on their current year's studies. On May 6, they became first classmen, or seniors. O'Rorke was named Cadet First Captain, the academy's highest honor.

During the next few weeks, they had been crammed with the senior year's program—hastily organized classes in military engineering, ethics, ordnance, and gunnery. It was decided to commission them after less than two months of the first class year. Finally, on June 24, 1861, thirty-four young men, all that remained of the 108 who had entered four years earlier, received their diplomas and commissions. To no one's surprise, Patrick O'Rorke, newly commissioned in the Corps of Engineers, stood number one in graduation order of merit.

By tradition, however, the loudest cheer at graduation goes to the class "goat." Hanging on by his nails, last man out of thirty-four, was George Armstrong Custer. He acknowledged their shouts with a grin and a jaunty wave; "Autie" Custer's search for glory had begun. In two years, when he was twenty-three, he would be a brigadier general. Two years after that he would lead a cavalry division and wear a second star. His fame would spread like quicksilver, and in 1876, his death at the Little Bighorn would stun the nation.

This was 1861, however, and these things were unknown. Who could have foreseen that twenty-one of the thirty-four graduates would see action in less than a month, or that in two years the gifted O'Rorke would be called on to make one of the most crucial split-second decisions of the Civil War?

In a few hours, the new lieutenants were on a train heading south. They left New York City and rattled through New Jersey and

Delaware and into Maryland. O'Rorke wondered what the future would hold. In general he was optimistic, but he also felt a measure of anxiety and found it hard to join in the general gaiety. For one thing, he had hoped to see a special girl in Rochester during his graduation leave. Now that leave had been canceled because of the war.

His departure from West Point reminded him of the day, four years earlier, when he had left Rochester. The proud marble cutters, who could ill afford such things, had even chipped in to buy him an ornate gold watch. He still had the watch, and now had a second piece of jewelry—a West Point ring. As the train headed south, the leading graduate of June '61 twisted his ring and studied its design. It was cut in sardonyx, from black to white. The crest showed an arm with sword in hand, interposed between the guns of a fort and the flag they were firing on. It seemed oddly prophetic, as did the motto "Per Angusta Ad Augusta," which meant, roughly, "To Honor Through Anguish." Among the class, however, the private joke was that their motto should be "Promotions or Coffins." This, too, had a rather chilling accuracy. After the next four years, one of every five of them would have become a general. Also, one of every five would be dead.

Their train passed through Baltimore; O'Rorke studied the other passengers. Some were businessmen heading for Washington, eager to be among the first to secure wartime government contracts. Here and there were families with a few women and children, but on the whole the passengers were masculine. Many were uniformed, as were O'Rorke and his classmates, in their new blue coats with the gold-bordered epaulets. They felt a bit conspicuous, but at least they knew how uniforms should be worn. This was hardly the case with some of their fellow passengers. Militia regiments were forming rapidly, and would-be colonels were competing for volunteers. Each felt free to modify his own regiment's uniform, and most felt that a colorful design would attract more recruits. Consequently the new soldiers wore a startling array of sashes, plumes, and colors. Now that they were actually under way, and had left behind the hometown ladies and their worshipful glances, some of the volunteers were feeling rather self-conscious. Others, however, particularly those convinced the rebellion would never come to serious fighting, were continuing to strut and pose.

O'Rorke noticed other men of military age who were not in uniform. Some, he suspected, were going south to join the Confederacy. Although a state of war technically existed, it was still relatively easy to cross over and find a Confederate recruiter. Some of the bolder recruiters, in fact, were operating in the very heart of Northern cities. They signed men up, gave them a small bonus, then told them to take the next train heading south.

This reminded O'Rorke of a comical incident concerning the class just ahead of his own. Back in May, the original class of '61 had headed for Washington on this same train, proudly responding to instructions sending them to the capital to learn their initial assignments. As they passed through New Jersey, however, someone started a rumor that they were really Union deserters of Southern sympathy, en route to join the Confederacy. The mayor of Jersey City had wired ahead. At Washington they were met by a forceful provost marshal and marched to jail. The elegant lieutenants were deflated rapidly. Their swords and revolvers were taken away; they themselves were shoved unceremoniously into cells. There they had stayed, until some time later Mayor Henry of Washington arrived, interviewed them, and became convinced of their identity. (In a happy ending, the class finally spent the night at the Continental Hotel, at the city's expense.)

O'Rorke and the others chuckled again over the reception afforded the lads of May '61. However, as their train neared Washington, they exchanged half-smiles and wondered if the same mistake could be repeated.

This time there was no slip-up. They were met at the depot by their special escort, a strapping lieutenant of artillery, who brought them directly to the offices of Winfield Scott, general-in-chief of all the Union forces. Scott greeted them cordially, then explained that they would be used at first to drill the new ninety-day regiments camped in the area.

There was a knock on the door and a whispered message from an aide. Scott, standing up, explained they had a visitor who had walked over from his office just for the pleasure of meeting them.

The door opened again. A tall, gaunt figure entered; Scott said, "Good evening, Mr. President."

Abraham Lincoln shook each man's hand, added his own words of welcome, then spoke briefly but sincerely of the importance of the coming struggle. It was a moment to remember, especially for O'Rorke. The lad from the orphanage had come a long way.

They stopped next at the office of the general commanding the defenses of Washington, who routed them to their respective training regiments. For the next three weeks, Lieutenant O'Rorke barked commands to sweating recruits in nearby Alexandria. Then he was told to report as special aide to General Daniel Tyler, commander of a division of Connecticut militia. A Confederate army was moving northward, and on July 20, less than a month after graduation, O'Rorke and twenty of his classmates were under fire at Bull Run. Leading the Confederates was General P.G.T. Beauregard, who had been their "supe" only six months earlier.

During the day, O'Rorke himself was unharmed, though a horse was shot from under him. In his report of the battle, Tyler praised Paddy's "prompt and gallant assistance," even mentioning some valuable reports sent from Paddy's "observatory" at the top of a tall pine tree. Acting as aide, courier, and tree climber, the new lieutenant had distinguished himself.

When the smoke from Bull Run had cleared, O'Rorke was given his first engineer troop assignment. Late in 1861, his unit joined an expeditionary corps on the Georgia coast. At the time, the Confederates had abandoned all coastal towns south of Charleston except Savannah. The latter town was defended by Fort Pulaski at the mouth of the Savannah River.

Soon O'Rorke, having gained the attention of the expedition's chief engineer, General Quincy Gillmore, was sent on a daring river reconnaissance. O'Rorke, one other officer, and a handful of volunteers started out just before dark. Their mission was to find locations suitable for gun positions. Wallowing through the marshland in the darkness must have been a wretched experience, yet O'Rorke's report was matter-of-fact, thorough, and remarkable for having been written by a green lieutenant with less than seven months' service.

Two weeks later, Gillmore, who continued to be impressed by O'Rorke, chose him for an even more vital night mission. This time the operation involved Venus Point, a marshland close to Fort Pulaski itself. So far no one had been able to find a way to position artillery in its soggy ooze.

On the night of February 20, Paddy and a group of engineers waded ashore. Then, with mud sucking at their boots, they worked silently and skillfully. First, O'Rorke outlined an area nine feet by seventeen feet in a spot generally level. The men dumped sand, spread it about, and managed to raise the level of the ground some five or six inches. On the sand foundation they laid thick planks, parallel to the direction of fire and not quite touching each other. They listened carefully; apparently they were still undetected.

Next came the deck planks, laid at right angles to the first ones. By this time they had a firing platform some eighteen inches above the ground's natural surface. They passed the word to the artillerymen, then started work on other platforms and a magazine. Lieutenant Horace Porter of the class of 1860 came with his men to push guns into position. With Paddy and his weary squad lending a hand, they struggled in the darkness, muddy, sweaty, and exhausted. It had been a weird construction project, but finally it was done.

At first light, the battery announced its presence to the startled defenders of Fort Pulaski. In honor of O'Rorke's efforts, Porter's artillerymen had him pull the lanyard to fire the first shot. The fort, whose masonry walls were no match for rifled cannon, surrendered a few days later. The Savannah River was open to the Union.

In May, the steamer *Mayflower* chugged up that river, stopping about three miles short of Savannah itself. A strange contraption was unloaded. Directing the operation was a civilian, pioneer balloonist John B. Starkweather. Some said he was a crackpot, but Starkweather insisted his "gas bag" had real military value. Now he was going to prove it.

Starkweather had been up before, of course, but no one had paid much attention to his observations. This time it would be different. He had found a professional soldier, Lieutenant O'Rorke of the engineers, who was willing to accompany him aloft.

Up they went, quite likely making Patrick O'Rorke the first American military man to "fly in combat." At any rate, the flight was a success, and early chronicles of aeronautics report it with gusto. Not only did Starkweather and O'Rorke get up and down safely but in the process they located four or five companies of previously undetected Confederates.

Paddy O'Rorke was becoming something of a legend. People spoke of his intelligence, his coolness under pressure, his judgment. In mid-1862, the day of his biggest decision was still a year away, but already the factors that would influence that decision were taking form.

In September of 1862, Paddy went home to Rochester. Probably this was the happiest month of his life, because at last he was able to claim as his bride the Rochester girl he had loved since boyhood. Her name was Clara Bishop; now it became Clara Bishop O'Rorke. Their honeymoon, however, was all too brief.

Although O'Rorke was just turning twenty-six his proud neighbors in Monroe County had no hesitation in asking him to take command of the local regiment they were forming. He accepted, and it was so ordered. The Monroe County regiment, officially designated the 140th New York Volunteers, resplendent in new red-

and-blue Zouave uniforms, marched to the station behind newly appointed Colonel Patrick O'Rorke. No doubt many of those who had known him as an apprentice marble cutter were puffing a bit and saying "We told you so!"

First stop was Washington. The regiment was assigned to the XII Corps; on the heights of Arlington, O'Rorke began to train them in earnest.

In December, arrangements were made to have the 140th New York assigned to a brigade in V Corps. The assignment was no accident. Brigade commander was the brilliant Gouverneur K. Warren, who had been assistant professor of mathematics at West Point while O'Rorke was a cadet. Obviously there was a bond between the two. Both men were topographical engineers; both had excelled scholastically. Warren, the number two man in the class of 1850, had fought to secure for his brigade the regiment led by the number one man of 1861.

The relationship was a good one. Through the winter and spring, the 140th did its work well. At Fredericksburg, it fortified positions in the town proper, and counted itself lucky to have been spared the bloody slaughter of Marye's Heights. O'Rorke was praised and brevetted for his conduct during the battle.

Warren, with a record of success, was promoted and pulled upstairs to become chief engineer for the Army of the Potomac. He suggested the colonel of the 140th as his successor, and O'Rorke was given command of the brigade.

Many watched the young colonel skeptically. He was now in a position qualifying him for promotion to brigadier general. Would he show he deserved his position or, without the support of Warren, would he be found wanting?

The test came quickly. In later days, Yankees liked to forget the name of Chancellorsville, where Fighting Joe Hooker, outgeneraled by the maneuvers of Lee and Jackson, had been beaten soundly. Toward sundown of May 1, however, near the close of the first day's fighting, O'Rorke gave the North one of its few bright moments.

On the Union left, II Corps was pulling back. The movement left O'Rorke's brigade uncovered. As the last division of II Corps passed, the division commander, no less a person than the distinguished Winfield Scott Hancock, sent word to O'Rorke that he'd better get his command onto the road and tag along behind.

It was a rough decision. Does one expose green troops to the enemy after an experienced senior officer has recommended withdrawal? Colonel Winslow, who had carried the message from Hancock, looked at O'Rorke expectantly, and no doubt shook his head when the younger man explained that since he had no orders from his own division, he guessed he'd hold his ground.

O'Rorke deployed his brigade in line of battle. Before the movement was even finished, someone gave a shout and pointed. To their front, Union pickets were seen scattering. On their heels was a line of Rebel infantry with fixed bayonets.

The gray line moved forward. Yankee soldiers, watching with fascination, found that their throats had suddenly gone dry. Rays from the setting sun gave the bayonets a ruddy glow. The Confederates dressed their line, continuing to shoot and to advance. O'Rorke moved laterally among his men, telling them to hold their fire until he gave the word.

The Southerners had appeared from behind a ridge. Now they were moving down a gentle slope toward O'Rorke's brigade. Behind them, a second wave of gray figures had appeared. Each line appeared to be a regimental front. Union men swallowed hard. "Commence firing!" yelled O'Rorke, and regimental commanders relayed his command.

The Federal fire was rapid and effective. Frantically, awkward fingers worked to reload and fire again. Although the Southerners had shot first, O'Rorke later sounded almost apologetic as he explained having his men fire while the enemy was at extreme range. "As the 140th and 146th N.Y. Vols. were under fire for the first time," he wrote in his report, "I thought it prudent to commence fire before the enemy got very close."

"Prudent" was an apt word for it—and the firing paid off. The Confederate line fell back, at first slowly, then with a scramble. O'Rorke's brigade was not attacked again, and in fact saw little action during the rest of the Chancellorsville battle. Their division commander told them they had "handsomely repulsed" the enemy advance, and O'Rorke's name figured prominently in the dispatches.

On the whole, however, Chancellorsville was a Union disaster. On May 5, the Army of the Potomac retreated through the mud of northern Virginia, back to its original bivouac at Falmouth, Virginia. Joe Hooker had lost 17,000 men and been defeated by an army half the size of his own. O'Rorke's brigade, part of the rear guard, felt disgruntled and confused. They had fought well, had beaten off the only Confederates they had seen, yet were now securing the tail of a defeated army.

Back in camp, the Army of the Potomac licked its wounds. Most men blamed Joe Hooker for the defeat. Deep down, he probably blamed himself. Once, years later, in a rare flash of insight and humility, he told a man who asked what went wrong at Chancellorsville: "Well, to tell the truth, I just lost confidence in Joe Hooker."

However, Hooker's engineer Warren felt that the disaster was more the fault of the corps commanders, and he said so rather openly. Warren was a man of controversy. He was undoubtedly brilliant; all could recognize that. He was also a man who could inspire fierce loyalty, both from above and from below. At the same time, he tended to be impatient with those whose minds moved more slowly than his own. No doubt this explained his respect for the quick-witted O'Rorke. It also explained his choice of engineer aides. One was Ranald Mackenzie, top graduate in the West Point class of 1862. Another was a young graduate of Rensselaer Polytechnic Institute named Washington Roebling, who'd one day go down in history as an architect of the innovative Brooklyn Bridge.

But Warren, for all his virtues, was also flawed. He could be opinionated and tactless; many thought him overambitious. Obviously he was a rising star in the Army of the Potomac, but just as obviously, he was a man whom others might resent.

Perhaps some of the resentment toward Warren rubbed off on O'Rorke. Even at the time, it would have been hard to say for sure. O'Rorke, in any event, although he had been brevetted and commended after both Fredericksburg and Chancellorsville, now found a strange reversal in his surging career. Captain Stephen H. Weed, former commander of the V Corps artillery, and another who had performed ably at Chancellorsville, was suddenly promoted to brigadier general and given command of O'Rorke's brigade. O'Rorke was returned to command of the 140th New York Volunteers, who by this time were calling themselves the "Rochester Race Horses."

Paddy took the demotion without murmuring. After all, he liked and respected Steve Weed, and the latter (West Point '54) clearly was his senior in the regular army. Nevertheless, he wondered what would come next. Warren, his friend and fellow engineer, was far removed on the staff of the army commander. Meade, his corps commander and another engineer, might also be moving up. Some said he was the logical successor to Hooker as army commander.

Near the end of June, it happened. A messenger from Washington arrived in the middle of the night. Meade was awakened and told to relieve Hooker and take command of the army. One of his first thoughts was to replace Hooker's chief of staff, a man whom he doubted, with Warren, whom he knew and trusted. Warren, by this time a thirty-two-year-old major general, was riding high. The army was on the move, however, and Warren protested that this was no time to change both commander *and* chief of staff. Meade yielded.

Two weeks earlier, in mid-June, Robert E. Lee had made his boldest and most threatening move. He had invaded the North—had pushed through Maryland, and was now into Pennsylvania. The Army of the Potomac was in pursuit, and by May 27, Meade's entire army was in Maryland. (The former commandant of cadets, Confederate cavalry general Fitzhugh Lee, was among those trying to learn its exact location.)

O'Rorke led his Rochester Race Horses, who were getting a chance to earn their name, on one hard day's march after another. The roads were hot and dusty. Moving north, however, where the people were friendlier and the fields seemed greener, they found their spirits rising. O'Rorke thought about the further changes caused by Meade's elevation. General George Sykes, formerly his division commander, had replaced Meade at V Corps. Romeyn Ayres had moved from a neighboring brigade to take over from Sykes at division. Was it mere coincidence, O'Rorke wondered, that now his three superiors in the chain of command—Weed, Ayres, and Sykes—were all former artillerymen? And was it his imagination that Ayres and Sykes were treating him with a certain coolness? In any case, he'd best watch his step.

On the first of July, Meade learned that advance elements of his I Corps had met the Confederates, almost by accident, near a Pennsylvania crossroads town called Gettysburg.

Meade hurried other troops forward. Neither he nor Lee would have chosen this site, but whether they liked it or not, the opening volleys were sounding for the mightiest battle ever to be fought in North America.

O'Rorke's regiment was one of those rushing forward. They marched all day—from Union Mills, Maryland, on into Pennsylvania. At twilight, when they thought their day's march was over, new orders had come. Under a full moon, they marched thirteen more miles. At one A.M. they halted. Some tried to sleep, but at four A.M they were roused and marched three more miles.

By the morning of July 2, Meade had deployed his army on the high ground south of Gettysburg. On the right, the XII Corps bent back at Culp's Hill, forming the famous "fishhook." Next, from right to left, the XI, I, II, and III corps stretched along Cemetery Ridge. The line angled south toward Round Top and Little Round Top, the two hills where the Army of the Potomac would anchor its left flank. Or would it?

On the left, General Daniel Sickles had marched his III Corps forward to what he considered better ground. In the process, he had given up the ridge line and was nowhere near the Round Tops. Lee sent Longstreet moving toward the dangling left flank. The envelopment didn't get all the way around. Instead, it caught on the sharp edge of Sickles's line. The Peach Orchard and the Wheat Field, pleasant patches of sleepy farmland, would soon become famous, bloody names in American history. Meade committed his reserve, sending word to crusty George Sykes to use his V Corps to support the crumbling left flank.

Back in the V Corps assembly area, O'Rorke and his men were finding the all-night march to have been a case of "hurry up and wait." All morning they had dashed from place to place, generally at quick time. Now, still having seen no action, they were ready to call it a day.

As the regiment rested on its arms in an open field, a rider arrived with a message for Colonel O'Rorke. It was a copy of the General Order written by Meade when he took command of the army. O'Rorke mounted a stump and read it to his regiment. All were called on to do their utmost to repel the invader; all were urged to fight "desperately and bravely." By now, however, these were troops rather unimpressed with rhetoric. Moreover, they smiled at their colonel's discomfiture. O'Rorke obviously took no pleasure in the role of stump orator. Loyally, however, he read the entire message, including the awkward final passage stating that commanders had the authority to order the instant death of any soldier who failed to do his duty in the face of the enemy.

As this was going on, Meade was becoming concerned about his exposed left flank. Warren, with Meade's approval, galloped off in that direction to see what he could learn. As a staff officer, Warren was technically only the commander's engineer advisor. Within the next few minutes, however, he would be full into one of the war's most dramatic combat missions.

Warren guided his horse toward Little Round Top. Unless he was mistaken, that was the critical piece of terrain in the area. Moreover, if the Confederates planned to strike the Union left, they would probably be massing in those woods to the west, on the other side of the Emmitsburg road.

Warren found a battery of rifled artillery and asked them to fire a round into the line of woods. The trees concealed John B. Hood's Texans. As the shot winged past, a thousand heads turned to follow the sound. The quick turning in unison, and the accompanying motion of guns and bayonets, made the woods ripple and come alive for an instant.

Warren had his answer: The attack was coming on the left. He sent young Ranald Mackenzie to ask that reinforcements be sent to Little Round Top. Then he pushed up the hill to get a better look. At the top, he found only a signal detachment. The Union's sole armament on the crest of Little Round Top was a pair of semaphore flags.

Just then the attack started on Sickles's men at the Peach Orchard. Time passed, and no reinforcements had reached Warren at the summit. He was beginning to feel rather naked. Musket balls began to fly past, and the signal team understandably decided it was high time they were folding their flags.

Warren asked them to stay, to keep waving their flags even if they had no further messages. The flags stayed and, as Warren put it, the signal officer kept waving them "in defiance."

By this time, as a result of Mackenzie's mission, troops had arrived on the lower slopes of Little Round Top, well to the left of Warren. A brigade under Colonel Strong Vincent, including Chamberlain's 20th Maine, was already locked in furious combat with hard-fighting men from Alabama. After much bloody work, including a desperate bayonet charge by the 20th Maine, the crisis there was temporarily averted.

Now, however, a new crisis was at hand. Other men in butternut began to appear, coming from a wild rock formation called Devil's Den. Lean Southern troops, emitting the spine-tingling Rebel yell and storming Little Round Top from a new direction, were smelling victory and coming on fast. If they could seize the crest, they could roll up the whole Union line on Cemetery Ridge and the battle would be theirs.

Warren, along with his aide Washington Roebling, pounded back down the hill, looking for help. Near the base of Little Round Top, he spotted a regiment moving toward the Peach Orchard. Could he divert them in time to beat the rebels to the crest? He might, if the commander would take an order from a mere staff officer.

It was a coincidence such as can happen in real life, but which no author would dare use in a work of fiction. The Union had more than 150 regiments at Gettysburg that day. Warren was galloping hard to meet one of them, and by chance, it was a unit from his old brigade. Coming along the Peach Orchard road was the 140th New York, and riding at its head was Patrick O'Rorke.

Warren began shouting while he was still fifty yards away, telling O'Rorke to take his men up Little Round Top. O'Rorke protested, saying General Weed was expecting him up ahead.

"Never mind that," said Warren. "Bring them up on the double-quick, Paddy! Don't even stop for aligning. I'll take the responsibility."

Both he and O'Rorke knew that was impossible. As a staff officer, Warren had no authority to divert troops from an assigned mission. Only their commander could do that—but there was no time to find the commander.

This was Paddy O'Rorke's moment of truth. No one could criticize him if he stuck to the orders of his brigade and division commanders. Moreover, if he failed to follow those orders, he might well find himself standing tall before a court-martial.

What if the absence of the 140th New York Volunteers led to a disaster in the V Corps sector? Ayres and Sykes would hardly be satisfied with a reply that he had gone off on the urging of his fellow engineer Warren. These were the men who had just dropped him back from brigade to regimental commander. Obviously they would look critically at any tampering with their authority.

On the other hand, O'Rorke trusted Warren's judgment. If Warren said this hill was critical, he knew it must be so. Some men are given months or even years to make a fateful decision. Patrick O'Rorke had about five seconds.

A century later, a leadership text would say: "The leader must be willing to accept responsibility and make decisions."

"Follow me," said O'Rorke, heading straight up the slope of Little Round Top. Roebling accompanied him as a guide, while Warren galloped off to seek more reinforcements.

Down the Peach Orchard road came a battery of six 3-inch rifles, led by Lieutenant Charles Hazlett, West Point '60. Warren urged them to head for Little Round Top. Hazlett agreed, adding with a grin that he might not be able to do much good with his guns, but that having them along would at least give the infantry some added confidence. Warren, followed by Hazlett's battery, hurried back up the hill. Years later, men of the 140th remembered the frantic race up Little Round Top. Wild-eyed horses from Hazlett's battery came breaking through the infantry as the gunners lashed them upward.

The ground became too rough for riding. O'Rorke jumped down from his horse and tossed the reins to his sergeant major. At his side was Captain Porter Farley, who described the scene later:

> As we reached the crest, a never-to-be-forgotten scene burst upon us. A great basin lay before us full of smoke and fire and literally swarming with riderless horses and fighting, fleeing and pursuing men. The air was saturated with the sulphurous fumes of battle and was ringing with the shouts and groans of the combatants. The wild cries of charging lines, the rattle of musketry, the booming of artillery, and the shrieks of the wounded were the orchestral accompaniments of a scene very much like hell itself—as terrific as the warring of Milton's fiends in pandemonium. The whole of Sickles' corps and many other troops that had been sent to its support in that ill chosen hollow were being slaughtered and driven before the impetuous advance of Longstreet. But, fascinating as was this terrible scene, we had no time to spend upon it. Bloody work was ready for us at our very feet.

The Confederates were just below the crest and coming straight for the top. There was no time to execute the maneuver that would put the regiment into proper line of battle. Nor was there time to load the muskets or even to fix bayonets. If the 140th hesitated at all, the enemy would be on them and pushing them from the crest.

Paddy didn't hesitate. He drew his saber and flashed it in the sunlight. As he gave the order to charge, only the thickness of his brogue showed that he was a little more excited than usual. He rushed straight at the enemy, the men of his regiment along with him.

It was as bizarre a counterattack as the war ever saw. The initiative was seized without bayonets or loaded muskets, merely by the force of running bodies. The Southerners paused, and the men of New York dropped into line, taking cover as well as they could among the rocks and brush. Now they began to load and to fire. The Confederate charge broke. The Texans fell back, leaving behind some riddled bodies. Others, too intermingled to withdraw, threw up their hands and surrendered.

The Southerners re-formed and charged again. From above, the guns of Hazlett's battery roared. At one point the firing was so intense that, in one of the battery's crews, three cannoneers in succession were killed before a fourth could discharge the piece. Nearby, Warren, talking to Hazlett, was grazed by a musket ball.

O'Rorke moved from place to place, disdaining the partial cover offered by the boulders. As the second charge was beaten back, a bullet caught him in the neck. Paddy O'Rorke dropped instantly, dead without a word.

The fighting continued, but the Rebel charge had reached its crest. By this time, the rest of Stephen Weed's brigade had arrived and gone into line. Weed himself, standing near Hazlett's battery, fell with a mortal wound. He gasped something that sounded like "my sister." Hazlett bent to catch his words—and just then he, too, was hit. He fell dead across Weed's body.

At last, however, the fighting slackened. Men in ragged gray staggered back into the valley. The peak stayed in Union hands. Gettysburg continued twenty-four more hours; the war lasted nearly two more years. From Devil's Den and Little Round Top, however, all roads led to Appomattox.

Meade, the Gettysburg victor, later said: "But for the timely advance of the 5th Corps and the prompt sending of a portion on Round Top, where they met the enemy almost on the crest and had a desperate fight to secure the position . . . the enemy would have secured Round Top, planted his artillery there, commanding the whole battlefield and what the result would have been I leave you to judge."

In his classic work *American Campaigns*, historian Matthew Steele wrote: "One can almost show that every defeat of the Civil War happened because someone was slow; somebody stopped to rest, or lost his way, or marched too slowly, or waited for somebody to join, or waited to get his orders."

Steele might have mentioned the corollary: We needed then, and shall always need, leaders who are not afraid to make decisions—leaders who will obey orders, but who are still willing to exceed those orders when the situation demands it. Men like Patrick O'Rorke.

In 1889, men of the 140th New York Volunteers climbed Little Round Top again. They met to dedicate a monument that still stands, a stone with a likeness of O'Rorke and the words

Col. Patrick H. O'Rorke
Killed July 2, 1863
FRATERNITY

The words of that generation seem flowery by our standards, but their sincerity shines through. His comrades sang his praises, and O'Rorke would probably have been embarrassed if he had heard the speaker that day as he referred to "the grace of form and carriage, the modesty, the purity and honesty of character, the amiable temper, the intellectual force, the commanding influence over others, the knightly accomplishments of his profession, and above all, the proven courage of Col. Patrick O'Rorke, who here died at the head of his regiment. . . . He was a very perfect, gentle knight."

Warren's tribute to Paddy was simpler: "He was glorious."

CHAPTER 7

# Decision at Abbeville

**B**y 1917, after three years of bloody trench warfare, France and England had nearly exhausted their manpower reserves. To the east, the once-potent Russian army was literally coming apart, succumbing as much to the revolutionary chaos at home as to the pounding of the Germans. The Allies watched in horror, realizing it was only a question of time until the massive German war machine was recombined and concentrated on the Western Front. Once that happened, the Germans seemed well capable of achieving a breakthrough, capturing Paris, splitting the Allied armies, and dictating a peace treaty on their own terms.

To the French and English, the Americans seemed to provide the only hope, and at this point it was a hope for mere survival rather than for all-out victory. They cheered as the United States declared war on April 6, cheered even louder as Woodrow Wilson, who'd once said Americans were "too proud to fight," now proclaimed the nation a full-fledged partner in a war to "make the world safe for democracy."

The Allies were understandably impatient. There were no American divisions ready for combat, and even if there had been, the United States had no means of transporting units to France or of providing logistic support once they arrived. The American Army had a mere 200,000 men, half as many as the British had lost in the 1916 battle of the Somme, or the French at Verdun. The United States had no tanks, its fifty or so planes were nearly obsolete, and its heavy guns had ammunition enough for only a nine-hour bombardment.

Meanwhile, the Western Front was a ditch running with blood, and after three costly years, the Allied manpower situation had become critical. Let the Americans come over as raw troops, said the Allies. The French and English could integrate them into their own armies, and were more than capable of providing all the leadership and training they might require.

On February 1, 1917, Germany had declared unrestricted submarine warfare and so brought the United States one step closer to war. Later that same month, on February 19, a young staff officer, telegram in hand, was faced with an unpleasant task. He had to tell Secretary of War Newton Baker and President Woodrow Wilson that General Frederick Funston, one of the nation's finest officers and a potential Army commander, was dead of a sudden heart attack.

The officer, then-Major Douglas MacArthur, never forgot their reaction: "Had the Voice of Doom spoken, the result could not have been different. The silence seemed almost like that of death."

Wilson asked Baker who would take Funston's place if the United States went to war. Baker turned to MacArthur. "Whom do you think the Army would choose, Major?"

"I cannot, of course, speak for the Army," answered MacArthur, "but my own choice would be without question General Pershing."

Wilson, who'd soon be faced with that decision, looked at MacArthur long and hard. Then he said softly: "It would be a good choice."

John Joseph Pershing, however, was but one—and the junior one, at that—of six two-star generals. Of the others, the most obvious candidate for the job was the popular Leonard Wood, not only younger than Pershing but several years senior to him in grade. The four other major generals on the active list, all in their sixties and nearing compulsory retirement, were probably out of contention.

On April 6, when Congress finally declared war, most observers agreed that the choice lay between Wood and Pershing. Both were good men, of course, but somehow Wilson felt unsure about Wood. This was a man who'd naturally take orders, as would any career soldier, but who might also be inclined to exceed those orders. Also—and this was something Wilson couldn't overlook—Wood had on occasion not only criticized administration policies, but had done so publicly.

Pershing, on the other hand, was one whose loyalty and discretion were never in doubt. Even when he was leading the Mexican Punitive Expedition and often felt frustrated by Wilson's policies, no word of public complaint had ever been voiced. For example, when given the order to pull out of Mexico, an order with which he violently disagreed, he'd said nothing to his staff, had merely paced around his tent and the surrounding bivouac for much of the night, then next morning given the order to withdraw without any complaint or explanation to anybody concerned. Wilson appreciated that.

Pershing, who wanted the expeditionary force appointment with all his heart, waited anxiously. The first inkling of success was a telegram from his father-in-law, the influential senator Francis Warren: "Wire me today whether and how much you speak, read and write French."

John Pershing might be the soul of honesty, but in this case he fudged a bit. Although his French was indifferent at best, he wired back: "Spent several months in France 1908 studying language. Spoke quite fluently; could read and write very well at that time. Can easily reacquire satisfactory working knowledge."

Next came a telegram from Army Chief of Staff Hugh Scott, directing Pershing to select four regiments of infantry and one of artillery for possible service abroad. "If plans are carried out," Scott added, "you will be in command of the entire force."

That made sense. The Army's current table of organization called for a division that size. Sadly enough, though, no such unit even existed. Pershing designated the 16th, 18th, 26th and 28th regiments, together with the 6th Field Artillery, as the nucleus of the 1st Division, "the Big Red One."

Pershing was summoned to Washington, and on May 10 he was ordered to take his provisional force to France as soon as he judged it ready. Two days later, however, Secretary of War Baker told him his orders had been changed. He would not be commanding that newly formed division. Instead, he would be going overseas at once as commander-in-chief of *all* American forces in Europe. He would learn more that afternoon, when he and Baker went to meet the President.

Pershing was curious—why had *he* been selected? It surely hadn't been for his personality. Even those who knew him best, such as General Robert Bullard, a West Point contemporary who was to be one of his key commanders in France, said Pershing lacked personal magnetism; troops might feel confidence and respect, but never affection. Others used words such as "cold," "humorless," and "dispassionate"—hardly terms of endearment—to describe him.

It hadn't always been like that, of course. As a cadet at West Point, even though he'd been something of a loner, Pershing had been elected class president four straight years, and upon graduation, when the gang had gotten together at Delmonico's to celebrate, they'd insisted he remain their class president. He'd even known how to let his hair down—like that time at Pine Ridge, South Dakota, after one of the Indian campaigns, when he'd had a mini-reunion with eight of his classmates and where liquor flowed freely. Years later, in his autobiography, he described the celebration with self-deprecating humor: "It would have been more pleasant, had two or three or four of the boys not gotten a little too full, one of whom I am which."

Later, too, when he was assigned to the University of Nebraska, there'd been a real rapport between him and the cadets, especially those on the crack drill team they called the Pershing Rifles in his honor. George Sheldon, a future Nebraska governor who was captain of that team, said later: "We all tried to walk like Pershing, talk like Pershing, and look like Pershing. . . . His personality and strength of character dominated us. We loved him devotedly."

He knew he'd changed, though, along the way, and he guessed it wasn't all for the best. He was a stern, aloof disciplinarian, a strict enforcer of rules and regulations, a man who demanded full, instant obedience. Men might respect him—he hoped they did—but he knew very few really liked him. Maybe, if his wife were still alive, she would have made him ease up a bit. . . .

Once again he relived the horror, recalling the moment he'd learned his Presidio home had gone up in flames, killing his beloved Frances and three of their four children. "My God. My God. Can it be true?" he'd cried out as his whole life came crashing down. After that, what mattered promotion, glory, or ambition? All that remained was work and duty—duty to his country, to his President, and now, above all, to the men he'd be leading.

John J. "Black Jack" Pershing had traveled a long way since his boyhood days in Laclede, Missouri. As a junior officer, he had fought on the American frontier and in Cuba, had taught at West Point and the University of Nebraska, had served in Asia as an attaché and military observer. Later, as a general, he had won distinction as a field commander, both in the Philippines and in Mexico. Now, at age fifty-six, he was about to meet the President of the United States.

Newton D. Baker, small and timid-looking, Wilson's unlikely choice for secretary of war, sat with one leg under his body, the other barely reaching the floor. Methodically, he explained the abrupt change, whereby Pershing would be going overseas as overall American commander rather than the leader of a single division. Baker, a former student of Wilson's at Johns Hopkins, a man of strong character and brilliant mind who'd turn out to be one of America's better secretaries of war, spelled out the current situation. For political purposes, as well as for morale, it had become necessary to establish an American presence overseas, and soon.

Pershing's role was being expanded, said Baker, mainly as a reaction to the Allied military missions now in Washington—a French group headed by Marshal Joffre, and a British team led by Arthur Balfour, Lloyd George's foreign secretary.

According to Baker, the missions were mostly interested in financial help. This was understandable; both of their countries were very near bankruptcy. The French were spending $133 million a month on armaments alone; the British even more. As for military help, the mission people frankly didn't think the United States would be capable of raising, training, and transporting an army sufficiently large to have much of an effect.

It seemed incredible to Pershing that the Allies didn't even *want* U.S. combat units. Indeed, he'd found it almost insulting when told that old Marshal Joffre, hero of the Battle of the Marne, had said rather begrudgingly that an American token force might be useful, but mainly "to cheer people up."

General Robert-Georges Nivelle, Joffre's replacement, seemed equally disdainful of American combat potential as he urged the United States to send thousands of laborers, railroad workers, drivers, stevedores, nurses, and doctors so as to free more Frenchmen for battle.

As for combat troops, Nivelle recognized, just as Joffre did, that the United States might need to provide some fighting men for the sake of American pride and morale, but only as replacements for the devastated French battalions, and only under French control.

Pershing wondered how the British felt about this, and was told that General Bridges of the Balfour mission in part agreed with Joffre, but also felt that any Americans coming over should be with the British, since so few of the French officers spoke English. The English were asking for 500,000 American recruits. When they got to Britain, Bridges said, they'd be issued British uniforms, trained in trench warfare, and then sent to France to join the line in Flanders.

Pershing asked if Mr. Wilson agreed with all this. The President, Baker replied, seemed rather impressed by Joffre and Bridges, but after all, he wasn't completely naïve. Wilson knew full well that the American people would support neither the French nor the British plan, and for him personally it'd be political suicide. Moreover, when the war was over, Wilson would want to take his place at the head of the peace table, and the only way he could do that would be for Americans to have had a major, *fighting* role in securing that peace.

At the White House, Wilson confirmed that Pershing was to form a staff, proceed overseas, and there prepare the way for the expeditionary force he'd be commanding. Wilson then said: "We seem to be laying great tasks on you, General."

"It is what we are trained to expect," Pershing replied, adding that he would give the job everything that was in him.

"General, I have every confidence you will succeed; you shall have my full support." Wilson meant what he said.

As Pershing began to consider his immediate needs, he may have recalled something which now seemed rather comic. Years earlier, with the Army as always laboring under a shortage of funds, the War College had been unable to afford good maps for its students. Someone had bought huge quantities of the cheapest maps he could find. The maps had come from Germany, and various exercises had been based on the terrain found on those maps, causing Pershing and others to complain about the senselessness of studying the Franco-German frontier over and over, and knowing the Moselle country better than their own. It now appeared that those Franco-German terrain studies had been a blessing in disguise, and Pershing was thankful for every bit of knowledge, for he, like President Wilson, was in a new and unexpected situation. (On his inauguration day, Wilson had told his wife, Ellen: "It would be an irony of fate if my administration had to deal with foreign affairs.")

On May 28, 1917, John Pershing and his staff sailed for Europe on the U.S.S. *Baltic*. In his briefcase Pershing carried a copy of his War Department orders. Paragraph Five of those orders read:

> In military operations against the Imperial German Government, you are directed to cooperate with the forces of the other countries employed against that enemy; but in so doing the underlying idea must be kept in view that the forces of the United States are a separate and distinct component of the combined forces, the identity of which must be preserved.

Reading that paragraph, Pershing knew he'd have a fight on his hands. The Allied armies, hungry for replacements, would be wanting to feed Americans into the line as soon as they arrived, and with little thought for "separate and distinct identity."

On July 4, Parisian civilians cheered and threw flowers as a handful of Yanks paraded through the Arc de Triomphe. They were expecting a great deal of the Americans, little realizing how little the United States was able to help at this point. Military men weren't so easily fooled. The Yanks looked like just what they were—untrained civilians in uniform. One French veteran, turning to his companion in the crowd, said: "And they send *that* to help us!"

Later that day, at Lafayette's tomb, when Colonel Charles Stanton uttered the stirring words "Lafayette, we are here!" Parisians went wild. Pershing was at the same ceremony, some reporters attributed the phrase to him, and so, as Pershing's, it passed into American and French folklore. (The phrase was first suggested for Pershing, who felt it would be "uncharacteristic." He did, however, agree to Stanton's using it.)

To this point, things had gone well, and Pershing hoped, when he spent the next few months training and getting his units up to strength, that the French wouldn't be too disappointed. He'd hold his men back until he knew they were ready, and if his allies complained, so be it. It might mean standing firm, and alone, but when a person felt he was right, he shouldn't be afraid to hold his course, even if everyone else disagreed. He'd learned that fifteen years earlier in the Philippines, when he was but a captain. . . .

His job had been to pacify the local Moros, fierce, primitive people who distrusted all foreigners. The local sultan, or *datto*, was Manibilang. Pershing's initial goal was to win Manibilang's trust. His ultimate goal, for which he'd need Manibilang's support, was to visit the Lake Lanao Moros in the interior of Mindanao—to enter the Forbidden Kingdom. No Spaniard or American had ever done so.

The Spanish, in fact, had once committed several thousand troops trying to force their way into the Forbidden Kingdom, but, after a year of fighting, had admitted failure and abandoned the effort. Later, when the Americans arrived, Pershing's predecessor, Captain R. S. Stevens, had asked permission just to visit the area, taking no soldiers, only interpreters. Angry Moros said it was impossible, and local *datto*s, saying they couldn't be held responsible for his safety, implied that Stevens would be waylaid along the trail. The Forbidden Kingdom remained forbidden.

"It was a human problem," Pershing said, not a military one, and he approached it in a human fashion. First, from his station at Iligan, he visited the nearby marketplace, mingling with the Moros, asking about their crops, their water buffalo, their leaders. He came to realize that theirs was a tribal society, where winning over leaders such as Manibilang was a necessary first step. With support from the *datto*s, he might be able to gain the Moros' confidence and eventually be able to open the interior to Americans.

Through his patient, low-key approach, Pershing managed to meet Manibilang's son, who'd become sultan when his father abdicated in his favor. Everyone knew, however, that Manibilang, although he remained aloof, was the real power. Through the son, Pershing invited Manibilang to visit Iligan. The invitation was accepted; when Manibilang arrived, along with a colorful retinue, he was treated with full, ceremonial courtesy; Pershing even provided a room in his own quarters. During their discussions, Pershing made the point that Americans were "a different and more friendly people" who would not interfere with Moro customs or religion, and who would, moreover, help Moros to get rich by building roads and by buying Moro products at good prices. After the visit, increasing numbers of Moros began coming to Iligan. Then came an unprecedented invitation—for Pershing to visit Manibilang in the interior.

Should he accept? Father Placido, the local Spanish priest, advised against it in the strongest terms. "No white man will ever go up into those forests and hills and come out alive," he warned. "The Sultans got fed up on all white men when they had the Spanish here before. These Mohammedans are waiting every day and every night to kill *you*!"

If Pershing visited the Forbidden Kingdom, said the priest, he'd stay forever, pushing up bamboo. "They say up there that Americans grow nice bamboo." Others, both Filipinos and Spaniards, said the same thing. Pershing would be traveling, alone and unarmed, among thousands of savage "Mohammedans." What if Manibilang betrayed him? And even if he didn't, who could say what the other *dattos* might do? Or what if even a single Moro, wielding a razor-sharp, deadly kris, ran amok and waylaid him along the trail?

Pershing, who'd been waiting for just this invitation, said it was a chance he'd have to take. You win trust by showing trust—and you show *complete* trust by going unarmed.

The visit was eminently successful. Manibilang arranged for Pershing to meet other area leaders; he even brought him to a *ranchería* on market day, and Pershing received permission to address the crowd. He took the occasion to assure the people of American friendship and, answering questions, managed to ease most of their fears. During much of the trip, Pershing was accompanied by Manibilang's son and an "escort of honor." (He'd seen Manibilang's occasional wary glances, knew much hostility still existed, and suspected the escorts were in fact serving as bodyguards.)

Well, he had gone in, and come out alive. He had gambled and won, becoming the first American to visit the Forbidden Kingdom and to return with information about its size and its people. His willingness to ignore the warnings, and to follow his own convictions, had paid off.

And now, in 1917, Black Jack Pershing would face a different kind of challenge. As an example, when Georges Clemenceau, the fiery French premier, visited the U.S. 1st Division, he insisted it be put into the line without delay. Told the Americans weren't ready, Clemenceau said it wasn't a question of being ready—no one is ever completely ready—it was a question of helping France, which was being bled white. The French people demanded to know when American troops would see action!

If full American divisions weren't ready, the Allies said, then "amalgamate" by putting smaller units with the French and British on a temporary basis. Pershing stood firm. If American troops went into Allied ranks, he predicted, "very few of them would ever come out." Moreover, "no people with a grain of pride would consent to furnish men to build up the army of another nation."

As weeks went by, the British and French, concentrating on trench warfare, helped to train Yanks arriving "over there." Pershing appreciated the help, but he insisted American units also learn skills useful in a war of maneuver. He abhorred the dehumanizing, often senseless war of attrition, consisting mainly of massed frontal attacks, and felt strongly Americans should not be fed aimlessly into what he called the "mincing machine."

The Allies remained skeptical of American military know-how. In Paris, a French general, referring to the officers with Pershing, asked, "Is this your personal staff?"

"No," said Pershing, "it is my General Staff."

The general persisted, explaining to Pershing that it took thirty years to form a competent General Staff.

"It never took Americans thirty years to do anything!" Pershing snapped back.

As soon as he was able, Pershing escaped the constant visitors and social distractions of Paris by moving his headquarters to Chaumont, a small village at the confluence of the Marne and the Suize, not far from the front. As the American buildup continued, Pershing made several courageous, ground-breaking decisions. On his own initiative, he contracted with the French government for 5,000 planes at a cost of $60 million, more than Congress had appropriated initially for the entire Spanish-American War. Next, when he realized U.S. purchasing officers were creating inequities and driving prices sky-high by competing against each other, he established the General Purchasing Board (GPB), going against the unanimous advice of a group of officers who said a central purchasing agency would be illegal.

"It was no time to discuss technicalities," Pershing said later. To head the GPB, Pershing named Charles G. Dawes, a close friend from University of Nebraska days. Dawes, in Pershing's words "the most unmilitary human that ever lived," who later became U.S. vice president under Coolidge, combined drive and business acumen to make the GPB highly effective.

Training, however, remained the main concern, and over the coming months Pershing continued to insist that arriving units always learn something about maneuverability. "We're not going to win this war by slugging it out in the trenches," he said. "At some point we must break through the Hindenburg Line, and when we do, I want us to know what to do when we get out in the open!"

As time passed, Americans participating in local actions proved themselves to be tough soldiers and good marksmen. Now more than ever, the Allies felt that such men should be fed into the line as replacements. Despite the complaints, and the pressure from Paris, London, even Washington, Pershing refused to break up his army. His goal, as he was forced to explain over and over, was to train an army that could fight as a unit, in a sector of the line distinctly American.

The situation was delicate. Premier Clemenceau warned that Americans might end up "trying in vain to organize on lost battle-fields over the graves of Allied soldiers." Another of Pershing's critics was British field marshal Sir Douglas Haig. Deep down, Pershing knew Haig's irritation was justified, but he also sensed a bit of jealousy. Haig understandably felt that the gallant, long-suffering British Expeditionary Force should receive the major credit for winning the war, and didn't feel any latecoming Americans should hog the glory.

Even James Harbord, Pershing's loyal Chief of Staff, believed that his boss "risked the chance of being cursed to the latest generation if, through failure to cooperate, the War were lost." Nevertheless, despite pressures, cajolery, even insults, as long as Pershing felt the Americans weren't ready, he refused to feed them into the meat grinder. When he could commit a full U.S. corps, then he would move—not before.

German commander Erich Ludendorff knew the buildup in American manpower and productivity could eventually be decisive. Time for a German victory was running short. As a consequence, in the spring of 1918 he launched a major offensive, one he hoped would win the war before large numbers of fresh Americans joined the fight.

On March 21, 1918, following a massive artillery barrage, thirty-two German divisions smashed into the British Fifth Army; twenty-eight supporting divisions followed, attacking under the cover of still more artillery and poison gas. The British collapsed into chaotic confusion, and Ludendorff had his breakthrough.

The Germans rolled forward, and a week later, by the time their attack lost momentum, they had advanced forty miles, inflicted 200,000 casualties, and taken 70,000 prisoners. Desperately, Haig tried to patch his line, but on April 9, Ludendorff struck again, south of Ypres. Two days later it seemed the whole British line was gone.

Marshal Foch, the newly appointed Allied commander, shifted reserves as well as he could and tried desperately to gather troops enough for a counterattack. In view of the crisis, Pershing knew he had to yield his position and offer American troops. He drove nearly all day over muddy, congested roads, to Foch's headquarters at Clermont-sur-Oise. Arriving late in the evening, he found Foch bent over a map spread on a kitchen table.

"I have come," Pershing said, "to tell you that the American people would consider it a great honor for our troops to be engaged in the present battle. I ask you for this in their name and my own."

Foch, gripping Pershing's arms, thanked him profusely. The five raw divisions under Pershing's control were loaned to the French and were sent into quiet sectors along the line, freeing ten French divisions for the relief of the British.

On April 16, as the 1st Division prepared to go forward, Pershing gathered its officers together and, for once dropping his characteristic reserve, spoke to them in emotional terms: "You are going to meet a savage enemy, flushed with victory. Meet him like Americans. When you hit, hit hard, and don't stop hitting. You don't know the meaning of the word defeat!"

Soon the Germans launched another major offensive, and this time the situation was even more critical. In May, the Allied Supreme War Council, including the French, English, and Italian heads of government, met at Abbeville. Clemenceau, Foch, and Pétain represented France; Lloyd George, Field Marshal Haig, and Lord Milner were the British contingent; Prime Minister Vittorio Orlando and General di Robilant were there from Italy. Pershing, along with General Tasker Bliss, represented the Americans. With a tear in his eye, Foch told the solemn assembly that, without further reinforcements, he doubted he could stem the tide.

After reviewing the situation, Foch proceeded to ask Pershing for the immediate use of every American in France. Pershing reminded Foch that by this time his five best U.S. divisions were already fighting under French and British control. The remainder, unfortunately, were still untrained and wouldn't be ready until August. Sending them in their present condition to fight under the French or British would neither relieve the emergency nor win the war.

Foch became more and more angry, and Pershing bore the brunt of that anger. Sir William Wiseman, one of the British participants, said

Pershing became "black as thunder." Wiseman considered Pershing "an odd man" who was supremely confident of his own opinions while minimizing those of others. Although Wiseman felt Foch was in the right, he still had to sympathize with the American. Pershing, he felt, "is much overworked and understaffed, and is called upon to discuss, indeed to decide, questions which should clearly be determined by civilian authorities."

Foch glared at Pershing. "You are willing to risk being driven back to the Loire?" he asked. This was a crucial moment for Black Jack Pershing. How easy, even how prudent, both personally and professionally, it would be to give in to Foch.

Over the years, John Pershing had proven his physical bravery; now his moral courage was being tested, and in a brutal fashion. He faced the challenge head-on, telling Foch: "Yes, I *am* willing to take that risk. The time may come when the American Army will have to stand the brunt of this war, and it's not wise to fritter away our forces in this manner. The morale of the British, French and Italian armies is low, while as you know, that of the American Army is very high. It would be a grave mistake to give up the idea of building an American Army in all its details as rapidly as possible."

"The war might be over before you are ready," said Foch.

"The war will not be saved by feeding untrained American units into Allied armies," said Pershing.

Lloyd George, who had frequently complained about Pershing to Woodrow Wilson, whispered to Lord Milner, "It's no use. You can't budge him an inch."

Pershing pounded the table. "I have thought this program over very carefully and will not be coerced!"

He was taking a grave risk, and he knew it. If the Allies lost the war and blamed it on the Americans' failure to cooperate, Pershing would go down in history as a scoundrel and a coward. He had, however, after much soul-searching, set a course he believed to be right. He had already given up his best divisions, and while committing more Americans might give a temporary lift to Allied morale, it would not by itself stop the Germans, nor would it win the war.

The day after the Abbeville conference, Lloyd George tried to shame Pershing, saying: "If the war is lost, it would be lost honorably by France and England as they would have expended their last in the struggle, but for Americans to lose the war without having put into it more than Belgium would not be in compatibility with American pride and tradition."

Pershing's answer was simple and to the point. "The United States will put troops on the battle line when it shall have formed an Army worthy of the American people."

In July, Bullard's American III Corps, containing the U.S. 1st and 2nd divisions, attacked near Soissons as part of the French Tenth Army. The momentum had shifted, and in many ways it marked a turning point in the war. During fierce fighting, the Yanks seized their objectives and proved their worth as fighting men.

"*Superbe! Magnifique!*" said French staff officers. "Without the Americans this would never have been possible. We owe it all to you."

By August, a true, distinct American army had been assembled. Careful planning over a period of weeks had set the stage for the first all-American offensive of the war. It was to be an attack against the St. Mihiel salient, a heavily defended area which Pershing referred to as "practically a great field fortress." In 1915, the French had suffered 60,000 casualties while trying to take the same area.

Marshal Foch, who had agreed to the assault, suddenly changed his mind less than two weeks before the attack was to start. Field Marshal Haig had convinced Foch that the time was right for a general offensive along the entire front, with the Americans again relegated to a supporting role.

On August 30, Foch told Pershing the St. Mihiel attack would be put on hold so as to give proper support to Haig's late-September push.

Pershing, gritting his teeth, told Foch: "I can no longer agree to any plan which involves the dispersion of our units."

Tempers flared as Foch shouted that Pershing had to rely on French tanks and artillery for support, so there was no such thing as an all-American attack.

Pershing coolly pointed out that this was true only because France had insisted America rush overseas as many men as possible, whether or not they had proper support.

Foch, with a sneer, then said: "I take it you do not wish to participate in the battle, *mon général?*"

The insult hurt, but Pershing was not to be baited. He replied: "Most assuredly, but as an American army and in no other way."

"I must insist upon the arrangement," said Foch.

"You may insist all you please, but I decline absolutely to agree to your plan. While our Army will fight wherever you may decide, it will *not* fight except as an independent American army."

It was a standoff. Foch stormed out, demanding that Pershing study the plans for general attack and then submit a written reply. Pershing, in his response, said: "There is one thing that must not be done and that is to disperse the American forces among the Allied armies; the danger of destroying by such dispersion the fine morale of the American soldier is too great, to say nothing of the results to be obtained by using the American army as a whole."

When Pershing's letter showed he would not back down, Foch agreed to a compromise. The St. Mihiel attack could go as planned. Two weeks later, however, the Americans would also have to participate in the wider offensive in the Meuse-Argonne sector. Unhesitatingly, Pershing agreed.

At dawn on September 12, following a four-hour artillery preparation, a mighty American army, 665,000 men in nineteen divisions, launched the St. Mihiel offensive. Participants included many who went on to fame in World War II, such as tank commander George Patton, and George C. Marshall, World War II Chief of Staff, who did much of the planning. First man "over the top" in the 84th Brigade of the Rainbow Division was Colonel Douglas MacArthur.

"Here at last," Pershing said, "after seventeen months of effort, an American army was fighting under its own flag."

The speed of the American attack took the Germans by surprise. Rather than the plodding, steady advances they had seen in the past, this time they were faced by Americans who came wildly forward in sudden rushes, rarely stopping to regroup.

Flying overhead, American ace Eddie Rickenbacker looked down and saw doughboys using what he called frontier tactics. "They scurried from cover to cover," Rickenbacker said, "always crouching low as they ran. Throwing themselves flat, they would get their rifles into action and spray the Boches with more bullets until they withdrew from sight. Then another running advance and another furious pumping of lead from the Yanks." Retreating Germans compared the Americans to "wild American Indians" and feared they might be scalped if captured.

By the afternoon of September 13, all objectives had been reached. The Americans pushed on, soon liberating 200 square miles of French territory and capturing 16,000 prisoners along with 443 guns and large stores of matériel and supplies. Moreover, the swiftness of the advance had caused U.S. casualties to be far less than anticipated.

The St. Mihiel offensive had been a stunning success. Congratulations poured in from President Wilson and Premier Clemenceau. Foch telegraphed Pershing to say that the United States had "won a magnificent victory by a maneuver as skillfully prepared as it was valiantly executed."

According to plan, the American forces now shifted north to take part in the Meuse-Argonne offensive. Despite problems caused by inadequate supplies, inexperienced staffs, and monumental traffic jams on incredibly muddy roads, American divisions were ready and in place when the offensive was launched on September 26.

It was hard, bloody work, but the attack pressed forward, ponderously but surely, with Americans playing a key role. By the end of October, Pershing was able to report that all main defense systems in his sector had been breached and the Argonne was clear of the enemy.

The constant assaults finally broke the Germans' will to resist. The Kaiser was deposed, the Germans asked for an armistice, and at eleven A.M. on November 11, the guns fell silent.

For the Americans, and for all the Allies, it was an exhilarating moment. For Black Jack Pershing, with St. Mihiel proving the wisdom of building a distinct American army, there was special vindication. When he wrote of St. Mihiel in his "Final Report to the Secretary of War," Pershing's formal phrasing could not conceal his satisfaction: "The material results of the victory achieved were very important. An American Army was an accomplished fact, and the enemy had felt its power."

CHAPTER 8

# Decision in Texas

I n 1898, soon after the United States declared war on Spain, eighteen-year-old Billy Mitchell dropped out of college, joined the army, and became a Signal Corps lieutenant, thanks in large part to the influence of his father, a U.S. senator. To young Mitchell's disappointment, however, his regiment did not sail for Cuba until December of 1899, four months after the fighting had ended.

Returning from Cuba, and over his parents' rather violent objections, he promptly volunteered for duty in the Philippines and became a participant in the hazardous two-year campaign against guerrilla leader Emilio Aguinaldo.

115

But should he commit to an Army career? He was still debating the question during his next assignment, when he helped construct a vital 1,700-mile Alaskan telegraph line. Finally he decided that Army life, with all its challenges, was where he belonged. He had found his niche; at age twenty-four, Billy Mitchell became the Army's youngest captain.

The challenges continued. Back in the Philippines, he volunteered for an undercover spy mission, a reconnaissance of Japanese activities in the islands between Formosa and the Philippines. Next he toured the battlefields of the Russo-Japanese War, took detailed notes, and sent Washington a full report describing Japanese military capabilities.

At age thirty-two, back from the Orient, Mitchell was chosen for duty on the Army General Staff, and after 1914, when U.S. involvement in the European war became all too likely, his was one of the voices warning of America's unpreparedness. The air service, part of the Signal Corps, became his special interest; while off-duty, he took flying lessons at his own expense. This experience was probably a factor when, in March of 1917, he was sent to France as an aeronautical observer.

Billy Mitchell arrived in Paris on April 10, 1917, exactly four days after the United States declared war on Germany. As one of the small group of officers laying the groundwork for the American Expeditionary Force, he needed to learn everything he could about aerial warfare. And quickly.

Was the man a spy, sending secret telegraph messages to the Germans from his hotel room? Night after night, neighbors had been hearing the sound of furious typing. Finally the mystery was solved: The typist was the young American, Major Mitchell, sending voluminous reports and bombarding the War Department with suggestions.

Boldly, Mitchell asked Washington for $50,000 for office expenses, only to be told it was "not customary" to send so much money to a junior officer. This caused one of Mitchell's lieutenants to remark wryly that it "was not customary to have a world war."

During that first month in France, Mitchell was in constant motion. He inspected French aerodromes; flew over the lines with a French pilot; took part in an infantry attack, becoming not only the first American under fire, but also the first to receive a Croix de Guerre. Before the month was out, he realized that American planes were inferior (he called the American-made Nieuports, with gas tanks mounted directly behind the pilot, "flaming coffins") and recommended that the United States rely on planes purchased from their allies.

In May, Mitchell drove himself to the headquarters of the British Royal Flying Corps, arriving in a cloud of dust and to the sound of screeching brakes. (He'd later acquire his own Mercedes racing car and drive even faster.) The young major walked smartly into the building and announced to a startled adjutant that he was there to see the commander, Major General Sir Hugh Trenchard.

The self-assured Mitchell, although respectful, was clearly not in awe of "Boom" Trenchard, who was already something of a legend. Starting from scratch, Trenchard had assembled a powerful RFC force of nearly 2,000 planes, and by this time was recognized as the Allies' leading authority on aerial warfare.

Sir Hugh, noted for his brusque manner, was leaving to inspect his various squadrons. Did the major have an appointment?

No, the major did not, but he still wanted to see as much of the organization as Trenchard was willing to show him, and not just the British equipment, supplies, and operating procedures; he'd also like to accompany some of the RFC flyers going against the Germans.

Trenchard, somewhat taken aback, said that this was a tall order and he really had more important things to do than to serve as a chaperon. Mitchell, with a disarming grin, said he knew Trenchard had a smooth-running outfit; surely it could get along without him for a couple of days.

Trenchard's aides expected an explosion, but the chief, rather amused, said Mitchell appeared to be the sort who usually got what he wanted and he might as well come along. For the next three days, Mitchell stuck to Trenchard's side, soaking up information like a hungry sponge. Before long, he had accepted Trenchard's conclusions—that planes should be used in massed formations and that air supremacy was a necessary prerequisite for victory on the ground. These were ideas that Mitchell was to promote, and to defend, for the rest of his life.

The two men, far different in personality, seemed to complement each other. Trenchard, a fine leader and organizer, had none of Mitchell's eloquence. (Winston Churchill once said of him, "He can't write and he can't speak but we can't do without him.") Mitchell, on the other hand, was the articulate, eager airpower advocate who was always ready to speak out with single-minded enthusiasm.

In the coming weeks, Trenchard kept his eye on Mitchell, liked what he saw, and remarked to one of his staff: "Mitchell is a man after my own heart. If only he can break his habit of trying to convert his opponents by killing them, he'll go far."

Fourteen months later, in July 1918, as General Erich Ludendorff prepared to launch his last great offensive, an American plane flew low over the battle area. In it was Mitchell, performing his own personal reconnaissance. He slipped down, through fog and low clouds, skimming along the Marne River. "Suddenly," he later wrote, "as I rounded a turn of the river east of Dormans, I saw a great mass of artillery fire hitting the south bank, and spanning the river, five bridges filled with German troops marching over."

Mitchell flew back and reported what he had seen. Ground forces were aligned to meet the threat, and Mitchell's airmen took part in the counterattack that stopped the German thrust. Elmer Haslett, one of Mitchell's pilots, who had seen him flying within 500 feet of the advancing Germans, thought this was one of the most remarkable flights of the war and said it was lucky that the man in that plane was "a rare tactician and strategist" who realized the significance of what he had seen. "When the fliers found out who had made that mysterious flight," wrote Haslett, "our morale was improved one hundred per cent."

Thanks mostly to Mitchell, American airpower had become a reality. On September 12, forty-nine squadrons, twenty-nine of them American, supported Pershing's St. Mihiel offensive. Nearly 1,500 planes under Mitchell's command—American, French, British, and Italian—strafed enemy positions and bombed the German rear areas. It was the finest example to date of airpower used in mass, and Mitchell organized it.

General Pershing, the AEF commander, was highly pleased with the support he had received and recommended Mitchell's promotion to brigadier general. He also wrote a warm commendation:

> Please accept my sincere congratulations on the successful and very important part taken by the Air Force under your command in the first offensive of the American Army. The organization and control of the tremendous concentration of air forces . . . is as fine a tribute to you personally as is the courage and nerve shown by your officers a signal proof of the high morale which permeates the service under your command. . . . I am proud of you all.

In the Meuse-Argonne campaign that followed, lasting from September 26 until the end of the war, General Mitchell commanded the Air Service, Army Group. His former teacher, Hugh Trenchard, now listened respectfully to Mitchell's ideas; for the action, he graciously consented to put his British squadrons under Mitchell's command.

Henry "Hap" Arnold, who became the U.S. Army Air Forces commander in World War II, visited Mitchell during this period. According to Arnold, Mitchell was "on top of the world. . . . The fliers around him would have done anything for him, and so would the boys out in the squadrons. . . . Billy was clearly the Prince of the Air now."

Consistently, Mitchell's airmen were able to gain aerial superiority and to render close support to the advancing doughboys. After the Meuse-Argonne campaign, Trenchard saluted Mitchell's achievement: "The most terrific exhibition I have ever seen—you have cleaned out the air."

Following the armistice, Billy Mitchell sailed for home on the Cunard liner *Aquitania*, thinking of peace in terms of planes. With supreme confidence and the tone of an evangelist, the handsome young airman told his fellow passengers that future wars would be won, not on the ground, nor on the sea, but in the air. Pershing was sending him home to become chief of military aeronautics, and Mitchell was determined to build an air arm more powerful than the Army and Navy combined.

As the *Aquitania* neared New York harbor, a flight of planes from Mitchel Field on Long Island circled the ship to welcome the general home. With a broad grin, Mitchell waved enthusiastically to his fellow flyers, all of whom saw him as their champion. And what better champion could there be? At age thirty-nine, Billy Mitchell had already spent twenty-one years in the Army, had come through three wars, seen fourteen major engagements in France, and was one of the most decorated men in the AEF. As a final recognition, Marshal Pétain personally had awarded him the Legion of Honor.

Understandably, it was a triumphant, glorious homecoming, and Billy Mitchell looked to the future with glowing confidence. Perhaps it was just as well he could not know what lay ahead, for soon after his arrival in Washington both his new title and his office would disappear in a postwar reorganization. In the following months, airpower's potential would be disparaged by those in authority, the Air

Service would be reduced to a handful of obsolete planes, and the number of air officers, once as high as 20,000, would reach a postwar low of 232.

More significantly, while Mitchell might have guessed he would spend the rest of his life crusading for airpower, he could never have foreseen the difficulty of that crusade.

Everyone knew the *Osprey*. It was Mitchell's favorite, an elderly blue-and-white De Havilland biplane sporting his own private Air Service insignia and flying a long blue pennant at the tail for identification.

On this day in July of 1921, the *Osprey* described lazy hawklike circles in the sky as Billy looked down at the German battleship *Ostfriesland*. The mighty *Ostfriesland*, a veteran of the World War I Battle of Jutland, was as formidable as any ship afloat. She had been built on orders from Admiral Tirpitz so as to be nearly unsinkable, and was protected by four skins plus a whole series of watertight compartments. Now, however, the once-proud warship was to be used as a target, testing Mitchell's belief that any surface ship, regardless of construction, could be sunk by attack from the air.

On hand to watch the test were hundreds of distinguished visitors, including General John J. Pershing and Secretary of War John Weeks, together with a small army of reporters and photographers. For Billy Mitchell, it was a moment of truth. For nearly three years, he had been insisting that airpower was now dominant over seapower. He had argued long and loud, in the process encountering strong opposition and personal resentment not only from the Navy but from many Army colleagues as well. Now it was put up or shut up.

There had been good moments during those years, of course, such as the time his friend Douglas MacArthur, the newly appointed superintendent of West Point, had invited him to speak to the Corps of Cadets. He had received a standing ovation; among his cadet listeners were many future leaders of World War II, including Maxwell Taylor, Lyman Lemnitzer, and future Air Force Chief of Staff Hoyt Vandenberg.

Mostly, however, those years had been full of frustration. Mitchell had inundated his superiors with suggestions and recommendations: Long-range bombers, capable of crossing the Atlantic, should be developed; a force of expert airplane mechanics should be trained; funds should be provided for aerial torpedoes and armor-piercing bombs; combined maneuvers should test coastal defenses against air attack; commercial aviation should be expanded so as to provide a pool of trained pilots in case of war; air routes should be set up immediately, not just across the country, but into South America and Canada.

The ideas were not all Mitchell's, but he had been the only one in authority pushing them. Regardless of their source, however, they had been met with silence. Secretary of War Newton Baker and the General Staff had more or less decided Mitchell's ideas were beneath serious notice; some said the poor man had been deranged by the war. According to one rumor, the War Department cellar had a special place, known as the Flying Trash Pile, for discarded Mitchell proposals.

Billy had kept speaking out, impressing, among others, certain members of Congress. At last the Navy, under pressure from both Congress and the public, had agreed to a series of tests—planes versus ships. Herbert Corey, a well-known war correspondent, returned from a Navy training cruise and wrote Mitchell, "You are throwing the Navy into convulsions. The entire fleet trembles with rage at the mention of your name."

Mitchell's outspokenness brought official Navy protests, causing the Air Service chief, General Charles Menoher, to write the secretary of war asking that Mitchell be fired. "He has given serious offense to the Navy Department by his public utterances and publicity. . . . It is recommended and requested that Brigadier General William Mitchell be relieved of duty as Assistant Chief of the Air Service."

Secretary of War Weeks was inclined to go along with Menoher. However, when word leaked out that Mitchell might be fired, veterans' organizations, aerial clubs, and even the press quickly came to his support. Bowing to public opinion, Weeks reached a compromise, leaving Mitchell in position but telling him to keep his maverick opinions to himself, to stop lobbying the Congress, and to stop baiting the Navy. Meanwhile, though, the bombing tests would proceed as scheduled and, as one paper reported, "Mitchell will get a chance to show whether a dreadnought is obsolete in the presence of a modern bombing plane."

The bombing tests, conducted in phases, had begun in June of 1921, using former ships of the German navy as targets. In the first phases, a submarine and a torpedo-boat destroyer were sunk by aerial bombs. Mitchell described the latter attack:

Bombs began churning the water around the destroyer. They hit close in front of it, behind it, opposite its side and directly in its center. Columns of water rose hundreds of feet into the air. For a few minutes the vessel looked as if it were on fire. . . . Then it broke completely in two in the middle and sank out of sight. . . . All our methods and systems of bombing had proved to be correct.

Next target, five days later, was the light cruiser *Frankfurt*. In morning attacks, the graceful cruiser resisted as planes struck with machine-gun fire and small bombs. That afternoon, however, when powerful six-hundred-pound bombs were used, the *Frankfurt* sank rapidly.

"So far, so good," Mitchell probably thought as he circled over the *Ostfriesland*. If he didn't sink the battleship, however, all the other tests would be forgotten. Nearby, on the observer ships, Navy experts felt confident. If a cruiser could resist so tenaciously, surely a battleship would be safe.

As the test began, hundreds of dignitaries looked through their binoculars. One of the guests of Secretary of the Navy Edwin Denby was Italian general (later marshal) Pietro Badoglio. Also on hand, grinding away with four different movie cameras, was a Japanese contingent led by a government official named Katsuda.

The first wave of attacks caused considerable damage to the *Ostfriesland*, but nothing mortal. Subsequent attacks were then delayed, both by weather problems and by changes in the administrative rules. (Mitchell was forever convinced that additional obstacles created by the Navy were deliberate attempts to make him fail.)

Finally the last wave of bombers took off from Langley Field in Virginia and approached the target. They were carrying 2,000-pounders, similar to the mighty "blockbusters" of World War II. The first bomb plunged downward, hit near the point of the bow, and caused a billow of smoke and flame. Five minutes later another bomb hit in the water near the mainmast, creating violent subsurface pressures and huge underwater fractures. This was followed by another hit, then another. Minutes later, the great ship pointed her bow to the sky and slid, beam first, beneath the water.

A reporter from the *Washington Times*, watching Secretary Denby and accompanying admirals, wrote: "Not a word was spoken by the men as the great rust-encrusted hulk took its final plunge. It seemed as though all in the little knot of onlookers were attending a funeral, as if one of their dearest friends was being buried, and they couldn't believe it." Other Navy officers, perhaps sensing the end of an era, were seen dabbing their eyes with handkerchiefs.

Especially significant, with ominous foreshadowing of that "day of infamy" twenty years later at Pearl Harbor, were the words spoken to a reporter by the Japanese observer Katsuda: "Very great experiment, profoundly exciting. Our people will cheer your great Mitchell and, you may be sure, will study his experiments. There is much to learn here."

Even Mitchell felt a twinge of sadness as he witnessed the death of a gallant ship. Still, as the *Osprey* returned to Langley, his mood became festive. Every available plane had been sent aloft to welcome him home. As soon as he landed, he heard the booming of cannon, music from a military band, and cheers from officers and men, mechanics, crewmen, and a host of bystanders. Hands pulled him from the cockpit; laughing and smiling, he was hoisted on the shoulders of husky pilots who proceeded to carry him around the field. That night, as people snake-danced around a bonfire and called for a speech, Mitchell said a few words: "In the war to come, and you'll see it, God will be on the side of the heaviest air force. What we did to the *Frankfurt* and the *Ostfriesland* is what will happen to all warships in future wars. And don't you forget it. Keep your eye on the sky!" It may have been Billy Mitchell's greatest moment.

The success of the bombing tests, and the attendant publicity, soon made Mitchell a national hero. As such, he was much in demand as a speaker; true to form, he continued to step on toes as he asserted the superiority of airpower, constantly derided the Navy, and called for a modern, well-funded, and independent air force.

Predictably, the friction continued between Mitchell and his immediate superior, General Menoher. When Menoher was transferred to another assignment, many expected Mitchell would be made chief of the Air Service. Higher-ups, however, including Army Chief of Staff Pershing, wanted to keep a tighter rein on the outspoken airman. Consequently, General Mason Patrick, a strong-willed nonflyer who had been Mitchell's boss in France, was given the job, along with instructions to tone down Mitchell's pronouncements and publicity.

Mitchell nevertheless continued to speak out, often recklessly, and soon he and Patrick had a showdown. After first threatening to resign, Mitchell backed down and promised to submit loyally to Patrick's authority.

An uneasy truce developed between the two. Patrick, an honorable, fair-minded West Pointer of the old school, sized up his assistant rather well:

> Mitchell is very likeable and has ability; his ego is highly developed and he has an undoubted love for the limelight, a desire to be in the public eye. He is forceful, aggressive, spectacular. He has a better knowledge of the tactics of air fighting than any man in the country. . . . I think I understood quite well his characteristics, the good in him—and there was much of it—and his faults.

Black Jack Pershing had a similar opinion. In 1923, he wrote on Mitchell's efficiency report: "This officer is an exceptionally able one, enthusiastic, energetic and full of initiative . . . an expert flyer. . . . He is fond of publicity, more or less indiscreet as to speech, and rather difficult to control as a subordinate."

That same year, more bombing tests were held; more ships were sunk; but once again the Navy downplayed the results. The admirals still insisted the battleship was supreme, although they were now also calling for aircraft carriers.

Divorced from his first wife in 1922, Mitchell married Betty Trumbull, a Michigan socialite, in October of 1923. With the blessings of his superiors, who were more than happy to have him out of the country, Billy Mitchell and his bride left on a seventeen-month combined honeymoon and inspection trip. The itinerary included Hawaii, the Philippines, India, China, Korea, and Japan.

As a result of the trip, Mitchell prepared a frank, full report on what he'd found, once again stepping on toes as he criticized U.S. air defense capabilities in both Hawaii and the Philippines. He was convinced that before long America and Japan would be at war, and he went into considerable detail about Japanese capabilities. One portion of his 1924 report predicted a surprise assault on Pearl Harbor by Japanese aircraft. He even included a possible attack scenario, forecasting actual events with chilling accuracy:

> The Japanese bombardment, 100 ships organized into four squadrons of 25 ships each. The objectives for attack are 1) Ford Island (in the middle of Pearl Harbor), airdrome, hangars, storehouses, and ammunition dumps; 2) Navy fuel oil tanks; 3) water supply of Honolulu; 4) water supply of

Schofield; 5) Schofield Barracks airdrome and troop estab-
lishments; 6) naval submarine station; 7) city and wharves of
Honolulu.

Attack will be launched as follows: bombardment, attack to
be made on Ford Island at 7:30 A.M. . . . Group to move in
column of flights in V. Each ship will drop . . . projectiles on
the targets.

(Mitchell was off in his prediction by twenty-five minutes, since the
actual assault on Pearl Harbor began at 7:55 A.M. Some Japanese
planes, however, waiting for slower torpedo planes to arrive, were
seen circling overhead at precisely 7:30.)

The voluminous study was passed among various staff sections, but
eventually was more or less ignored. A few people admired specific
portions of the report, but in general Mitchell's visionary flamboy-
ance only served as an irritant. He was baffled. With all his heart, he
wanted to convince his brother officers of airpower's vital role in
national security. He would have preferred to do so while observing
proper military protocol, but conventional methods seemed ineffec-
tive, even pointless.

While Mitchell was away, General Patrick, working through proper
channels, as was his wont, had tried to help the airpower situation,
but he too had failed. "The Air Service is practically demobilized and
unable to play its part in any national emergency, or even to meet the
many peacetime demands for service," Patrick wrote the War Department. The only response was a further reduction of air strength.

Mitchell, in his zeal, would not keep quiet, nor would he limit
himself to military channels. He continued to speak out publicly,
wrote a series of inflammatory articles for the *Saturday Evening Post*,
and, in testimony before Congress, broadened his attacks on the
Navy and the War Department. Consistently, he stressed the need for
a greater and more independent air force.

At one point, his friend Hap Arnold said, "Billy, you've got to take
it easy. We need you. Don't throw away everything just to beat out
some guy who doesn't understand airpower is coming."

Mitchell only smiled. "When senior officers won't see the facts,
you've got to do something unorthodox. Remember, I'm doing it for
the good of the country, for the future of the air force, for the good
of you fellows. I can afford to do it. You can't."

The uproar continued as Mitchell kept making headlines, bringing
not only more criticism from above but also a host of new fans,

among whom was Will Rogers, at the time perhaps the most popular man in America. In 1925, Mitchell gave Rogers his very first airplane ride, a swing around Washington in the *Osprey*. When they landed, Mitchell told Rogers it had been his last time in the air as a brigadier general; he was being reduced to the grade of colonel, relieved as assistant chief of the Air Service (over the objection of General Patrick, who wanted him retained), and reassigned to a lonely job at Fort Sam Houston, Texas, near San Antonio.

Rogers, like many others, was outraged. Even *The New York Times*, not always friendly to Mitchell in the past, said, "Gen. Mitchell has done more by example and initiative to advance military aviation than any other officer in either the Army or the Navy. . . . To get rid of him by demotion or exile would be a scandalous misuse of authority."

Mitchell knew that he was at a crossroads when he arrived in San Antonio. On the one hand, he could watch what he said, carry out his rather undemanding duties as aviation officer for the VIII Corps Area, and retire after three years in relative comfort and security. This would mean, however, that his airpower crusade would be put on the back burner.

Alternatively, he could continue to speak out and risk the consequences. He knew, of course, that people in Washington, even President Coolidge, were watching to see his reaction to this out-of-the-way assignment. To Mitchell, the ethical choice was clear.

He might now be in Texas, and far from the Washington seat of power, but editors and publishers, thirsting for controversy, continued to pursue him. Soon he wrote an article for *Liberty* magazine, again deriding battleships. "Why have treaties about battleships, the most expensive of all war equipment, when planes can destroy them?" In San Diego, while inspecting an aircraft plant, Mitchell added more fuel to the flames by saying U.S. airpower was "almost extinct" and predicting the country, as usual, would only learn, by bitter experience, from the "disaster of war."

Next his book, *Winged Defense*, appeared; it contained mostly previously published material, and Mitchell himself saw it as a "little book" of small consequence, although his publisher proudly hailed it as "a bomb in the lap of American complacency." It served, however, to throw down the gauntlet rather plainly: "The truth of our deplorable situation is going to be put before the American people, come what may. If the War Department wants to start something, so much the better[;] . . . then we will have a chance to remedy this unfortunate situation."

Mitchell continued to hammer away, calling for air force independence, better planes, better funding, all the while praising (and sympathizing with) the men who were doing the flying and coping with bureaucratic blunders. Official Washington bided its time, knowing one more act of blatant insubordination would give the moral high ground to both the the War Department and the White House.

The triggering event came after two aerial mishaps that followed each other in rapid succession. First, a Navy PN-9 aircraft disappeared in the Pacific during an attempted flight between the West Coast and Hawaii. Then the dirigible *Shenandoah* crashed after running into a lightning storm over Ohio. Both flights had been undertaken for publicity purposes, and both were subject to justifiable criticism. The PN-9 had been flying a course against prevailing winds which seriously limited its range. The *Shenandoah*, en route to state fairs in the Midwest, had taken off against the advice of its capable young skipper, who lost his life in the crash, and who had warned his superiors of the danger of flying over mountains during storm season.

Reporters, hoping for a controversial statement, gathered at Mitchell's Texas headquarters. They were not disappointed. What they received was a scorcher—nine mimeographed pages with more than 6,000 words. It was clearly a calculated attempt to force a showdown. Mitchell, with intemperate anger, wrote: "These accidents are the result of the incompetency, the criminal negligence, and the almost treasonable negligence of our national defense by the Navy and War Departments."

Fliers were "bluffed and bulldozed," he said, until they dared not tell the truth. The services' conduct of aviation had been "so disgusting as to make any self-respecting person ashamed of the cloth he wears." Only patriotism kept men flying despite the bureaucrats, who "have passed all bounds of national decency. . . . This condition must be remedied. . . . It concerns us all. The American people must know the facts, and with their unfailing common sense and ability they will surely remedy it."

Mitchell had finally done it—brought about the court-martial, and the showdown, he had courted for years. Now he would have a chance to tell his story on a national stage, but at a price.

The press at first was generally favorable to Mitchell, but there were hostile comments as well. "Permit this violent outburst to go unpunished," said the *New York World*, "and every private in the Army and enlisted man in the Navy will feel at liberty to denounce his superior officers. Armies and navies are not made that way."

Mitchell continued to speak out, his challenges to authority becoming ever more direct. The press, sensing that he had gone too far, became increasingly critical. *The New York Times* referred to his "insubordination and folly"; the *Herald Tribune* said he "shockingly violates military standards."

The *Kansas City Star* summed it up rather well: "How can you punish a man who wants nothing more than to be punished and is deliberately inviting court martial? . . . Mitchell is a zealot, a fanatic, a one-idea man, he will go to any limit to make his case . . . but with all that, he sincerely believes in what he preaches."

Hoping to appease the public, Calvin Coolidge convened a board to examine the entire field of aviation, naming as chairman Dwight Morrow, a prominent banker and the future father-in-law of Charles Lindbergh. Soon the Morrow Board called Mitchell to Washington as an expert witness. Just before he appeared, the Army announced that Colonel Mitchell would be tried by court-martial while he was in Washington, rather than at his post in Texas.

Billy Mitchell testified before the Morrow Board for a day and a half. Publicity was only moderate; everyone knew the big show would be the upcoming court-martial. The Morrow report, full of compromises, was basically inconclusive. Airpower was important, it said, but a buildup such as Mitchell recommended would be far too costly; the Army and Navy should control the air services; a separate Air Force Department was not needed. (Only after World War II did the Air Force become a separate service.) President Coolidge called the report "reassuring to the country, gratifying to the service, and satisfactory to the Congress." People noted, with some annoyance, that the report was released during the court-martial, neatly timed to divert attention from Mitchell's recently completed defense.

The court-martial had been convened on October 28, 1925, to consider charges that Mitchell was guilty of "conduct prejudicial to good order and discipline" as well as "conduct of a nature to bring discredit upon the military service." The generals on the nine-member court, including Douglas MacArthur, were all comrades of long standing. None of them relished the task at hand.

Mitchell's primary defense counsel, who had volunteered his services free of charge, was Representative Frank Reid of Illinois, a lawyer who had formerly practiced with Clarence Darrow. In many ways, the outcome was a foregone conclusion: Obviously Mitchell's conduct *had* been "prejudicial." Some even felt he should plead guilty, then say why it was necessary to act as he had. Instead, he and Reid chose to put on a lengthy defense, calling witnesses to support Mitchell's charges of bureaucratic incompetence and mismanagement. Defense witnesses were a Who's Who of airpower past and future, including World War I's "ace of aces," Eddie Rickenbacker, and Carl "Tooey" Spaatz, World War II strategic air commander in both Europe and the Pacific.

Reid conducted a sparkling defense. There were even moments of humor, as when Reid asked General Hanson Ely, a hostile witness, what he thought of the statement "The development of aircraft indicates that our national defense must be supplemented by, if not dominated by, aviation." Ely said he could not agree.

"You think it is absurd?"

"Yes."

"That is the statement of President Coolidge."

"I don't care what it is." The court ordered the remarks about Coolidge stricken from the record.

By December 17, both prosecution and defense had presented their cases. The government had had no trouble proving the matter of insubordination, foiling Mitchell's and Reid's efforts to make the issue only the truthfulness of Mitchell's position.

When it came time for closing arguments, Mitchell asked Reid to remain silent. Then he spoke on his own behalf, saying: "My trial before this court-martial is the culmination of the efforts of the General Staff of the Army and the General Board of the Navy to depreciate the value of air power. . . . The truth of every statement which I have made has been proved by good and sufficient evidence before this court. . . . To proceed with the case would serve no useful purpose. I have therefore directed my counsel to entirely close out our part of the proceeding without argument."

The chief prosecutor said that since the defense had made no closing statement, the prosecution would waive its own. Major Allen Gullion, however, one of the assistant prosecutors, plainly trying to make a name for himself and curry favor with his superiors, launched forth with a lengthy, vicious attack, calling Mitchell a "loose-talking megalomaniac . . . an all too familiar charlatan and demagogue type," one who was "never overly careful as to the ethics of his methods." Conveniently, Gullion had mimeographed copies of his remarks ready for the press.

When Gullion was finished, and the courtroom became still, Will Rogers, one of the spectators, came forward, put his arm around

Mitchell, and said: "The people are with you, Billy. Keep punching. You'll rope 'em yet."

Mitchell called it "a moment of tenderness—the one moment of all that nightmare which I'll never forget."

It took very little time to reach a verdict: "Guilty on all charges and specifications." Mitchell was sentenced to be suspended from all rank, command, and duty, with the forfeiture of all pay and allowances, for the next five years.

Congressman Reid told the press: "They may think they have silenced Mitchell, but his ideas will go marching on, and those who crucified him will be the first to put his aviation suggestions into practice." For a while, there was public indignation about the verdict. In Congress, bills were introduced to reinstate Mitchell and even to punish those who had attacked him. Ultimately, however, Congress took no action and the furor subsided.

Mitchell, unwilling to stay in uniform at the cost of silence, resigned his commission six weeks later. In the coming years, and even as a civilian, he continued to crusade on behalf of American air-power. As for the court-martial, he had known what was coming, accepted the results, and remained friendly with members of the court for the rest of his life.

When Mitchell died in February 1936, at age fifty-six, General Frank McCoy, one of the court-martial judges, served as one of his pallbearers. Douglas MacArthur, another of the judges and a lifelong Mitchell friend, wrote of Billy: "That he was wrong in the violence of his language is self-evident; that he was right in his thesis is equally true and incontrovertible. . . . Had he lived through World War II he would have seen the fulfillment of many of his prophecies."

CHAPTER 9

# Decision in Sicily

**I**t was in July 1942, at Camp Claiborne, Louisiana, that the normally unflappable Matthew B. Ridgway received one of the biggest shocks of his life. The 82nd Division, *his* division, the infantry outfit he'd been whipping into shape over the past few weeks in the searing summer heat, was being converted from infantry to airborne! Not only that, the cohesive, smooth-running team he'd been building was about to be split in half.

Army Chief of Staff George Marshall had decided to make the 82nd an airborne division—and without delay. Moreover, to complicate matters, the 82nd was also being asked to provide the nucleus of a second airborne division, the 101st.

131

Inwardly, Matt Ridgway groaned at the prospect of splitting up his division. Still, he was a soldier; he would do what he was told. He was even somewhat flattered to be chosen for this unique assignment. On the other hand, he knew almost nothing about being a paratrooper. For that matter, few Americans did; no U.S. airborne division was even in existence, and except for the Germans, the whole airborne concept was pretty much in its infancy.

Crete, Ridgway supposed, had changed everything. In May 1941, German airborne troops under General Kurt Student had assaulted that British-held Mediterranean island. Student's force, without benefit of sealift, had dropped from the air, almost as if by magic, and had used parachutists and glider-borne infantry to score a dramatic victory. Understandably, U.S. planners had been impressed, and as a consequence had concluded that airborne forces had "arrived."

What American planners did *not* know, however, was that Student's forces had suffered an appalling 44 percent casualty rate on Crete. Air losses had also been heavy—some 170 out of 530 planes. Ironically, as America was using the "lesson of Crete" to justify an emphasis on airborne units, Hitler was calling Crete a disaster and saying "The days of the paratrooper are over."

In the days and months that followed, Ridgway's paratroopers would know both triumph and disaster. Along the way, they would also learn just how difficult airborne warfare could be.

Forty-seven-year-old Matt Ridgway had made a decision. If people in the 82nd were going to have to start jumping out of airplanes, he wanted to be first. "Wanted" might not be quite the proper word, of course. After all, there was the question of his trick back. Years earlier, when he was a West Point cadet, part of his training had involved jumping a horse over hurdles with his eyes closed. Doing so, he'd taken a nasty fall and landed on one of the hurdles, injuring his back rather severely. At the time, he'd been afraid to turn himself in to the hospital, fearing it might cause him to be washed out of the Academy. He'd just gritted his teeth and stuck it out; but ever since, the back had been a problem and at times he felt as though someone had stabbed him there with a bayonet and neglected to remove it.

Well, he still had to show the way and make that first jump, but, as he later wrote: "It occurred to me that this was an idiotic enterprise that might well get me a broken leg, or worse, and that I was a damned fool to be such an eager beaver, breaking the first rule of an old soldier—which is never to volunteer for anything."

Best place for that first jump, he decided, was the Airborne School at Fort Benning. Several of his staff volunteered to go along and do the same, but he turned most of them down, saying it would be foolish to take an unnecessary risk. (And just what did that say about *him*?) Some he did bring along, though, including General Bud Miley, one of the few senior officers with parachute experience, and General Max Taylor, who, like Ridgway, would become one of the outstanding airborne leaders of World War II.

At Benning, Ridgway's group was given a brief orientation, followed by a few minutes in a suspended harness, some practice jumps from a raised platform to simulate landing shock, and a quick briefing on maneuvering the chute while in the air and collapsing it once you were on the ground.

Ridgway, Miley, and a few others loaded up. Their C-47 would be first over the drop zone, or DZ. As they approached the DZ, "old hand" Bud Miley offered to act as the "wind dummy": If the wind pulled him away from the DZ, the pilot, on his second pass, could make a correction.

The green light came on and Miley jumped. Matt Ridgway, watching from the open door, saw Miley float gracefully to earth, smack into a cluster of tall pine trees. Novice jumper Ridgway felt his stomach give an extra twitch. If that was what happened to an *experienced* jumper . . .

The pilot, correcting for the wind, made a second pass. Ridgway, next up, leaped from the plane and seconds later felt the opening shock, "like the blow of a club across the shoulders." Then, after a few moments of beautiful, peaceful silence, the ground came rushing up at him and he forgot everything he'd been told. He landed with an impact he compared to "jumping off the top of a freight car traveling at thirty-five miles an hour onto a hard clay road-bed." However, he *was* safely on the ground, and his trick back had held up.

Moments later, Max Taylor and a few others jumped from a second plane. As Taylor neared the ground, a gust of air caught him, lifted him up a few feet, then threw him to the ground with a crash. To observers, he seemed to have landed on his head. However, Taylor, a good athlete in fine physical condition, got up unhurt and even offered a weak smile.

As Taylor's comrade Bill Moorman put it, Max "really didn't like to jump out of airplanes, but he liked to be *around* people who jumped out of airplanes."

\* \* \*

In the following months, Ridgway once again took a group of individuals and units of varied backgrounds and welded them into a tight-knit organization. At Fort Bragg, in North Carolina, his paratroopers, with their bloused trousers, jump boots, and airborne patches, became a proud, swaggering, feisty group. Nevertheless, when orders came ordering the 82nd overseas, Ridgway wished he'd had more time to get them ready. "No division that left the States for battle," he said, "had been torn up and put back together so frequently," and none "had less time to train."

Ridgway was also concerned about the Troop Carrier Wing, the inexperienced people who'd be called on to fly the 82nd into battle. Mass airdrops required precision flying at a level of skill that green American pilots had not yet achieved. In practice maneuvers, parachutists had been scattered all over North Carolina rather than landing on proper DZs. Night exercises had been particularly disastrous, and Ridgway annoyed his superiors by saying that at this stage night airdrops were just not feasible.

Meanwhile, plans were under way for the 82nd to support Operation Husky, the Allied invasion of Sicily, and despite Ridgway's advice, they'd enter combat by jumping at night.

On May 10, 1943, after eleven days at sea, the 82nd landed in North Africa. Supposedly their arrival at Casablanca was a closely held secret, but that very evening, Axis Sally on her nightly broadcast said cheerfully: "Welcome to Africa, Matt Ridgway and your bad boys." The Germans knew too damned much, and it came as a shock.

Exactly two months later, American and British parachutists and glider troops were dropped at night in support of Husky. The attempt was every bit as disastrous as Ridgway had feared. Most pilots failed to find their navigational checkpoints, and fewer than 20 percent of the paratroopers landed anywhere near their designated drop zones. Parachutists landed as far as sixty-five miles off target, and few units were able even to assemble. The glider forces were similarly jumbled. Many British gliders, for example, were released too far from shore and at too low an altitude. Sixty-nine gliders, carrying 1,100 men, came down in the sea; about 200 men drowned. Other men, both British and American, were killed as their gliders broke apart on impact.

It took days before Ridgway's scattered 82nd Division could become organized, and even then, more tragedy was in store. On the night of July 13, American anti-aircraft crews, both Army and Navy, mistakenly fired on a formation of troop carrier C-47s. Sixty planes were hit; twenty-three went down, either crashing into Sicily or falling into the sea. Total casualties exceeded three hundred, including more than a hundred killed. The episode was the greatest friendly-fire catastrophe in airborne history.

Eventually, however, as the Sicily campaign continued, the 82nd gathered itself together and Matt Ridgway proved to be a superb combat leader. Always he was at the point of attack, leading, coaching, inspiring his men, with courage that became legendary throughout the 82nd. At Trapani, for example, as Italian artillery zeroed in on a truck convoy, Ridgway brought guns forward to silence the enemy batteries. Then, when heavy shellfire caused one of the gun crews to take cover, Ridgway, ignoring the bursting shells, calmly strode up to the abandoned gun. "His brave example," said an officer who witnessed this, "rallied the crew back into action." The officer felt it was one of the boldest acts he'd ever seen. Finally, after several such incidents, George Patton, who was himself notorious for taking risks, scolded Ridgway for exposing himself too recklessly. Actually, Patton's reprimand didn't much bother him; Ridgway considered the rebuke to be "more of a compliment."

By mid-August 1943, American and British forces had overrun nearly all of Sicily. Ridgway's paratroopers had played a prominent part, having at one point advanced 150 miles in six days while capturing 15,000 prisoners.

In Italy, meanwhile, Allied air attacks were bringing the war closer to home and causing the people to lose faith in their leaders. The Grand Fascist Council, convening for the first time since 1939, had voted to remove Mussolini and to replace him as premier with seventy-three-year-old Marshal Pietro Badoglio. Eisenhower issued a statement applauding the removal of Mussolini and saying he stood ready to deal with the Badoglio government. However, in view of the "unconditional surrender" doctrine announced the previous January at Casablanca, he knew that this might be politically difficult.

Badoglio, hoping to remove Italy from the war with no further damage, had sent a representative to Lisbon to begin secret negotiations with the Allies. Publicly, however, he and King Victor Emmanuel insisted Italy would keep fighting alongside the Germans. Hitler, himself a master of deceit, wasn't fooled, nor was the Desert Fox, General Erwin Rommel, who wrote in his diary: "In spite of the King's and Badoglio's proclamation we can expect Italy to get out of the war."

Regardless of what Italy might or might not do, it was clear the Allies would soon be launching an invasion of the Italian mainland.

\* \* \*

All his life, Matthew Ridgway had fancied himself as a team player. That was why it bothered him so much when Walter Bedell "Beetle" Smith, Eisenhower's Chief of Staff, implied otherwise in a stern lecture that Ridgway felt sure was delivered on orders from Ike himself. Eisenhower, Bedell said, demanded the utmost cooperation between the British and American forces. Any senior American officer who acted otherwise might as well start packing up, for he was going home.

Ironically, the trouble had come because of friction between Ridgway and a man he admired greatly, the distinguished British lieutenant general Sir Frederick "Boy" Browning. Browning, the airborne advisor on Eisenhower's staff, had often been condescending toward the newly arrived Americans. It was understandable. The British by now had been fighting for four years, much of the time standing alone. The latecomer Americans were still untested and unproven. Nevertheless, the patronizing attitude of the British rankled.

The trouble between Ridgway and the British started when an airborne battalion commander received a note telling him that General Browning would arrive the following day to inspect his unit. This was discourteous to Ridgway, since properly the note should have come through him and should have asked if an inspection at that particular time would be convenient.

On another occasion, Ridgway was told that Browning would be arriving to review Ridgway's plan for the Sicily invasion. Ridgway had fired back a rather blunt note, saying there were no official plans for the Sicily invasion until such time as they had been approved by Ridgway's boss, General Patton. Until then the plans were not available for inspection by anyone, except on General Patton's orders.

George Patton, who admired straight talk, liked Ridgway's response and approved his sending it. Up the line, however, it created a stir. Although Bedell Smith was an old friend, he made it plain that Matt Ridgway needed to get along with the British if he wanted to keep his job.

By late August, with most of Sicily secured and the Germans heading for safety across the Strait of Messina, the Allies needed to know whether the Italians were ready to talk peace. Tentative contacts were made, and on August 31 Italian special agent Giuseppe Castellano arrived clandestinely at Cassibile, a Sicilian village that had fallen into Allied hands but a few days earlier. He was resplendent in a uniform that, dripping with medals and golden braid, showed him to be a general in the Italian army. Underneath that handsome uniform, however, Castellano was sweating, and with good reason. As soon as he revealed Italy's willingness to surrender, he would become a traitor to the Axis cause and a marked man in the eyes of his German allies. Giuseppe Castellano, like his boss, Marshal Badoglio, was far more afraid of the Germans than of any Englishman or American.

The Cassibi le meeting would launch an incredible chain of events, which Dwight Eisenhower later described in his classic memoir, *Crusade in Europe*, as "a series of negotiations, secret communications, clandestine journeys by secret agents, and frequent meetings in hidden places that, if encountered in the fictional world, would have been scorned as incredible melodrama."

Giuseppe Castellano, unaware of the events he was about to set in motion, and wearing his most ingratiating smile, entered the Cassibile conference room. In response, the Allied representatives, led by "Beetle" Smith, were courteous but businesslike. Smith introduced Eisenhower's political advisor, Robert Murphy of the U.S. State Department, as well as Britain's representative, the future prime minister Harold Macmillan.

Smith said he presumed that Castellano knew the purpose of the meeting. Now that Sicily had been secured, the Allies would soon be landing on the Italian mainland. Obviously it would help if Italy announced its surrender prior to those landings. Was Castellano empowered to sign an immediate armistice on behalf of his government?

Rather than giving a direct answer, the wily Castellano, referring to a paper he took from his pocket, began giving a pessimistic description of the situation. The Germans had been strengthening their positions around Rome; if they learned of these negotiations (and German informers were everywhere) their retaliation against the Italians would be swift and brutal. The Italian army, with inferior equipment and limited fuel supplies, was in such a weakened state that it would be able to do little to defend itself.

What Castellano was saying, then, was that the threat of German retaliation, particularly against Rome, made it impossible to make any public announcements until the Allies had landed in force and could guarantee the security of the Eternal City.

Smith said that was quite unacceptable. He then proceeded to explain the "facts of life"—that in view of the Allies' unconditional-surrender policy, the Italians had very little leverage. The only way the Badoglio government could obtain favorable terms would be to announce a surrender *before* the landings, and then to provide full military cooperation.

The smile disappeared from Castellano's face as Smith continued. General Eisenhower, he said, had very little maneuver room. If the Italians did not comply with the American demands, Eisenhower would undoubtedly decide to turn the matter over to the Allied governments, who would be sure to insist on the harshest conditions.

Castellano, more than a little flustered, said he would have to return to Rome for further instructions. Evidently the Italian leaders feared what the Germans might do, particularly to the city of Rome. Although Castellano did not know it, Operation Avalanche, a landing at Salerno, was set for September 9. To support Avalanche, Eisenhower felt it essential to make the Germans divert forces to neutralize the Italians. Perhaps, thought the Allied planners, if plans were made to safeguard Rome, Badoglio might come to terms.

Eisenhower's staff discarded their previous ideas for employing the 82d Airborne Division and drew up a new plan, Giant II, involving an airborne assault near Rome by the 82nd, with the paratroopers then helping the Italians defend the city until such time as the Germans were forced to give full attention to the seaborne invasion.

On September 1, Ridgway and Taylor were summoned to the headquarters of the army group commander, British general Sir Harold Alexander. There they learned of the plan to use their division for an air assault on Rome. At first glance, it seemed like a brilliant concept; not only could they ease Badoglio's concerns over the safety of Rome, they might also be able to block highways the German commander, Field Marshal Albert Kesselring, would use to send reinforcements south to strike the Salerno beachhead.

Upon reflection, however, and after giving Giant II a hard look, Ridgway and Taylor were not so sure: Further examination showed the plan to have many drawbacks. First, there was the long overwater flight at night, by pilots who still lacked the necessary training and who might well produce navigational nightmares similar to those of Husky. Secondly, Rome was out of fighter support range, either from North Africa or from the fields in Sicily; going in without fighters meant they would be at the mercy of enemy air. Moreover, after landing they would have to rely on either bombers or their own light parachute artillery, but without the dive-bombers who could at least pinpoint enemy guns and serve as a form of heavy artillery. Finally, even if they were lucky the first night, after that all enemy guns and fighters would be alerted—ready to intercept any possible resupply missions.

On September 3, Castellano, once more back in Sicily, signed an armistice agreement on behalf of the Badoglio government. Under the terms proposed by Eisenhower, Italian ships and planes would be turned over to the Allies, and all Italian soldiers would lay down their arms.

That same day, Ridgway and Taylor met with Castellano and the Allied staff to complete plans for the jump on Rome. It was an ambitious undertaking. Five airfields north of Rome would be used for both parachute and air landing operations. As this was happening, friendly ships would move up the Tiber River, bringing artillery and antitank weapons. Because of a shortage of transport aircraft, the first assault wave would consist of only 2,000 paratroopers.

In a Sicilian olive grove, Ridgway, Smith, and Taylor sat up all night with the Italian military representatives, asking pointed questions about the extent of Italian cooperation. At one point, the Italians suggested that U.S. planes approach their drop zones from north of the city. At night, however, this would make it difficult to identify the routes; it would be far better for planes to navigate up the Tiber.

"If we do that," Ridgway asked, "can you guarantee they won't be fired upon?"

"Well, it's always possible the cease-fire might not be *total*," said one of the Italians.

Ridgway and Taylor looked at each other. Their skepticism was increasing by the minute, and it continued to grow as the Italians glibly promised to provide several hundred trucks, along with gasoline, rations, and support services.

As the meeting broke up, Ridgway decided the Italians had been much too ready to give their assurances about nearly everything. Looking into their faces, he could just read their fear of the Germans, and in his heart, he felt sure they either couldn't or wouldn't honor their commitments.

Taylor, who felt the same way, asked Ridgway what he was going to do next. Ridgway said he was going to go talk to Beetle.

Soon Ridgway and Smith were sitting together under an olive tree, out of earshot of anyone else. As Ridgway voiced his concerns, his friend Smith listened, very quiet, very grave. "Well, Matt, if that's the way you feel about it, I think the only thing for you to do is request an appointment with General Alexander, and tell him personally how you feel. I'll arrange it for you if you want."

The implication was clear. For this operation, Ridgway was under the command of Sir Harold Alexander, who would be calling the shots, and Ridgway had best behave accordingly.

The meeting with Alexander did not go well. Sir Harold, one of the great soldiers of World War II, no doubt preoccupied with the main Salerno landing, had little desire to discuss the problems of a single American division involved in a secondary diversion. He brushed off Ridgway's concerns rather cavalierly, ending the meeting by saying: "Don't give this another thought, Ridgway. Contact will be made with your division in three days—five at the most."

It seemed to Ridgway and Taylor that too much depended on the Italians. Would they, as promised, be able to light the airfields, suppress the anti-aircraft fire, and provide all that logistic support? After a few hours of brooding, Ridgway talked to Alexander again, making the suggestion that someone go into Rome to check on the Italians' situation.

"Too dangerous, too risky" was Alexander's response. To Ridgway, risking the lives of one or two officers did not seem unreasonable when his whole division was being risked on what he considered a shot in the dark.

As a career soldier, Matt Ridgway knew that further argument might be interpreted as insubordination. Not only that, it would be insubordination to a highly respected British superior. Ike had made it clear how he felt about such things; if Ridgway kept fighting the problem, he would be putting his career on the line.

Showing great moral courage, Ridgway refused to let it drop. Bypassing Alexander, he again appealed to Bedell Smith, who spoke to both Alexander and Eisenhower. Ike himself decided to send two men into Rome to evaluate the situation. Maxwell Taylor courageously volunteered for the job. Accompanying him would be Colonel William T. Gardiner, a former governor of Maine and an Air Force intelligence officer.

On September 6, Taylor flew from Bizerte to Palermo, where he met up with Gardiner. Details of the mission were discussed, including how much the Italians should be told about the Salerno plans. On the fourth, Castellano had asked Bedell Smith when the landings would take place and when the armistice would be announced. Smith feared a leak, so rather than give the actual date of Avalanche—the ninth—he said only, "Within two weeks."

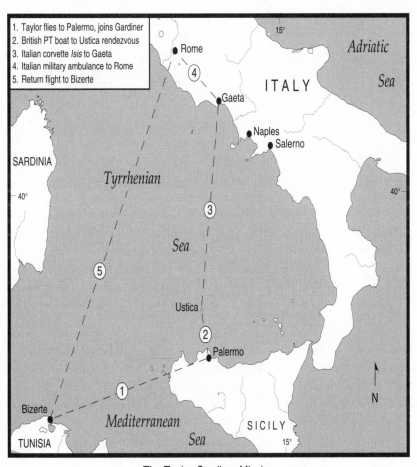

1. Taylor flies to Palermo, joins Gardiner
2. British PT boat to Ustica rendezvous
3. Italian corvette *Isis* to Gaeta
4. Italian military ambulance to Rome
5. Return flight to Bizerte

The Taylor-Gardiner Mission

Taylor and Gardiner, not wanting to be shot as spies if they were captured, decided to go in uniform, but without wearing any insignia of rank. At a final briefing, they were told that unless Taylor sent word to cancel, the Giant II airdrop would take place the night of September 8–9. Coded messages would be sent using Italian facilities, but as backup, Taylor and Gardiner would carry a small radio of their own. If any message contained the code word "innocuous," it would mean that Taylor recommended the operation be scrubbed.

Meanwhile, presumably in support of Giant II, Italian army Chief of Staff Mario Roatta (a man characterized by Harold Macmillan as a "travelled and intelligent conversationalist" but also "a natural coward") was moving two divisions toward Rome, but in a leisurely fashion so as not to arouse the Germans.

At two A.M. on September 7, Max Taylor and Bill Gardiner went aboard a British PT boat, which moments later shoved off from Palermo into the dark waters of the Tyrrhenian Sea. Fifty miles to the north, as they reached their rendezvous point near the island of Ustica, a blinker on the Italian corvette *Isis* flashed a recognition signal.

The PT boat skipper tried coming alongside the *Isis*, but choppy waters made steering difficult and a collision all too likely. Finally Taylor and Gardiner climbed awkwardly into a small boat and, in the darkness, were rowed across to the *Isis*. After a handclasp from the British sailors, along with a "Cheerio and good luck," they were on their own.

Welcoming them aboard the corvette was Rear Admiral Franco Maugeri, the chief of Italian naval intelligence, who later hosted Taylor and Gardiner at a private luncheon where he discussed the details of their mission, complained about the "perfidious English," and assured them of his friendship toward all Americans.

"I don't like this," Taylor told Gardiner. "If this fellow knows so much about what's going on, how many others have been told about our mission?"

Throughout the day, the corvette moved steadily eastward. In late afternoon, after picking its way carefully through mine fields, the *Isis* docked at the port of Gaeta. Under the cover plan, Taylor and Gardiner were to be treated as downed Allied airmen who had been rescued from the sea. Accordingly, they were pulled off the *Isis* and, as curious Italians looked on, two escort "guards" shoved them roughly into a navy automobile.

On a back road outside Gaeta, the two Americans and their escorts were transferred into a waiting military ambulance. The four men huddled uncomfortably in the back of the vehicle as it sped north toward Rome along the historic Appian Way. The only light came through a tiny window in the panel next to the driver, making it impossible to see much of where they were going. Taylor and Gardiner felt like cooped-up mice in a cage, but they kept telling themselves the two escorts and the driver were all fine, brave, trustworthy chaps. At least, they sincerely hoped so!

They came to a roadblock; the tension increased, but moments later they were waved on. Another roadblock, and once again they were allowed to continue. Then the ambulance slowed to a crawl. They had caught up with a German patrol, close enough that had they wanted to—which they did not—they could have reached out and shaken hands.

Finally, around 8:30 P.M., they arrived in Rome at the Palazzo Caprara, across the street from the Italian War Office on the Via Firenze, where they were greeted warmly on behalf of General Giacomo Carboni, commander of the corps assigned to defend Rome.

Back in Sicily, Ridgway fidgeted and waited for word. The 82nd's troopers were scheduled to take off in about twenty-four hours, and Ridgway watched anxiously as men started leaving for their departure airfields.

In Rome, Max Taylor told his hosts he needed to see General Carboni immediately but was informed that General Carboni was not available at the moment. Neither was General Vittorio Ambrosio, Carboni's superior, who had gone to Turin on private business. For now, though, dinner was ready. "Please join us, gentlemen."

The Americans kept looking at their watches as an elegant meal was served in leisurely fashion. Taylor, growing impatient, again said he needed to see General Carboni. Shortly after ten P.M., Carboni finally appeared, resplendent in a beribboned tunic and highly polished boots. To the Americans, he appeared something of a dandy.

When they finally got down to business, Carboni produced a map on which he showed the disposition of his four divisions around Rome. "The Germans," Carboni said, "mistrusting us ever since the change in government, have been moving thousands of troops south through the Brenner Pass. They now have twelve thousand men north of Rome with one hundred and twenty heavy and one hundred and fifty light tanks, plus another twenty-four thousand men to the south of us. They have cut off our gasoline, we are short of ammunition, and frankly, if they decide to occupy Rome, there is nothing we can do about it."

"Then what do you recommend, General?"

"It is not up to me to recommend," Carboni said unctuously. "I am saying, however, that the arrival of airborne troops will only provoke the Germans to very drastic action. In my opinion, my men cannot secure the airfields, cover the assembly areas, or provide anything like the logistic support you want."

Taylor began to get a sinking feeling in the pit of his stomach. What had happened to all those assurances? Trying not to show his anger, he stood up.

"I want to be taken to Marshal Badoglio at once," he said.

"Please, gentlemen, it's the middle of the night. We cannot very well disturb the marshal at this hour."

Although Taylor was a rather young and junior American officer, and Badoglio a head of government, this was no time for niceties. "I insist," Taylor said. "Call the marshal and tell him we're on our way."

Carboni, in his own car, drove the Americans through blacked-out streets to Badoglio's villa on the edge of Rome. Pietro Badoglio, rubbing his eyes and showing every one of his seventy-three years, came downstairs in his pajamas to receive his visitors. After acknowledging the Americans' presence, Badoglio withdrew with Carboni to another room. The Americans grew more and more restless.

When the marshal reappeared, still in his pajamas, he fully backed what Carboni had said, repeating Carboni's pessimistic estimate almost verbatim. Obviously, during the private meeting, Carboni had brought the old marshal over to his way of thinking.

"The armistice will have to be postponed," Badoglio said.

"Let me remind you, sir, that the armistice has already been signed on your behalf."

"I recognize that, but the situation has changed. There is now no way we can defend Rome."

Taylor, trying to stay calm, tried again. "Marshal, your government has made some very serious commitments. How, may I ask, do you expect the Allied leaders to react to your change of heart?"

"I am sure, General Taylor, that you can return to General Eisenhower and explain our situation so he will understand and sympathize with us."

In a cold voice, Taylor replied, "No sir, I won't do that. We are *not* couriers. I will, however, convey to General Eisenhower whatever message you wish to send."

The crafty Badoglio—who still hoped to mollify the suspicious Germans, those Italians who were eager to surrender, and now the angry Americans—penned a message to Eisenhower saying that since the airfields could not be defended, Giant II would not be feasible. Therefore, it was "no longer possible" for his government to accept an armistice.

Taylor and Gardiner conferred. The Italians did not know, nor could they be told, that 2,000 American paratroopers would soon be strapping on their chutes. Lives were hanging in the balance. Taylor followed Badoglio's message with one of his own:

> In view of the statement of Marshal Badoglio as to inability to declare armistice and to guarantee fields GIANT II is impossible. Reasons given for change are irreplaceable lack of gasoline and munitions and new German dispositions. Badoglio requests Taylor return to present government views. Taylor and Gardiner awaiting instructions. Acknowledge.

Taylor and Gardiner returned to the Palazzo Caprara and gave their messages to Carboni for transmission. Allied Headquarters in Bizerte acknowledged Badoglio's message, but there was no response to Taylor's. Although Taylor's first message had been sent at 1:21 A.M., by eight A.M. there was still no reply. In some fourteen hours, the paratroopers might be on their way to potential disaster. Impatiently, Taylor sent a second message at 8:20 A.M., again stating the Italians' inability, or unwillingness, to follow through on their commitments.

The clock kept ticking. As the morning wore on, Taylor and Gardiner wondered if there had been a problem with decoding. Badoglio's message was still the only one which had been acknowledged. Finally, at 11:20, Taylor could stand it no longer. He sent a third message containing but two words: "Situation innocuous."

At Bizerte, Eisenhower was livid as he read Badoglio's message and the first one from Taylor. There was no doubt about it, Badoglio was guilty of the worst kind of double dealing. Fuming, Ike took up a pencil to write a reply, broke it, took up a second pencil and broke that too. Finally he gave up writing and dictated his scorching reply to Badoglio:

> I intend to broadcast the existence of the armistice at the hour originally planned. If you . . . fail to cooperate as previously agreed I will publish to the world the full record of this affair. Failure now on your part to carry out the full obligations to the signed agreement will have the most serious consequences for your country.

Then, gritting his teeth, Eisenhower reluctantly canceled Giant II. At 3 P.M., Taylor and Gardiner received a message telling them to return. Once more they were driven by ambulance through the enemy-held streets of Rome, and at Centocelli airfield on the outskirts of the city, they boarded a trimotor Savoia-Marchetti bomber for their flight to Bizerte.

Taylor had been assured that the flight plan had been cleared with both Italian and Allied air forces, but considering the nature of other Italian assurances, he and Gardiner were more than a little apprehensive. The trimotor took off and headed for North Africa, on what Taylor felt could be the most dangerous part of the trip. Tension increased as they reached the Tunisian coastline and a U.S. fighter plane made a pass at their aircraft. Fortunately the pilot held his fire.

At Allied headquarters, Taylor made a brief report to General Eisenhower, then headed for a bunk. He tossed his musette bag into a corner where, as he later wrote, "the sound of smashing glass from my forgotten bottle of Scotch provided a fitting end to a disappointing mission."

By this time, Allied ships were in the water and nearing the Salerno beaches. Over the radio, the landing forces heard Eisenhower announce the Italian surrender. This forced the Italian premier's hand; as Eisenhower noted: "Badoglio, in fear and trembling, finally decided an hour and a half later that he had to follow suit."

Meanwhile, at Bizerte, Allied staff officers worried that their message to Ridgway might not be decoded and delivered in time to cancel the airdrop. To make doubly sure, American general Lyman Lemnitzer squeezed in behind the pilot of a British fighter plane and headed for the departure airfield at Licata to deliver the message in person. At first the pilot's navigation was faulty, and only after he spotted Sicily's Mount Etna did he set a proper course for Licata. Because of the delay, sixty planes carrying paratroopers were already in the air and circling by the time Lemnitzer touched down. Finally, just as a radio message with the same information was received,

Lemnitzer was able to tell Ridgway the airdrop was off. It was a near thing.

In later years, a few critics would claim that Taylor backed off too soon, that he should have browbeaten Badoglio into fighting the Germans. However, since Badoglio and his ministers left Rome soon after he made his surrender announcement, abandoning the people to cope with the Germans as well as they could, it is doubtful if anything Taylor said or did could have changed Badoglio's mind or stiffened his spine.

One person who never doubted the correctness of Taylor's actions was Ridgway, who wrote:

> When the time comes that I must meet my Maker, the source of most humble pride to me will not be accomplishments in battle, but the fact that I was guided to make the decision to oppose this thing, at the risk of my career right up to the top. . . . When all is said and done, the most precious asset any nation has is its youth, and for a battle commander ever to condone the needless sacrifice of his men is absolutely inexcusable.

"The hard decisions," Ridgway wrote, "are not the ones you make in the heat of battle. Far harder to make are those involved in speaking your mind about some hare-brained scheme which proposes to commit troops to action under conditions where failure is almost certain, and the only results will be the needless sacrifice of priceless lives."

Ridgway was forever convinced that if Giant II had proceeded, his division would have been chewed up. Later he recalled Alexander's assurance of a linkup within three to five days, and noted: "It was nearly seven months before the advanced elements of the ground forces, in spite of every possible effort on their part, finally took Rome."

Matthew Ridgway, who was relatively unknown that day in Sicily when he chose "the harder right instead of the easier wrong," would go on to become one of the twentieth century's greatest, most successful, and most respected military leaders.

CHAPTER 10

# Decision at Atsugi

With one of World War II's
great ironies, cynical GIs in the Pacific often referred to Douglas
MacArthur as Dugout Doug, implying that the general might be a
rear-area type concerned for his own personal safety. The truth, of
course, was that throughout his life MacArthur was a man of remarkable courage, both physical and moral. Indeed, those who knew him
best often considered his bravery to be downright foolhardy. When
the first Japanese bombs fell on Corregidor, for example, and others
were taking cover, MacArthur, almost defiantly, was out in the open
counting the number of enemy planes. After the all-clear sounded,

148

Filipino president Manuel Quezon chided him for risking his life needlessly.

Smiling, MacArthur said, "Oh, you know, the Japs haven't yet fabricated the bomb with my name on it." Then, growing serious, he added: "Of course, I understand what you mean, and I have no right to gamble with my life, but it is absolutely necessary that at the right time a commander take chances because of the effect all down the line, for when they see the man at the top risking his life, the man at the bottom says, 'I guess if that old man can take it, I can too.'"

Soldiers referring to "Dugout Doug" would have been surprised had they talked to doughboys of the World War I Rainbow Division, where MacArthur's bravery was well known, and even more surprised had they known what he'd done years earlier at Veracruz.

At dusk, under an overcast sky, thirty-four-year-old Douglas MacArthur, moving cautiously, slipped silently past an American outpost and into enemy territory. A storm was coming up, so visibility would be limited. Thank heavens for that—it wouldn't do to get caught. Just recently an American private, wandering forward of the lines, had been seized and executed. Moreover, General Funston, who didn't want to risk an incident, knew nothing of his mission, so if MacArthur *were* captured, Funston could do nothing for him. MacArthur must have wondered at the dramatic, improbable series of events which had led up to this moment. . . .

In the spring of 1914, the United States and Mexico were drifting close to war. Following the Mexican Revolution, outrages had been committed by both federal and rebel soldiers, including threats to American citizens and insults to the American flag. On orders from President Wilson, Navy ships had blockaded Veracruz to prevent the landing of war matériel, and the town itself had been seized by U.S. Marines. Although Veracruz was now held by a U.S. brigade under General Frederick Funston, the Americans actually were under siege—bottled up by some 11,000 angry Mexicans under General Victoriano Huerta.

If hostilities broke out, and it became necessary to mount an American expeditionary force, Army Chief of Staff Leonard Wood had been told he'd be in charge. Wood, in turn, had selected young Captain MacArthur to act as his own special agent. MacArthur, acting more or less as a spy, was told to make a reconnaissance of the potential area of operations and to find "all possible information which would be of value."

As Wood's independent representative, and not part of Funston's brigade, Captain MacArthur was very much on his own. Thinking strategically, he decided to learn what the transportation capabilities would be if Wood were to arrive with troops who needed to maneuver inland. His first order of business, therefore, was to check out the rail situation. At Veracruz, there were plenty of freight and passenger cars, but no locomotives. Without engines to haul men and supplies, an American landing force would be immobilized. MacArthur needed to find those missing locomotives.

At a Mexican bar, MacArthur mingled with the patrons and learned that a drunken civilian was bragging about engines hidden somewhere in the interior. When the man sobered up, it turned out he was a railroad fireman and engineer. What about it? MacArthur asked him. If the price was right, could he show him where those engines were hidden? He could, and he even had two friends, fellow railroad men, who'd also like to earn some Yankee dollars. After some haggling, an agreement was reached. So far so good; special agent MacArthur was making progress. In the back of his mind, though, he wondered if this might only be a trick to get an American off alone so he could be killed and robbed.

Once forward of the lines, MacArthur, moving quickly, met the Mexican engineer, who was waiting with a handcar at the appointed place. MacArthur, in uniform, carried nothing except an identification tag and a loaded revolver with plenty of ammunition. Before they proceeded, he insisted on searching his companion. Despite some whiny protests, MacArthur, still fearing treachery, confiscated the man's .38 revolver and hidden knife. Then he had himself searched to prove he carried nothing of value. In other words, the men could gain the promised reward, some $150 in gold for each of them, only by getting MacArthur back safely.

They traveled several miles by handcar to Boca del Rio, making good time. However, at the Jamapa River, they found the railroad bridge was down. Hiding the handcar in some brush, they searched the riverbank, found a small native canoe, and used it to paddle across. After landing, they located two ponies that had been tethered near a tiny shack. Mounting up, they followed a trail running alongside the tracks until they neared the town of Paso del Toro.

Cautiously, they eased their ponies around the town, then trotted back to the rail line. Waiting there with a handcar were the other two men. They hid the ponies and, before proceeding, MacArthur insisted on searching his companions for hidden weapons once again.

The group, now four in number, pumped the handcar vigorously and pushed on. All went well until they came to a shaky-looking bridge. The railroad men said they couldn't cross without first examining the bridge's condition. No, said MacArthur, time was too short—they'd have to keep going.

Again the men protested: It was too great a risk—they wouldn't do it! MacArthur drew his revolver, and in a firm voice said he guessed they would. This "persuasion" worked, and the protests ceased. "In fact," MacArthur later wrote, "after getting into the spirit of the thing their conduct was most admirable."

The handcar kept going. As they came to the next town, MacArthur knew that either his uniform or his Anglo features could mean immediate detection. He dismounted, tied himself to one of the men to keep from being separated, and sent the other two ahead with the handcar. After skirting the town, he and his partner rejoined the men on the handcar. At village after village, the process was repeated.

Shortly after one A.M., they reached the town of Alvarado; just as advertised, there were the missing locomotives, five of them. MacArthur made a careful inspection. Two were switch engines, useful only in rail yards, so they wouldn't be much help. The other three, however, were fine, powerful machines, which with the addition of a few spare parts would do just fine. With that, he gave the word to start back.

So far all had gone well, but on the return trip, near the town of Salinas, their luck changed. As before, two men had taken the handcar on ahead. Then, as MacArthur and his companion skirted the town, they were confronted by one of the gangs that had been prowling the countryside, looting and killing at random. Five armed men in civilian clothes called for them to throw up their hands. The captain and his companion decided to make a run for it; maybe, in the darkness, they could get away.

Minutes later, they had outdistanced all but two of their pursuers. Looking back, they saw that the last two, gaining ground, had taken out their pistols. Shots rang out, and bullets snapped overhead.

MacArthur drew his revolver and returned fire. One of the men dropped. MacArthur fired again and the second man fell. For the moment, they were safe. Now to find the handcar—and they just hoped their companions hadn't been frightened away by the gunshots.

Understandably, the men on the handcar had scuttled on ahead, a full mile beyond Salinas. Eventually, however, the group was reunited and the mission continued. Then, at Piedra, disaster nearly struck again. Because of a wind-driven mist, which obscured their vision, they suddenly found themselves in the middle of fifteen mounted guerrillas. A general mêlée ensued, and one of the horsemen crashed against the handcar, knocking MacArthur off his feet. The outlaws began firing wildly as those on the handcar pumped furiously, trying to outdistance their attackers.

The chase began in earnest, and the night's silence was shattered by pounding hoofbeats, raucous shouts, and the crack of pistol shots. MacArthur, getting to his feet, drew his revolver and returned fire, hitting four of the horsemen in rapid succession. Wisely, the pursuers decided to abandon the chase. Once they were clear, MacArthur found three bullet holes in his clothing, though he himself was unharmed; he felt he must be leading a charmed life. One of his companions hadn't been so lucky. Fortunately, though, the man's wound didn't look too serious.

The party's travails weren't over yet. Near Laguna, they ran into three more mounted men, who not only began firing but also kept up a running fight with the handcar. MacArthur, hoping to outrun the bandits, did not return fire; after several anxious minutes, all but one of the men had been outdistanced.

The third man, however, on a particularly fine horse, refused to give up. He raced ahead of MacArthur and the others, turned, and fired. One bullet clipped through MacArthur's shirt. Two other shots, hitting within inches of his feet, ricocheted off the floor of the handcar. As the man charged, MacArthur drew his revolver, took careful aim, and fired. The man dropped, and the gallant horse was also killed as it went crashing into the car. MacArthur and the others, by this time bone-tired, were forced to drag the carcass off the rails before they could proceed.

At Paso del Toro, as he left the rail line and said good-bye to two of the men, MacArthur assured them they'd definitely earned their reward, which he'd be happy to pay when and if he ever got back to American lines.

He and the first man then found their ponies and, after riding back to Boca del Rio, returned the animals to the place where they'd found them. (Next morning, the ponies' owner must have been truly puzzled to find his normally vigorous animals acting so bedraggled.) The canoe was where they had left it, near the banks of the Jamapa River. The weary American helped his companion into the boat; by this time the man's wound was making him increasingly weak. MacArthur began to paddle across. Tired as he was, it was hard going, and in the darkness he failed to see a hidden stump.

The bottom was ripped; the boat began to fill with water, and within seconds, it sank beneath their feet. MacArthur managed to get clear and to grab his companion. Fortunately they were fairly close to shore and the water was only five feet deep. This was a good thing, by this time both men were so exhausted they would have had a hard time swimming. With difficulty, MacArthur held his companion's head above water as together they struggled onto the muddy riverbank. On hands and knees, they crawled a few feet farther, then collapsed, gasping for breath.

A half-hour later, as it began to get light, they staggered to their feet, found the first handcar, and again started back. Once close to Veracruz, they abandoned the car and managed to cross unobserved into American lines. Mission accomplished.

In a later report, MacArthur would write: "None of the men we encountered were Mexican troops. All were guerrillas undoubtedly bent on general mischief. Owing to the darkness I was not recognized as an American soldier and in consequence no alarm was ever felt for the engines. Months later when traffic was partially resumed I saw one of them running to Tejar from Alvarado."

When he learned of the incident, Leonard Wood recommended MacArthur for the Medal of Honor, the same award his father, Arthur MacArthur, had won during the Civil War at Missionary Ridge. (A board studying Wood's recommendation eventually turned it down, citing the fact that MacArthur had not been acting in an official capacity.)

Fortunately the crisis with Mexico was solved peaceably. Douglas MacArthur returned to Washington and to his position on the General Staff. Before long, as America's entry into the European war grew ever more likely, he was instrumental in the formation of the 42nd Infantry "Rainbow" Division, a National Guard unit drawn from several states. When the division went overseas, MacArthur, now a colonel, went with it as chief of staff.

Soon he was distinguishing himself by his hard work, his military competence, and his courage. In February 1918, even before

American units were in the line, MacArthur, disdaining to wear a helmet or carry a gas mask, accompanied French troops on a trench raid armed only with a trench knife and a riding crop. After savage fighting, the party returned at daybreak escorting a large number of German prisoners. Frenchmen crowded around the American colonel, shaking his hand, slapping him on the back, offering him cognac and absinthe. Later, General Bazelaire, after kissing him on both cheeks, pinned a Croix de Guerre on his chest.

Next, as the Rainbow Division came on line to do its part in the ghastly, nightmarish trench warfare, MacArthur time after time accompanied various units on their most dangerous raids. To steady the men as they prepared to go "over the top," he often walked the line in his eccentric apparel—on his head a visored cap rather than a helmet, around his neck a four-foot muffler knitted by his mother, and, as an outer garment, a West Point sweater with the "A" he'd won in athletics. Soon his division commander, General Menoher, would tell a *New York Times* reporter: "Colonel MacArthur is one of the ablest officers in the United States Army and one of the most popular." By this time doughboys were calling him the American d'Artagnan, the Fighting Dude, or even the Beau Brummell of the AEF.

Father Francis Duffy, regimental chaplain of New York's famous "Fighting 69th," wrote in his diary: "Our chief of staff chafes at his own task of directing instead of fighting, and he has pushed himself into raids and forays in which some older heads think he had no business to be. His admirers say that his personal boldness has a very valuable result in helping to give confidence to the men."

One of MacArthur's West Point classmates, trying to find him, once asked soldiers wearing the Rainbow Division shoulder patch if they knew their chief of staff when they saw him. The indignant answer was that "every soldier in the 42nd Division" knew MacArthur.

Over the years, the MacArthur legend continued to grow, and in the early days of World War II, his Japanese opponents were well aware of MacArthur's importance both as a military leader and as a symbol. That made him a prime target, and as his greatly outnumbered forces on Bataan retreated before the powerful Japanese war machine, Tokyo Rose was making an ominous prediction. "We will capture General MacArthur," she announced, "and when we do, we will bring him to Tokyo, where he will be publicly hanged in the Imperial Plaza!"

MacArthur evaded capture, of course, having been ordered by President Roosevelt to leave the Philippines, go to Australia, and organize the offensive against Japan. A main object of that offensive, he announced, would be the liberation of the Philippines. "I came through," he said, "and I shall return."

Some people criticized the first-person nature of that pledge, saying it merely indicated a massive personal ego. Filipinos suffering under the cruel Japanese occupation knew better. American guerrilla leader Ed Ramsey explained it this way: "America had failed to defend the Philippines and the promised relief had never appeared. A trust had been violated, a confidence betrayed. In its place MacArthur offered the Filipino people a personal pledge, and they accepted it unquestioningly. 'I shall return' was more to them than a promise; it bespoke a covenant."

Now, in July 1945, less than four years after making that pledge, Douglas MacArthur was on board the U.S.S. *Boise*, his temporary headquarters, and talking to General George Kenney, his Air Force commander in the South Pacific. By this time MacArthur had fulfilled his promise of returning to the Philippines. Soon, he believed, the ugly war with Japan would be brought to a close.

Together, he and Kenney reviewed the events of the past few months. In March, Marines had captured Iwo Jima; on April 1 they landed on Okinawa. At this point the Japanese government had proclaimed that Okinawa, not Leyte or Luzon, would be the war's decisive battle, reminding the people that samurai warriors let "the enemy cut one's skin to eat his flesh." Not until 110,000 Japanese had been killed in bloody combat did Okinawa fall. And now, with Okinawa secure, the Allies were at last ready to plan the final act: invasion of the Japanese homeland.

Kenney was convinced, he told MacArthur, that soon, despite the propaganda they'd been fed, the Japanese would realize the end was near. B-29s from Iwo Jima and Saipan were hitting Japan around the clock, and by this time U.S. warships were even shelling coastal cities at point-blank range.

Kenney was wrong about the Japanese perception. Many people still believed the Home Islands, having fallen as drops from the sword of a god, were so sacred that foreign invasion was unthinkable. Even the leaders, who admitted that American landings were imminent, remained optimistic. The Chinese mainland remained in Japanese hands, and the bulk of the Japanese army was still undefeated. As for repelling invaders, they had 10,000 kamikaze planes at their disposal, along with some 250,000 garrison troops and 32 million civilian militiamen. All males fifteen to sixty years old and all females seventeen to forty-five years old had been conscripted. Even little children had been trained to strap explosives around their waists, roll under tank treads, and blow themselves up.

Meanwhile, people were being told that Americans were hairy barbarians who would be sure to mistreat women if they got the chance. Many female plant workers were given cyanide capsules to swallow if American rapists threw them to the ground. Nippon was indeed a nation ready for hara-kiri—determined to prevail, or if not, to go down fighting.

Now that Germany had surrendered and more troops from Europe were becoming available, MacArthur more than ever felt that Allied victory was almost inevitable. It might, however, come at the cost of a million or more casualties.

The question, of course, was what it would take to bring about a Japanese surrender. The signal, MacArthur had been telling his staff, would originate from the Imperial Palace. All along, he said, he'd been urging the Pentagon and the State Department to be on the lookout for conciliatory gestures.

MacArthur didn't know it, but as early as May, Japanese envoys in Moscow had made overtures toward an armistice. Harry Hopkins had cabled President Truman that "peace feelers are being put out by certain elements in Japan." Truman, new in office and perhaps not as politically astute as Roosevelt might have been, decided to ignore the signals. Advisors such as Dean Acheson, as well as Hopkins himself, convinced him that negotiations would be pointless, that unless Hirohito was dethroned, the war would have been in vain.

To MacArthur, however, Hirohito was the key. He was convinced the Japanese would never renounce their emperor, equally convinced the Japanese would never submit to an Allied occupation unless Hirohito ordered it.

Planning was under way for Operation Olympic, a landing on Kyushu scheduled for November 1, also for Coronet, the main assault on Honshu, which was to follow four months later.

MacArthur, as he talked to Kenney, made a surprising prediction. It was now mid-July, and he thought that by September the Japanese would sue for peace, making Olympic unnecessary. Kenney disagreed, citing the recent Potsdam Declaration, which told Japan to surrender unconditionally or face "utter destruction." That implied deposing the emperor; surely the Japanese would never consent to abandon Hirohito. MacArthur said he, too, was appalled by the Potsdam communiqué, but still felt that, when the time came, the Allies would have the good sense to let the Japanese keep their emperor.

A few days later, the general learned for the first time about a powerful new weapon. The following week, on August 6, an atomic bomb called Little Boy was released over Hiroshima. Now that Japan's fate was obvious, the Soviets lost no time in seeking their share of any spoils. Two days later, in Moscow, Foreign Minister Molotov told the Japanese ambassador that Russia was declaring war on Japan. Within hours, three Russian army groups rolled over Japan's Kwantung Army and swept into Manchuria.

Events were now moving rapidly to a climax. On August 9, a second bomb known as Fat Man was dropped on Nagasaki, and Hirohito told members of the Supreme War Council: "I cannot bear to see my innocent people suffer any longer."

On August 10, the council, bowing to the inevitable and swayed by the emperor's guidance, agreed to the Allies' terms, asking only that Hirohito be retained as emperor. The Allies, despite the Potsdam Declaration, were quick to accept.

On August 15, the Japanese people heard Hirohito's voice for the first time. In a radio broadcast, he said the Japanese would have to "endure the unendurable and suffer the insufferable." It was time, he said, to "pave the way for a grand peace for all generations to come."

The Russians cynically ignored Hirohito's announcement and continued their offensive. Port Arthur in Manchuria was seized, as were southern Sakhalin and the Kurile Islands. In the process, some 80,000 Japanese were killed, against some 8,000 Russians.

On Honshu, meanwhile, many senior Japanese officers, unwilling to face the dishonor of surrender, were committing hara-kiri with their little disemboweling knives. In Tokyo, one group of outraged young officers, convinced Hirohito's broadcast was a fake, fought their way into the emperor's palace, where thirty-two were killed before the rest were turned back. At nearby Atsugi air base, the base commander told his pilots it would be treason to surrender. "Join me in destroying the enemy!" he cried, and they shouted back, "Banzai!"

This was the mood as MacArthur directed the imperial government to send a delegation to him in Manila to discuss the surrender ceremonies. "By way of preparation," he told them, "I want you to remove all propellers from the aircraft at Atsugi, where I will be landing. Be ready with transportation from Atsugi to Yokohama, and reserve the Yokohama New Grand Hotel for Allied use. My temporary headquarters will be at Yokohama, and the battleship *Missouri* will be the scene of formal surrender ceremonies."

The Japanese, fearful of all the fanatics who might hope to assassinate MacArthur, argued about only one thing. They urged him not to land at Atsugi, saying it was much too dangerous. Atsugi, after all, was home to the kamikaze pilots, many of whom had not only refused to surrender but had even invaded the palace grounds, firing on the house of the prime minister and killing the commanding general of the Imperial Guard Division.

In Manila, MacArthur's staff was equally opposed to an Atsugi landing. "It's too much of a gamble," they said. "Don't forget, there are thousands of armed Japanese still in place, including some twenty-two divisions on the Kanto plain of Tokyo alone. You've come too far to risk everything at this point."

Only MacArthur seemed unaware of the danger. "Don't worry," he told Kenney and the others, "the Emperor is divine, and he has told them to lay down their arms."

"There's a flaw in that argument, General. Divinities aren't supposed to lose wars!"

MacArthur's Chief of Staff, General Dick Sutherland, was even more adamant. "My God, General, the Emperor is worshiped as a real god, and we have a report they tried to assassinate him. What kind of target does that make *you*?"

"Frankly, I doubt anyone tried to kill the Emperor. I suspect that report was false." (MacArthur was right, but at the time no one could be sure.) "I *shall* land at Atsugi, as announced, and will ride into Yokohama." The staff realized that further argument was useless; the "Old Man" had made up his mind. While conventional wisdom might suggest that the United States enter Japan in force and prepared for treachery, MacArthur felt that peace could be attained more rapidly by a show of confidence. It was a courageous decision, but he felt it was the right one, and he had the moral courage to act accordingly.

As it came time for the flight into Japan, MacArthur noticed several of the officers strapping on shoulder holsters with pistols. "Take them off," he said. "If they intend to kill us, sidearms will be useless. I know the Oriental mind, and nothing will impress them like a show of absolute fearlessness. If they don't know they're licked, this will convince them."

Despite his confident air, and his claim to know "the Oriental mind," surely Douglas MacArthur must have had doubts. Experience had shown the Japanese to be capable of deceit, and he knew much hatred still existed. In Tokyo, teams of youths wearing white headbands and calling themselves the Righteous Group for Upholding Imperial Rule and Driving Out Foreigners were said to be seeking an "honorable death." They had burned the homes of two senior ministers, had seized post offices, power stations, and newspaper offices, and had even laid siege to the home of the prime minister. As the journalist John Gunther wrote: "Professors who studied Japan all their lives, military experts who knew every nook and cranny of the Japanese character, thought that MacArthur was taking a frightful risk."

Throughout his life, MacArthur's critics accused him of egotism, of being a "performer" over-concerned with showmanship. Undoubtedly there was much truth in this, but it was also true that Douglas MacArthur, more than any other American before or since, knew the advantages of drama, of ceremony, of "face." This was especially true in Asia, where his courage and showmanship were about to have a remarkable effect.

At two o'clock on the afternoon of August 30, MacArthur's C-54, the *Bataan*, soared past beautiful Mount Fuji and approached the Atsugi airfield. One of MacArthur's companions, General Court Whitney, was understandably apprehensive. "It was difficult not to let my mind dwell on Japan's recent performances," Whitney later wrote.

> The war had been started without a formal declaration; near-ly everywhere Japanese soldiers had refused to give up until killed; the usual laws of war had not been complied with; deadly traps had frequently been set. Here was the greatest opportunity for a final and climactic act. The anti-aircraft guns could not possibly miss at this range. Had death, the insatiable monster of the battle, passed MacArthur by on a thousand fields only to murder him at the end? I held my breath. But as usual, he had been right. He knew the Orient. He knew the basic Japanese character too well to have thus gambled blindly with death. He knew and trusted that national spirit of chivalry called "Bushido."

The *Bataan* landed and rolled to a stop. MacArthur stepped from the plane, paused, looked at the blue sky, and smiled. Then, after returning the salute of General Robert Eichelberger, who had arrived earlier with a small detachment, he said, "Well, Bob, it's been a long road from Melbourne to Tokyo, but as they say in the movies, this is the payoff."

MacArthur entered a decrepit-looking Lincoln sedan, the best the Japanese were able to provide. Then he and the other Americans, in a ramshackle motorcade, began the fifteen-mile drive into Yokohama. Japanese soldiers stood in a long line on each side of the route, their backs to the roadway in a gesture of respect. It was their custom not to look upon the face of the divine emperor, and the two divisions on hand, 30,000 fully armed men, were guarding the Supreme Allied Commander in the same deferential manner used to protect the emperor himself.

That evening at the New Grand Hotel, MacArthur was served a steak dinner. As he started to eat, Whitney put a hand on his arm. "Better have someone taste that food, General. There's a good chance it may be poisoned."

MacArthur just laughed. "This is a good steak, and I don't intend to share it with anyone!"

The hotel staff had also expected MacArthur to request a precautionary tasting. When he did not, Yozo Nomura, the hotel owner, came to the table to express gratitude for this expression of "great trust," saying he and his employees were "honored beyond belief."

A delighted MacArthur beamed his appreciation, and Americans at the table wondered why he made such a fuss over Nomura's little speech. What the general knew, of course, was that word of everything he said and did would soon be spread throughout Japan.

On September 2, 1945, the historic, formal surrender took place on the battleship *Missouri*. During the ceremony, MacArthur told the assemblage it would be inappropriate to meet "in a spirit of distrust, malice, or hatred." Rather, both the victor and the vanquished should rise "to that higher dignity which alone benefits the sacred purposes we are about to serve." It was his "earnest hope and indeed the hope of all mankind" that "a better world shall emerge, one founded upon faith and understanding—a world dedicated to the dignity of man and the fulfillment of his most cherished wish—for freedom, tolerance, and justice."

Japanese representatives on the *Missouri* were amazed by the lack of vindictiveness. Toshikazu Kase, one of those representatives, wrote of MacArthur in his report to the emperor:

He is a man of peace. Never has the truth of the line "peace has her victories no less renowned than war" been more eloquently demonstrated. He is a man of light. Radiantly, the gathering rays of his magnanimous soul embrace the earth, his footsteps paving the world with light. Is it not a piece of rare good fortune . . . that a man of such caliber and character should have been designated as the Supreme Commander who will shape the destiny of Japan? In the dark hour of our despair and distress, a bright light is ushered in, in the very person of General MacArthur.

Six days after the surrender ceremonies, MacArthur established his headquarters in the Dai Ichi building in downtown Tokyo. His concern, he told the Japanese, was "not how to keep Japan down but how to get her on her feet again." Although he was a supposedly "all-powerful" supreme commander, he was still faced with as many problems as any military figure in history. "I had to be," he wrote later, "an economist, a political scientist, an engineer, a manufacturing executive, a teacher, even a theologian."

High on the list of problems were the Russians, who despite being latecomers in the war against Japan, were quick to present their demands. General Kuzma Derevyanko, head of the Russian mission, insisted that Soviet troops be allowed to occupy Hokkaido, the northern island of Japan, thus dividing the country in two. Their forces, he also stipulated, would be entirely independent of General MacArthur's authority.

MacArthur refused point-blank, whereupon Derevyanko became grossly abusive and insulting. When MacArthur refused to yield, Derevyanko began to bluster, saying that the Soviet Union would see to it that MacArthur was dismissed as supreme commander.

"Furthermore," said Derevyanko, "Russian forces will move into Hokkaido whether you approve or not!"

Once again MacArthur's moral courage was put to the test. Looking Derevyanko straight in the eye, he said: "If a single Soviet soldier enters Japan without my authority, I shall at once throw the entire Russian mission into jail, beginning with you, General."

Derevyanko acted stunned, as though he couldn't believe what he was hearing. Then, in a subdued voice, he said: "My God, I believe you would." He turned and left, and nothing more was heard of the matter.

Several symbolic events were soon to set the tone of the occupation. Foremost was the courtesy call on MacArthur by the emperor himself. Hirohito's unprecedented deference had monumental significance for the Japanese people, as did the well-publicized photo of a vigorous MacArthur towering over the diminutive emperor. Equally symbolic, at least to Douglas MacArthur, was the first review of occupation troops. It was staged in the plaza outside the Imperial Palace, on the very spot that Tokyo Rose had once named as the site of the general's scaffold.

For the next five years and more, Douglas MacArthur oversaw the rebuilding of Japan in what became perhaps the outstanding military occupation in recorded history. Later success owed much to how it all began.

Some months after Japan's surrender, at a dinner in New York, Winston Churchill was seated next to Winthrop W. Aldrich, later the U.S. ambassador to Great Britain. "Tell me, Ambassador," said Churchill, "what would you consider the outstanding accomplishment of any commander during World War II?"

"I would hesitate even to guess," said Aldrich. "But tell me, sir, what do *you* think?"

Churchill, lighting a cigar, paused for effect. "I am convinced," he said, "it was the landing in Japan by General MacArthur, accompanied only by a small force of troops, and in the face of several million Japanese soldiers who had not yet been disarmed."

Winston Churchill, arguably the greatest statesman of World War II, had paid a sincere, magnificent compliment to the moral courage of a man who may have been that war's greatest general.

Aldrich wrote MacArthur of the conversation, adding: "It is my belief that this opinion is shared almost unanimously by the people of this country."

CHAPTER 11

# Decision in Berlin

By December 1941, the war in Europe was already more than two years old. For many Americans, however, direct U.S. involvement still seemed but a remote possibility, and in most communities business was carried on more or less as usual. In Washington, D.C., however, things were different. The nation's capital had become a bustling boomtown of government activity, with most of its effort devoted to an urgent military buildup.

Even in Washington, however, people found time to relax, and on Sunday, December 7, 1941, as bombs fell on Pearl Harbor and a stunned America learned it was at war, thousands of Washingtonians were watching a football game at Griffith Stadium between the

163

Washington Redskins and the Philadelphia Eagles. The stadium crowd that day included a certain member of the U.S. Army Corps of Engineers, forty-four-year-old Colonel Lucius Dubignon Clay.

Clay was already known as one of the Army's brightest stars. In the Philippines, Dwight Eisenhower had called him "a superior officer . . . of unlimited capacity for advancement." Ever since his 1918 graduation from West Point, Clay's reputation had been tested in a series of increasingly difficult assignments. Finally, in the late 1930s, he had supervised the construction of the powerful hydroelectric dam at Denison, Texas, after which he had been summoned to Washington to head FDR's newly established airport-construction program. Once again he had performed with distinction; in his efficiency report, he was described as "full of energy . . . brilliant and original in thought . . . able to get a mission accomplished . . . a strong character who can be politely firm without being hard boiled."

Now, as a hushed stadium crowd learned the nation was at war, Lucius Clay braced himself for what would undoubtedly be new and even greater challenges. As he expected, he was given a war-related task almost immediately. Within days, wearing civilian clothes for secrecy, he was sent to Brazil to determine whether the United States should have airports there, and if present facilities were inadequate, whether neutral Brazilians would let the North Americans build new ones.

By the end of December, Lucius Clay's first wartime mission was completed. He'd found, in effect, that the United States could depend on Brazilian cooperation. Now, back in Washington, he was impatient, wanting to render his report so he could start promptly for either Europe or the Pacific, presumably as commander of a combat engineer unit.

He made his report to Dwight Eisenhower, newly appointed chief of the War Plans Division. "That's fine," said Ike, who remembered Clay from their time together in the Philippines. "I think you should give this to General Marshall, and I will arrange it."

After the report was delivered to Marshall, however, Eisenhower said: "Now, before we determine your next assignment, you can sit down here [in War Plans] and take one of these desks and help us out right here."

"I don't think that's my talent," said Clay.

"Well, in any event, you take a desk right here for the time being until we see what's happening."

Clay, who had never seen combat, feared he might end up fighting World War II from behind a desk—an unhappy prospect for a career soldier. That very afternoon, however, opportunity came knocking in the person of "Vinegar Joe" Stilwell, a pugnacious general who was on his way overseas, and who asked Clay if he'd like to go along as Stilwell's engineer. Lucius Clay jumped at the chance.

Next day, however, Clay learned it was not to be. He groaned inwardly as Eisenhower told him, rather mysteriously: "I'm sorry, but you're not going with Stilwell. You'll just have to stick around here. I can't tell you any more than that, but you're not going with Stilwell."

Later that week, the mystery was solved. George Marshall, the Army Chief of Staff, announced the creation of the Services of Supply, under General Bill Somervell. As chief of matériel (whatever that was) Clay would be promoted to brigadier general and made a member of Somervell's team.

The promotion was fine, but it didn't ease Clay's disappointment about staying in Washington. Nevertheless, he set to work vigorously. His job, Somervell said, was "to find out what the Army needs and get it!"

It wasn't much by way of guidance, particularly since the Army itself wasn't sure of its requirements. Nevertheless, Clay began assembling a team and establishing priorities.

On January 6, 1942, a month into the war, Franklin Roosevelt, in his message to Congress, announced dramatic production goals: 60,000 airplanes a year, 45,000 tanks, 8 million tons of shipping. FDR had pulled the numbers pretty much off the top of his head, as much for civilian morale as anything else, but to people in Washington, Roosevelt's objectives were soon almost sacred.

Could the objectives be met? Was it possible, for example, to build 45,000 tanks in 1942? Clay's calculations showed it might be possible, but only by slighting other requirements. Besides, tanks would be no good without proper ammunition. And what about crews for those tanks? Or trained mechanics to service them? His boss was not at all pleased when Clay said the numbers would have to be amended.

"The new Services of Supply," said Somervell, "will be judged, to a considerable extent, by the success or failure in meeting the objectives laid down by the President." Even if that weren't the best way to do things, Clay was told, one couldn't "take any such attitude toward the instructions of the Commander in Chief."

Clay persisted. FDR's 45,000 tanks were half again as many as the Army required in 1942. On the other hand, some of the President's figures, such as those for antitank guns, were well *below* what the Army needed. Moreover—and this was a telling argument—the tanks now being manufactured were already inadequate; why waste precious material on producing too many of them?

Eisenhower in War Plans lent his support to Clay's argument, and even Donald Nelson, chairman of the War Production Board (WPB) who regularly tried his best to avoid telling Roosevelt anything unpleasant, was finally won over.

Clay wrote a memo for George Marshall to send the White House, explaining why FDR's announced goals would have to be modified. Roosevelt reluctantly swallowed the bitter pill and, in a letter drafted by Clay, told Donald Nelson of the amended goals. The balanced procurement program (officially the Army's Supply Program) was alive and running. For Lucius Clay, it was the first of many major wartime struggles.

Over the next three years, as America's soldier in charge of defense production, Clay worked tirelessly. He was at his desk by 7:30 each morning, seldom leaving before ten or eleven at night, and it was not unusual for him to work seventy-two hours at a stretch in his determination to give the Army what it needed. His hard-nosed, selfless efficiency won the respect not only of the military but also of key administration figures such as Harry Hopkins, Bernard Baruch, Henry Morgenthau, and Secretary of War Henry Stimson. "The most able fellow around this town is General Clay," Morgenthau was heard to say. Also impressed was South Carolina's Jimmy Byrnes, FDR's overall home-front coordinator, who later in the war became Clay's boss.

All the while, however, and despite the importance of his work, the idea of staying in Washington continued to rankle. Clay wrote Somervell requesting to be relieved as director of matériel, saying "a fresh mind" would be of more value in the transition times ahead.

"I believe that I am qualified to command an Engineer regiment in the field," he wrote Somervell, "and such an assignment in the grade of colonel would be welcomed." Never mind that by this time he had become a major general; to get a combat assignment, he'd willingly take off the two stars.

His request was denied, and a frustrated Clay wrote his classmate Pat Casey, who was in Australia with MacArthur: "Washington is filled with families with husbands at various fronts, and I am beginning to feel like a draft dodger every time I walk down the street!"

Stay in Washington he did, however, except for a brief stint in France, at Eisenhower's special request, to unsnarl a bottleneck of massive proportions at the port of Cherbourg. Clay tried, with Eisenhower's help, to stay overseas, but once he'd solved the immediate supply-line problems and had things rolling smoothly, he was again recalled to Washington.

By early 1945, as the Allies were driving into Germany and victory in Europe seemed imminent, a paramount question became that of establishing a postwar military government. Who would head such a thing? And should he be military or civilian?

Roosevelt, thinking it over, decided the able assistant secretary of war John J. McCloy, a former Wall Street lawyer, was just the man for the job.

"I've made up my mind," he told McCloy. "You're going to be the first High Commissioner for Germany."

McCloy protested, telling Roosevelt it'd be a mistake to choose a civilian for the job: "It will be primarily a military problem at first, and the person who goes there is going to find himself in a situation like a Mississippi River disaster. Where are the rations going to come from? How are the people to be fed? Basic logistics. And with all of the armies there, with the military conquest so recent, I think a civilian might be submerged."

And who would McCloy recommend for the job? His own choice, he told Roosevelt, would be General Lucius Clay, the man who was doing such an outstanding job as Jimmy Byrnes's assistant. Secretary of War Stimson also favored Clay. He approached Byrnes, who agreed to Clay's release, but with great reluctance. Clay, he said, was the most able man he had ever worked with, and he didn't know how he could get along without him.

During the following month, other names were proposed, including that of Supreme Court Justice Owen Roberts. After considerable procrastination, FDR followed Stimson's advice, choosing Clay even as Stimson was saying it would "break Jimmy Byrnes's heart to lose him!"

Clay, meeting with FDR to receive the word officially, was shocked by the President's obvious ill health. Two weeks later, while on his way to Europe, he learned Roosevelt had died.

As Clay sat in the plane flying over the Atlantic, he knew nothing of the top secret policy paper still being written which would be his official guidance, nor did he know of its severe, punitive wording. JCS 1067, much of it written under the influence of Henry Morgenthau, contemplated the harshest possible treatment for Germany, with policies that in effect would reduce the country to a pastoral society whose industrial capacity would never again be able to threaten world peace.

It's doubtful that Clay ever harbored thoughts of punishing the average German, but if he did they were soon dismissed. Upon arriving in Berlin soon after Germany's surrender, he was struck by the depth of misery. "It was like a city of the dead," he later wrote, "and I must confess that my exultation in victory was diminished as I witnessed this degradation of man. I decided then and there never to forget that we were responsible for the government of human beings."

He had inherited a nightmarish situation. German government had collapsed; millions of POWs needed to be processed for discharge; countless thousands of displaced persons, with more arriving daily, were crowding the highways, desperately searching for food and a place to live; school buildings were destroyed; hospitals were filled with wounded German soldiers; farms and factories were mostly idle.

"I think," Clay wrote, "that if we had then realized the confusion and chaos which existed we would indeed have thought ours a hopeless task."

Clay decided it was essential, not only for Europe but for the entire free world, that Germany be rebuilt so as to take its proper place among nations. Although the harsh JCS 1067 said he shouldn't do anything to rehabilitate the German economy, those words had been written by people back in the States. To Clay, on the scene, JCS 1067 was plainly wrong. Obviously the Germans must be able to produce for export; otherwise they would starve.

In the coming months, Clay was firm, correct, even aloof, in his dealings with the Germans, but all the while he was guiding them on the road to recovery. Meanwhile, he used every trip to Washington to get the Germans more food.

In the absence of a functioning German government, Clay used his best judgment, made the necessary decisions, and assumed personal responsibility for those decisions. If he received orders he considered unwise, he was always willing to say so, even if it meant laying his career on the line. At one point he told a shocked secretary of the army: "Of course I will carry out the instructions given me in this teleconference; then I will cable requesting my immediate retirement." The instructions were quickly changed.

Soon after the war's end, the U.S. Army gained custody of perhaps the greatest single art collection in the world. In Thuringia, men of Patton's Third Army had discovered a huge trove of priceless paintings which had been stored in dehumidifying salt mines for safekeeping. Some were Nazi loot, which had been stolen from private collections in Western Europe and needed to be returned to the rightful owners. The truly great masterpieces, however, including fifteen paintings by Rembrandt, came from the Kaiser Friedrich Museum of Berlin. In addition to the awe-inspiring Rembrandts, there were works by Rubens, Botticelli, Dürer, Manet, and others, 202 of the world's greatest art treasures.

In general, the victors' mood at the time, Americans included, was one of retribution. Make the Germans pay for what they had done! Consequently, there was a real possibility this art would be seized and shipped off as a form of reparation. Clay, however, was determined to preserve those paintings for their rightful owners, the German people. He reasoned that the paintings should go initially to America. The Kaiser Friedrich Museum, he knew, with a bombed-out roof, crumbling walls, and standing water in the basement, was in no condition to receive them. Moreover, the museum was in the Russian sector of Berlin, and if the Soviets ever got their hands on those paintings, no one knew what might happen. No, the best plan would be for America to serve as the paintings' trustee until, as Clay put it, Germany had "re-earned the right to be considered a nation."

Shrewdly, Clay approached President Harry Truman during the Potsdam Conference in July 1945 and secured his approval, not only for shipping the paintings to the States for display and safekeeping, but also for announcing publicly, especially to the German people, the plans for their eventual return.

By playing the presidential card, Clay was preempting several key Americans, including members of the State Department, who were eyeing those paintings as possible reparations trophies. Others were proposing that eventual disposition "be subject to future Allied discussions," thus leaving their future return to Germany seriously in doubt.

Claiming such paintings for America was an offense to Clay's sense of honor. "I sincerely believe," he said, "that cultural objects belonging in Germany should be left in Germany if we expect to be successful in implanting democratic processes."

The battle was far from over. The paintings by this time were stored in Washington at the National Gallery, and despite Clay's recommendation, no public showing was held. By 1948, Clay was hearing rumors about the National Gallery wanting to retain the paintings indefinitely. Not coincidentally, about this time Senator William Fulbright of Arkansas introduced legislation "to retain and display" the Kaiser Friedrich collection in the United States. The Army, at Clay's prodding, asked Fulbright to drop the bill. Fulbright refused.

Clay, appalled at what he considered a breach of honor, said he "could not understand how a United States Senator could have such an elastic conception of America's international obligations." Then, pulling no punches, he spoke out frankly. To General David Noce, chief of the Army's Civil Affairs Division, he wrote: "From the very beginning, I have had serious doubts as to the real desires and intent of the directors of the National Art Gallery. . . . I am afraid their desire to increase the prestige of the National Gallery lies behind the Fulbright measure."

A teleconference was arranged between Clay and three powerful members of the Senate Armed Services Committee. The senators agreed with Clay's logic—that any legislation would imply a legal right to control the paintings. The senators supported Clay, as did the President. Consequently Fulbright, the State Department, and the National Gallery were all bypassed rather neatly. Before the paintings were returned to Germany, a hugely successful public exhibition was held, with proceeds going to a German children's relief fund. For American interests in Germany, it was a public relations triumph.

Years later, Clay said that to keep those paintings would have been to behave just like the Russians, and he'd never understood "how anybody in the U.S. Senate could have such a low conception of the responsibilities and duties of the U.S. government."

In March 1947, Lucius Clay became overall U.S. Commander in Chief for Europe (CINCEUR) replacing General Joseph McNarney. Events leading up to the change in command were rather ticklish, and at one point it appeared McNarney would balk at his next proposed assignment, with Clay being put in the awkward position of replacing a superior who didn't want to be replaced. To Clay, this smacked of disloyalty. The War Department said the change was definite, and Clay should so inform McNarney. This he refused to do, saying: "During my entire service in the Army I have had but one standard, and that was complete loyalty to my immediate superior. I am unwilling to have any suspicion cast on that standard as long as I am in the Army . . . self-respect is the most precious possession one can have." McNarney, who appreciated Clay's predicament, exited gracefully, leaving Clay free to become CINCEUR.

Ever since the war's end, it had become increasingly clear that far too many questions had been left open for postwar settlement. In hindsight, wartime planners appeared to have been remarkably naïve. No doubt, in the exhilaration of victory, they'd convinced themselves that wartime cooperation and goodwill would somehow carry over.

Nowhere was this naïveté more evident than in a 1943 talk by then–Secretary of State Cordell Hull, who promised the U.S. Congress: "There will no longer be need for spheres of influence, for alliances, for balance of power or any other of the special arrangements through which, in the unhappy past, the nations strove to safeguard their security or to promote their interests." Like Hull, unfortunately, too many leaders, both military and civilian, seemed to have felt that written guarantees were mainly superfluous.

A prime example of wartime trust was the question of Allied access to Berlin. All plans and proclamations accepted a common occupation of the German capital, but not one of them contained any guarantee of access or specific provision for road, rail, or air right of way. The omission was not accidental, for the subject had been raised with Ambassador John Winant, U.S. representative on the European Advisory Commission. Winant, however, felt that the right to be in Berlin carried with it the right of access, and feared that to raise the question would only confuse the issue, perhaps arousing Soviet suspicion and making mutual understanding more difficult to attain. According to Clay, Winant "believed it possible to develop a mutual friendly understanding in which differences would disappear."

By 1948, after three years of wrangling, it was evident that Winant and others had been wrong. Clay and General Sir Brian Robertson, his British counterpart on the Allied Control Council, had tried mightily to make things work and to establish a free Germany under quadripartite supervision. But the Soviet Union, as Clay saw it, did not want "to permit the message of freedom and economic security to reach the borders of its satellite countries." Stalin wanted nothing less than a unified, Communist Germany, which, like Hungary, Poland, Czechoslovakia, and other satellites, could be dominated by the U.S.S.R. Under this plan, the first step would be to drive the Western Allies out of Berlin.

When it became evident the Russians would never cooperate in establishing a true quadripartite government, the British and Americans announced plans to join together in a bizonal arrangement. The French, not wanting to antagonize the Russians, had initially held back, but eventually they agreed to consider linking their own sector to that of the British and Americans.

The Soviets, infuriated by this show of Western unity, initiated several harassing tactics to make Berlin uncomfortable for her former allies. It was not hard to do. Berlin, with a population of 3.3 million, was 110 miles inside the Russian zone. Berlin's western sector, containing two-thirds of the population, was dependent on a slender rail and highway pipeline; any disruption of that pipeline could cause immediate problems.

In January 1948, the Russians suddenly demanded to inspect a British military train en route from Berlin to Hamburg. The British refused, and the train was turned back. Clay and Robertson promptly put armed guards on trains to prevent entry. Subsequently, trains were often stopped for several hours before being allowed to proceed.

More annoyances followed, and people in Washington, both in the Pentagon and at State, were becoming nervous. Their anxiety reached new heights in March, when Clay, who personally felt that Americans in Berlin had little to fear, nevertheless wrote an alarming message, one intended for closed-door Congressional testimony, and perhaps designed mainly to stiffen Congressional support for continuing Universal Military Training. In any case, he said Russia was becoming increasingly hostile, and "war may come with dramatic suddenness."

Unfortunately, and to Clay's disgust, the message promptly was leaked to the press. Almost at once, people at home began worrying about American dependents and civilian workers. If they were in danger, shouldn't they be evacuated? That might be logical, Clay said, but politically it would be ruinous. "We are here now and must take the consequences."

To his officers, Clay said: "If any of you are nervous—and I don't want anybody who's nervous about his family around here—you may certainly send them home. But on one condition. You must go with them." It wasn't a fair decision Clay was putting to them, nor did he intend it to be.

The Control Council meanwhile had become merely a forum for Soviet propaganda. Finally, on March 20, the Russian representative, Marshal Sokolovsky, read an insulting prepared statement and stormed out of a meeting. The Council for all practical purposes ceased to exist.

The Soviets stepped up the pressure. On March 31, they claimed the volume of rail traffic between the occupation zones and Berlin had increased so much that more control was required. Henceforth, they said, there'd be no freight shipments without Soviet approval and inspection. By this time, people in Washington were even questioning the feasibility of staying in Berlin. Again Clay was asked about evacuating American dependents; he replied that the stopping of trains was "aimed at driving us from Berlin, and immediate evacuation of dependents would be considered a Soviet success."

On June 10, the Russians tried to remove the locomotives and rolling stock from rail yards in the American sector. Clay posted armed guards, and the Soviets backed off. To Clay, it was clear the Russians would keep applying pressure, especially if they sensed weakness. As someone said, "Stalin is like a man probing with a bayonet. When he feels mush, he'll continue to probe. When he feels steel, he'll pull back."

Then, on June 24, the Soviets closed the last rail link and cut off all electric power from the Russian sector to the three Western sectors. By the twenty-sixth, all highways and canals had been blocked. The Berlin blockade was a reality.

Lucius Clay, who all along had felt the Soviets might install a full blockade, knew what he wanted to do. Earlier, he had flown to Heidelberg and made plans for a 6,000-man armored task force, complete with artillery, bridging equipment, and an air cap. The column would move along the autobahn from Helmstedt to Berlin. Personally, Clay was convinced the Soviets did not want war, and he felt that a determined effort would succeed. If, on the other hand, they *did* want a war, it would come eventually whatever the Western Allies did.

"I am convinced," he told Washington, "that a determined movement of convoys with troop protection would reach Berlin . . . [and] might well prevent rather than build up Soviet pressures which could lead to war. Nevertheless, I realize fully the inherent dangers in this proposal since once committed we could not withdraw."

Back in April, Omar Bradley, noting that the U.S. position was militarily indefensible, had said he doubted whether America was prepared to start a war in order to save Berlin and Vienna. To that, Clay had responded: "Why are we in Europe? . . . After Berlin will come western Germany, and our position there is relatively no greater and

our position no more tenable than Berlin. . . . If we mean to hold
Europe against communism, we must not budge. . . . If America does
not know this, does not believe that the issue is cast now, then it
never will and communism will run rampant."

However, neither the State Department nor the Pentagon wanted
to test Soviet resolve. For Secretary of Defense James Forrestal, who
for months had been warning about the way the United States was
shrinking its conventional forces, this was a horrible situation, the
sum of all his fears.

Clay was told to forget the idea of an armored column, which
meant that for him there would always be a lingering "what if."
Would, for example, American resolution at this point—the summer
of 1948—have forestalled the Korean War of 1950? He'd never
know.

It was a time for decision. "You cannot live surrounded by force
and bluff," Clay would say, "without showing that you have no fear
of the first and only contempt for the latter." Very well then: If he
couldn't test the issue on the ground, he'd do it in the air. Clay consulted with his British colleague, General Robertson, who was in full
agreement. Then he asked the European air commander, Curtis
LeMay, if he could carry coal on his airplanes.

"General, we can carry anything!"

"You'd better start doing it," said Clay. "I want you to take every
airplane you have and make it available for the movement of coal and
food to Berlin."

Biographer Jean Edward Smith once asked Clay: "What was the
War Department's response when you began the airlift?"

"I never asked," Clay said. It was vintage Clay—taking action and
assuming full personal responsibility.

To supply Berlin, it would take at least 4,500 tons per day.
LeMay's C-47s couldn't provide that much. However, with British
help, and if C-54s with twice the capacity of the C-47s were brought
in from all over, the airlift just might work.

A key, of course, was the Berliners themselves. Clay spoke frankly
to West Berlin's courageous mayor, Ernst Reuter, telling him his people were going to be short of fuel and electricity, but probably not of
food. Nevertheless, they'd be very cold and feel very miserable.
"Unless they're willing to take this and stay with us, we can't win
this. . . . And I don't want to go into it unless you understand that
fully, unless you are convinced that the Berliners will take it."

Reuter's answer was loud and clear: "General, I can assure you, and I *do* assure you, that the Berliners will take it."

As others wavered, Clay remained firm, each day going to Tempelhof airfield to see how the lift was going and to make his presence felt. Ever the engineer, he even had work started on an additional landing field.

On paper, there was no way an airlift could feed Berlin, let alone supply coal for the coming winter months. Nevertheless, the air armadas began their flights. In West Germany, new airfields were pressed into service. Personnel records were searched to find more air controllers, mechanics, drivers, electricians, and men experienced in loading.

The airmen themselves were magnificent, working around the clock without grumbling. Pilots flew every hour the weather would permit, often taking frightening risks to land in minimum visibility. Truck drivers often worked for twenty-four hours without a break. But the airlift was beginning to come together; daily tonnages were increasing, especially when larger-capacity Air Force C-54s were assigned to the fleet. "We were proud of our Air Force during the war," said *The New York Times*. "We're prouder of it today."

A strong supporter of the airlift was British foreign secretary Ernest Bevin, who remembered all too well from Hitler's day the dangers of appeasement. Bevin told a cheering House of Commons: "We are in Berlin as of right and it is our intention to stay there." It was Bevin's contention that no negotiation should take place until the blockade was lifted; when he heard that U.S. State Department people were in Moscow talking to the Soviets, he asked: "What the hell is going on?"

In Washington, some were still faint-hearted. In mid-July 1948, Assistant Secretary of the Air Force Whitney told the National Security Council that the Air Staff was convinced the airlift was doomed to failure. Even President Harry Truman had his doubts, particularly when some on the Army staff said we should leave Berlin before being forced out.

Ultimately, though, with his usual decisiveness, and despite conflicting advice, Harry Truman said firmly that the U.S. was in Berlin to stay.

By late summer, Americans were united in their resolve to remain in Berlin. George C. Marshall, now the secretary of state, said: "We will not be coerced or intimidated in any way under the rights and responsibilities we have in Berlin." These were brave words, but no one knew if Marshall was merely whistling in the dark. Airlift tonnage was increasing, but with winter coming on, and thus also bad weather and increased need for coal, one wondered if Berlin could truly hold out.

With the massive volume of air traffic, safety became a problem, and the Russians did all they could to complicate the situation. Fighter planes continually buzzed incoming transports; mock air battles were staged over the city; and at one point, three and a half hours of anti-aircraft practice were held in the northern air corridor.

The first fatalities came on July 8. Three Americans on a return flight from Berlin were killed when their plane hit a hill northeast of Wiesbaden; two more died on July 25 when their C-47 crashed as it approached Tempelhof. At the crash site an unknown Berliner put up a plaque reading: "Two American officers became victims of the blockade here. You gave your lives for us. The Berliners of the Western sectors will never forget you. We stand deeply moved on this spot dedicated by your death. Once we were enemies and yet you gave your lives for us." Day after day, fresh flowers were laid on the scene. Before the airlift was over, more than forty American and British flyers were to lose their lives in aerial mishaps.

Throughout the fall and winter, with shortages of fuel, and electricity rationed to four hours per day, Berliners suffered but carried on. By this time, however, they knew they would not be abandoned. In October, a poll had nine out of ten Berliners saying they'd willingly endure the sufferings of the blockade rather than surrender to communism.

Both in the West and in Berlin, people were learning to adjust. Fassberg air base, in the British zone, was operated jointly by British and Americans, with Yanks grumbling about meager English rations and English food, which they claimed was mostly overcooked beef and broiled sprouts. When U.S. colonel John Coulter was given overall responsibility, matters improved—not only in supplies but also in morale, especially with the arrival of his glamorous wife, screen actress Constance Bennett, who enticed Hollywood friends to come entertain and also bring along the latest films.

By the spring of 1949, with Berlin having survived the winter and daily airlift tonnage at new levels, it was obvious the airlift was working. The Russians were on the defensive. Omar Bradley, Chairman of the Joint Chiefs, who'd initially been skeptical, wrote that "Clay's brainchild, the airlift, worked out far better than anyone dared hope" and called Clay "a logistical genius."

Finally, resigning themselves to the inevitable, the Soviets announced the blockade would be lifted on May 12. On the evening of May 11, the lights came on all over Berlin for the first time in over a year. A few seconds after midnight, the gates at Helmstedt were opened and a procession of cars and trucks drove smartly onto the autobahn. Then, at 1:23 A.M., a British military train set off carrying occupation officials, soldiers returning from leave, and a swarm of enthusiastic journalists.

For more than a year, Lucius Clay had been telling his superiors he wanted to retire. Working long hours under constant pressure, sustained mostly by black coffee and cigarettes, he was plainly worn out. However, as long as the blockade was in effect, he knew his leaving might be misinterpreted. Now that it was over, the way was clear, and Clay resubmitted his retirement request. With Washington's concurrence, his Berlin departure was set for May 15, 1949.

On the thirteenth, with traffic moving normally, Berliners celebrated. Schools and businesses were closed, and a special session of the city assembly commemorated the airlift and saluted the departing military governor. Ernst Reuter, concluding the ceremony, said:

> In our great struggle in the summer of the past year, we called on the world for help. The world heard our cry. . . . We are happy to have here in our midst as a guest the man who took the initiative in organizing the airlift at that time. The memory of General Clay will never fade in Berlin. We know for what we have to thank this man [prolonged stormy applause, the members rising], and we take advantage of this hour in which he bids farewell to Berlin to say we will never forget what he has done for us.

On the fourteenth Clay paid a farewell visit to Ernst Reuter in Berlin's city hall. It was a symbolic gesture he knew the Germans would appreciate—the military governor calling on a German politician. Next day, a half-million cheering townspeople lined the streets to say farewell to Lucius and Marjorie Clay. By the time stern, aloof Lucius Clay waved good-bye from the steps of a waiting plane, tears were streaming down his cheeks.

Shortages still existed, and the airlift continued in a reduced version for several more weeks. Finally, when the last RAF Dakota cargo plane flew into Tempelhof, it carried not only a payload but an inscription: "Positively the last load from Lübeck—73,705 tons—

Psalm 21, verse 11." People found the reference in their King James Bibles: "For they intended evil against thee: they imagined a mischievous device, which they are not able to perform."

Clay returned to the States and retired from the Army with appropriate ceremony, including a New York City ticker-tape parade. In the following years, he went on to further successes in both private and public life. For most Americans, however, General Lucius Dubignon Clay will always be associated with one pivotal event: the remarkable Berlin airlift.

In 1978, when Clay died and was buried at West Point, a marker was placed at the gravesite by the citizens of Berlin:

WIR DANKEN DEM BEWAHRER UNSERER FREIHEIT.

We thank the defender of our freedom.

CHAPTER 12

# Decision in Korea

On Saturday, June 24, 1950, things were quiet in the nation's capital. President Truman, in fact, had gone home to Missouri for the weekend. On that same day in South Korea, members of the American mission, both military and civilian, were relaxing in the sun; in the afternoon some even went by rail to a tiny beach resort a few of them were building into a vacation spa.

Later that day in Japan, the officers' club in Kokura held a costume party. The commander of the U.S. 24th Infantry Division, Major General William F. Dean, came as a Korean elder, or *yang-ban*; his wife, Mildred, was dressed as a proper Korean lady. Everyone

179

enjoyed seeing their hardworking boss in a playful mood. Dean himself, however, thought he looked a bit ridiculous in his long white robe and black stovepipe hat, souvenirs from his time as deputy commander of Korean occupation forces. Still, it was all in fun.

Bill Dean, six feet tall, 210 pounds, a self-proclaimed physical fitness nut with a bristling crew cut, was a month shy of his fifty-first birthday. He was known as a bluff, no-nonsense, "can-do" career soldier, an ROTC graduate who had little use for hypocrisy or showmanship. In the years preceding World War II, he had climbed slowly but steadily up the military career ladder. He had then performed with distinction during the war itself, and in the war's final stages he had commanded the U.S. 44th Infantry Division during tough fighting in southern Germany.

Now, in his present peacetime assignment, he was doing his best to bring the U.S. 24th Infantry "Taro Leaf" Division up to speed. It wasn't easy. In Japan's comfortable, relaxed atmosphere, it was almost impossible to keep men charged up. Moreover, peacetime economies, reflecting general U.S. complacency, forced him to operate at greatly reduced strength and with inferior equipment. His infantry regiments, for example, had but two battalions instead of three. Similarly, everything else was at two-thirds capacity or less. Still, Bill Dean did his best with what he had. His men trained hard, and even had he known what lay just ahead, there wasn't much he could have done differently.

On Sunday morning, June 25, after attending church, General Dean headed for the post office near his division headquarters building. Maybe there'd be some mail waiting for him, possibly a letter from his son, Bill, or his daughter, June. Bill was taking the West Point entrance examinations; June was en route to Puerto Rico with her husband, an army captain.

A duty officer, looking rather excited and waving a message, caught up with him. North Korean forces were reported to have crossed the 38th Parallel—it might be a full-scale invasion! A thought flashed across Dean's mind: Was this the beginning of World War III?

For a time, as information trickled in, it looked as though the South Korean army, said to be counterattacking, might have the situation contained. Dean asked MacArthur's headquarters about the South Korean officers now training with the 24th Division in Japan. Should they return home at once? No, he was told, have them complete their training; also, prepare to receive another group in July. Evidently higher-ups expected this to be a short war.

Within days, they learned that initial reports had been wrong. The South Korean army, after a brave initial resistance, was now being overwhelmed. Dispirited South Korean soldiers were straggling into Seoul, and American civilians were being evacuated.

At the United Nations, upon orders from President Harry Truman, U.S. Ambassador Warren Austin recommended to the Security Council that "Members of the United Nations furnish such assistance to the Republic of Korea as may be necessary to repel the armed attack and to restore international peace and security in the area." The motion was carried; fortunately the Soviet Union's representative, Jacob Malik, did not attend the meeting. If he had, he might well have exercised his right to veto.

President Truman made the crucial decision to commit U.S. forces. Within hours, American planes were flying support missions. A serious Bill Dean, summoned to a hastily called meeting in Tokyo, started out by sedan but was halted en route. Orders had been changed: He was now to go back to Kokura and await teletyped instructions.

The message came in around midnight. Dean read that his 24th Division had been selected to provide the first American combat troops for Korea. One battalion should head there as soon as possible. Dean himself was also to go, and once there, he'd assume two jobs—as overall U.S. ground commander and as commander of his own 24th Division.

Bill Dean, a skilled professional, was well aware that his division was in no way prepared for combat. Nevertheless, the 24th was probably as good or better than anything else MacArthur had available. Dean called Colonel Richard Stephens, commander of the 21st Infantry Regiment, and told him to put together a battalion task force and select someone to lead it. Stephens, in turn, called on thirty-four-year-old Lieutenant Colonel Brad Smith.

Military air transport was limited, so initially Smith's force would consist of just two rifle companies and one artillery battery. They'd go at once by air and report to Brigadier General John Church, who was already on the ground with a small detachment. The remainder of the division would follow as soon as possible by surface transportation.

At 3 A.M. on July 1, Smith's group, mounted in trucks, rode the seventy-five miles from Camp Wood to the air base at Itazuke.

General Dean was there to meet them. As transport planes warmed up, Dean told Smith, "When you get to Pusan, head for Taejon. We want to stop the North Koreans as far from Pusan as we can. Block the main road as far north as possible. Contact General Church. If you can't locate him, go to Taejon and beyond if you can. Sorry I can't give you more information. That's all I've got. Good luck to you, and God bless you and your men."

Smith and his group landed in Korea and headed north. Next day, more of Dean's 24th Division began to arrive. As each contingent made its way through Pusan, people lined the streets, laughing, waving, and cheering them on. A band played and the mood was festive; flags, banners, and streamers were everywhere. The prevailing attitude seemed to be that the Americans had landed and would soon have the situation well in hand.

Dean himself started out on July 2, aboard a four-engine C-54, which also carried a jeep and several members of his staff. Once over Pusan, however, they learned the mud airstrip had been torn up so badly that no more big planes could land. Back in Japan, they transferred to a smaller C-45 and started out again. This time they landed successfully at Pusan and, after a brief stop, took off for Taejon so Dean could assume command. It was nearly dark when they arrived over Taejon, and the pilot, after seeing the small unlighted field, just shook his head. Back they went to Itazuke Air Base in Japan. After a quick meal and about three hours' sleep, they again took off.

This time they found their destination socked in. Fog covered the whole area, and they couldn't even *see* Taejon. "But I was desperate," Dean later wrote, "so we finally flew out over the Yellow Sea, bored down through the fog bank, then came back east, following the Kum River line and dodging mountains under the high fog, and eventually landed. I never thought I'd have so much trouble in getting to a war!"

Task Force Smith, meanwhile, had moved north and taken up positions near Osan. Many people at this point, both in Korea and in the States, felt a mere American show of force would be enough to turn the tide. Surely the North Koreans, once they learned America had joined the fight, would stop their aggression and head home.

Dean, beginning to operate from his headquarters in Taejon, next sent elements of his newly arrived 34th Infantry Regiment to blocking positions near Pyongtaek, a few miles south of Smith's men at Osan.

On the morning of July 5, at Osan, Brad Smith spotted a North Korean tank column heading his way. Recoilless-rifle and rocket-launcher "bazooka" teams coolly held their fire. Then, as the lead tank closed to within range, Smith gave the word to open up. Several direct hits were made, but to the Americans' horror, the rounds bounced harmlessly off the thick armor plate of the Soviet-made T-34s. When the tanks came abreast of Smith's position, they began firing their cannons and machine guns, thereby inflicting the first American casualties of the war. The tanks, seemingly undamaged, then kept moving south.

An hour later, more tanks arrived, this time accompanied by a long truck convoy carrying North Korean infantry. Smith's men opened up with everything they had: Mortar shells landed among the trucks; machine-gun bullets raked the column; trucks burst into flames; men were blown into the air. However, as other troops arrived on the scene—a full two regiments, as it turned out—Smith saw hundreds of men maneuvering so as to surround and cut off the Americans.

Reluctantly, Brad Smith gave the order to withdraw. Within moments the situation became chaotic. Abandoning the position, men fled in confusion. The first tanks, meanwhile, had continued to advance and, a mile farther on, had overrun the supporting artillery battery. Adding to the problem, tank treads had torn up the signal wire that had been laid, effectively cutting off U.S. communications.

Bill Dean knew something bad had happened, but there was no way of telling *how* bad. Even though it was dark by this time, he started forward by jeep. At Pyongtaek, finding there was no word from Smith, he realized that the first American contact with the enemy had resulted in disaster.

Next day the 34th Infantry's position at Pyongtaek, which Dean had considered crucial, was also abandoned. The situation was deteriorating rapidly, and to Dean's mind some of the Pyongtaek problem had been caused by poor leadership.

On July 7, Dean gave command of the 34th Infantry to an old friend, Colonel Bob Martin. He and Martin had been together in Europe, and as soon as he'd received orders to go to Korea, he'd asked for Martin by name. GHQ, in turn, had released Martin from his staff assignment and made him available to the 24th Division. With the capable Bob Martin on board, Bill Dean felt he could breathe a little more easily. The two understood each other, liked each other, and when they'd been together in combat previously, it had been almost as though Martin could read Dean's mind and anticipate what he wanted. Under Martin, the 34th Infantry took up position near the town of Chonan.

Next day, the Eighth Army's new commander, stocky, pugnacious Walton Walker, arrived on the scene. That was good news; now Dean, relieved of the overall responsibility, could concentrate on his own 24th Division. Meanwhile, another report had been received. Intense fighting was under way near Chonan; Colonel Martin had gone forward to take personal charge of the situation. Walker and Dean went to see for themselves. South of Chonan, they watched the action from a hillside observation post. It appeared the Americans were falling back. Just then a breathless, sweating officer arrived with heartbreaking news.

Scrappy Bob Martin had been caught in Chonan as enemy troops and tanks entered the town. Rather than retreating, he had obtained a rocket launcher and posted himself in a house on the main street. An enemy tank had driven up; Martin, aiming the rocket launcher, had prepared to fire. As he did so, the tank's cannon had blasted away point-blank, cutting Martin in half.

For Bill Dean, it was a wrenching moment, both personally and professionally. Still, with the situation worsening, he had little time to mourn the loss of his friend. Other troops were arriving and new missions had to be assigned. Trying to stem the enemy advance, Dean ordered Colonel Richard Stephens to deploy his 21st Infantry Regiment in a blocking position near Chochiwon.

The last of the 24th Division regiments to arrive in Korea was the 19th, the "Rock of Chickamauga." In a way, they had a special place in Dean's heart. In the mid-1930s, as a young captain, he'd served with the "Chicks" in Hawaii. Now, still hoping to establish a firm line, he told his old regiment to set up and dig in along the Kum River.

By this time, the main 24th Division headquarters was back at Yongdong. Dean himself, however, with a small group, remained at Taejon in the schoolhouse serving as the 34th Infantry's command post. Some might have argued that Taejon was no place for a division commander. Later, Dean himself wondered if it was a mistake. At the time, though, he felt his big problem was communication. If he'd been in touch, perhaps the position at Pyongtaek would not have been given up so readily. He'd always been a hands-on kind of leader, one who felt that only by being up front, close to the action, could you make timely decisions in a fast-moving situation. For now, Dean and his aide, Lieutenant Arthur Clark, threw their sleeping bags on the schoolhouse floor and tried to catch a bit of rest. Dean felt confident that General Pearson Menoher, his capable assistant division commander, could run things back at Yongdong.

By 6:30 next morning, July 20, Dean was awake and hearing sporadic gunfire. Clark told him enemy tanks had already been sighted entering Taejon. As Dean later wrote: "There was only one difference between this report and many previous ones like it—this time there were no immediate decisions to be made, for the moment no general officer's work to be done." What should he do, then? Well, he wasn't about to turn tail and run; that surely wouldn't do the soldiers' morale much good. Moreover, if there *were* tanks in the town, maybe he could take a personal hand and hunt one down.

The Americans heard that a lone tank was parked at an intersection in the town's business area. Dean and his small group, along with a soldier carrying a bazooka, headed in that direction. Soon they came under rifle fire from snipers accompanying the tank. They returned the fire, probably knocking out one or more snipers, and kept going. Dean and the soldier with the bazooka went through one of the buildings on the main street and came out onto a rear courtyard. After circling, they entered the building closest to the tank. To get upstairs from the courtyard, Dean and the soldier chinned themselves on a window ledge, then climbed inside. Cautiously, Dean looked out a window, directly into the muzzle of a tank cannon no more than a dozen feet away.

Motioning to the bazooka man, Dean pointed to a spot at the base of the cannon where the turret joined the tank's main body. The bazooka fired, and screams could be heard coming from inside the tank. "Hit them again!" Dean yelled. Again the bazooka fired, the screaming stopped, and the street grew quiet.

By this time it was evident that Taejon could not be held. Enemy soldiers were throughout the town; to the south, other North Koreans were already starting to block the exit roads. Dean returned to the schoolhouse and gave orders for the 34th Infantry to start withdrawing. Even so, he knew they'd have to fight their way out.

A terse message was sent to headquarters: "Enemy roadblock eastern exit Taejon. Send armor immediately. Dean." With grim humor, he later said that if he'd known this would be his last official communication, he'd have tried to say something more memorable and dramatic.

A group of vehicles was organized into a rough convoy. Outside town, they ran into the tail of a previous column that had been ambushed. Trucks were on fire; streets were blocked; rifle fire poured from the buildings on both sides. Dean's jeep, and the escort vehicle following it, turned onto a secondary road, bypassing the stalled trucks. Soon they came upon wounded men on foot; they piled as many as possible into the two jeeps. Unhappily, they soon hit yet another roadblock. As machine gun fire swept the road, everyone dove into a ditch and tried to crawl to safety.

After dark, and on foot, the little group—more than a dozen strong by this time—began working their way south along a ridge. It was slow going, especially since one of the men was badly wounded. Dean, ignoring his general's "dignity" and forgetting his fifty-one-year-old legs, tried to carry the wounded man by himself. He was soon too exhausted to maintain the solo effort, but continued to take his turn of a two-man carry. Finally the group halted, and in the darkness, weary men slumped to the ground. The man they were carrying, delirious, had drunk all available water and was calling for more.

Around midnight, Dean thought he heard water running just off the ridge to one side. He started in that direction, and before he knew it, he was stumbling headlong down a steep slope and couldn't stop. He tripped, fell, and lay unconscious.

The Americans, now led by Lieutenant Clark, started out again, and in the darkness didn't realize the general was missing. When they did, they turned back and waited, hoping he'd return. Finally, after several hours, they decided it was no use and went on.

When Dean finally came to, he had no idea how long he'd been knocked out. There was a deep gash in his head, and when he tried to raise himself onto his hands and knees, he realized he had a broken shoulder. Bit by bit, he began crawling up the tricky slope that had been his undoing, but before long he passed out again. When he came to this time, it was just beginning to get light. A North Korean patrol was moving along the ridge, just a few feet away. How they missed him he'd never know.

Walking, staggering, sometimes crawling on all fours, he tried working his way south. He was thirsty, hungry, and suffering constant pain, which often made him semi-delirious. Over and over he kept telling himself he must never, under any circumstances, allow himself to be captured. With a general officer as prisoner, the Communists would have a field day, might even try to convince the world Dean had "seen the light" and gone over willingly.

Some time later, he saw another American lurching along. "Who are you?" Dean said. "What outfit are you from?"

"I'm Lieutenant Tabor—Stanley Tabor—from the 19th Infantry. Who are you?"

"Well," said Dean, "I'm the S.O.B. who's the cause of all this trouble." With Tabor's help, Dean kept going, slowly and painfully. Frequently he told Tabor to go on ahead and save himself, but Tabor always refused, saying two together had a better chance. About three days later, they met two Korean civilians who spoke a little English; they gave the Americans food and led them to a hut where they could rest. Thankfully, the two took off their boots, relaxed, and were soon asleep.

Suddenly a rifle shot rang out in the night air. They had been betrayed! Dean and Tabor, instantly awake, heard a voice call out in surprisingly good English: "Come out, Americans! Come out! We will not kill you. We are members of the People's Army. We will not kill you."

"Come on," said Dean. "Get your boots on in a hurry. I'm not going to surrender, Tabor. There'll be no surrender for me."

"That's the way I feel too," said Tabor. The two Americans slipped out a back door and began crawling away through thick weeds that offered some concealment. As shots were fired in their general direction, they reversed their course, going back through the village, then through a series of rice paddies. With Dean leading the way, they crawled snakelike through shallow paddy water. At the end of each paddy section, they inched their way carefully over low intervening dikes.

After traversing one of the fields, Dean looked back and called softly for Tabor. There was no reply. Somehow the two had become separated in the darkness. Bill Dean would not see another American for the next three years. (The gallant Tabor, who had refused to abandon Dean and go on alone, was eventually captured. He later died in prison camp.)

Dean, mostly hiding by day and traveling at night, somehow managed to avoid the enemy for a total of thirty-five days. It was a remarkable display of courage and willpower. At times he was given food by friendly Koreans; more often they ignored him; and more often yet, people gave the alarm, called out the home guard, and tried to seize him. Each time, he managed to escape. As the days went by, however, his injuries, plus the lack of food, made him increasingly weak.

On the thirty-fifth day, he met two men who offered to guide him to a place where he could be sheltered and fed. It was a trap. As they neared a village, Dean was surrounded by about fifteen men. He tried to pull his pistol, but as he did so, one of the men grabbed his arm and wrestled him to the ground.

"This is it," thought Dean, still determined not to be taken alive. "Shoot! Shoot, you sons of bitches! Shoot!" Instead, his arms were twisted and tied behind his back. He tried to run, hoping they would kill him, but in his condition, he was able only to stumble a short distance. Someone shoved him from behind and he fell on his face in the dust. Everyone laughed. By this time his shoulder hurt unmercifully. The greatest pain, however, came from knowing that, despite his best efforts, he was now a prisoner.

For the next several weeks, and as his identity became known, Dean was moved from place to place and subjected to a series of interrogations. He refused to cooperate, steadfastly refusing to sign anything or to go on the radio, even to tell his family he was safe.

Over and over, he was asked why he had come to Korea, and each time he would infuriate his questioner by saying he had come so as to help South Korea repel the illegal aggressors from the north. Mostly, though, he thought the questions were rather stupid, as when the interrogators asked about the South Korean army's defense plans, which by this time were hardly relevant. On matters of any significance, such as infantry tactics or organization, or the defense plans for Japan, he simply refused to answer.

If he'd only cooperate, one officer told him, by admitting the merits of communism and the evils of American policy, they would then leave him alone. Finally the officer gave up, saying: "General, you're a brave man, but you're very ignorant politically!"

He was passed from one captor to another, always closely guarded, at first retracing his way through Taejon and Osan, then continuing farther north, through Seoul and on into North Korea, passing through the capital city of Pyongyang. So far the treatment had been crude and uncomfortable, with little consideration for health or living conditions. However, there had been no outright cruelty. Then, a few weeks later, when he was given over to an unpleasant North Korean colonel named Kim, things changed dramatically.

At first Kim was rather friendly, even kind, and seemingly interested in Dean's welfare as he produced documents for the prisoner to sign. They were all of a type: a request for the misguided Americans to stop fighting; a letter thanking the North Koreans for their kind treatment of prisoners; another letter blaming the South Koreans, especially the "no-good crook" Syngman Rhee, for starting the war. When Dean refused to comply, the mood changed abruptly.

"These statements," said Kim, "are my minimum requests. If you sign these, you won't be tortured." As Dean stood firm, Kim grew increasingly hostile. In session after session, the questioning continued for hours on end; even when Kim paused, Dean usually was unable to rest. Often he would be awakened in the middle of the night and taken to an interrogation room, where Kim insulted him, threatened him, and told him that he'd never yet failed to get what he wanted from a prisoner, even "ones tougher than you."

After the American landing at Inchon, of which Dean was unaware, Kim and his henchmen grew even worse. Once, for example, Dean was made to sit in a straight chair and face three different questioners, Kim plus Lieutenant Colonels Choi and Hong. They took turns, spelling each other when one grew tired. The first questioner was Choi, who asked for military information that Dean didn't have and wouldn't have given if he did have.

How many airfields were in Japan? How did planes home in on a target? Was the United States going to use the atomic bomb? When Dean protested, saying that under the Geneva Convention he could be asked only his name, rank, and serial number, he was told the Convention didn't apply. Dean, they said, was a war criminal, and therefore considered a special case.

This particular session had started around nine in the morning, being interrupted only for food and for frequent dashes to the latrine because of Dean's dysentery. On and on it went, even as day turned into night. In the early-morning hours, Kim became aware that Dean's teeth were chattering.

"What are you shivering for, making your teeth go that way? Are you cold?"

"Yes, I'm a little chilly."

"This isn't cold," said Kim. "Take off your coat. Take off your shirt. Take off your trousers and your undershirt. I'll show you what it means to be cold."

Although the room temperature was near freezing, Dean was made to strip to his undershorts. At one point, the frustrated Colonel Kim threatened to have Dean's tongue cut out, to which Dean replied: "Go ahead and cut it out. Then you won't be able to make me talk." That was the end of that particular threat.

Finally Kim called a temporary halt, after using the last hour to harangue his prisoner, telling Dean that since he wouldn't cooperate, he was a dog and a robber, and would therefore be treated like a dog. "No more washing. You can't wash, you dog! You can have one blanket and sleep over there in a corner on the floor. . . . You want to remember that it's getting colder. If you fail to cooperate, we not only won't give you any clothes, we'll keep you outdoors."

Dean was allowed to sleep on the floor for a few hours; then the ordeal started again, with the three interrogators, Kim, Hong, and Choi, taking turns. Dean, forced to stay awake and respond, answered mechanically and unemotionally. Once, however, he lost his composure when Kim started to rant about American planes killing innocent people.

"Listen," said Dean, "I've seen atrocities committed by your troops worse than anything you've mentioned! At Chochiwon, I saw men murdered in cold blood while they had their hands tied behind them. And I talked to a lieutenant who saw your men drive prisoners ahead of them, to try to get others to surrender—then shoot them when we opened fire to repel an attack."

Kim became so angry that he yelled: "Close your eyes! I'm going to spit in your face!"

"Go ahead and spit," said Dean. "You've been spitting in my eyes for the last half-hour!"

"All right," said Kim. "This is the end. We're going to torture you." He then went on to describe certain ghastly measures, including the driving of bamboo splinters under the fingernails and then setting fire to them. Another possibility was to force water into the body through the rectum, causing, in Kim's words, "everything in you, everything, to come out through your mouth. It's very sickening."

Dean said: "That sounds good to me. The shape I'm in, you won't have to use much pressure. I think that'll kill me quickly. That sounds all right."

After more of this, Kim said Dean would be taken to the torture building early the next morning. "Under torture," said Kim, "you will probably die, but not before you've given us the information we want." He then asked Dean if he wanted to write a last message.

At first Dean declined the offer; then he changed his mind. "Okay," he said, "I'll write a last letter to my family." They gave him a pencil and paper, and he proceeded to write:

Dear Mildred, June, and Bill, I was physically captured on 25 August and have been a prisoner of war ever since. I did not surrender but was physically overpowered. Before I was captured I wandered in the hills for 35 days without food. As a result I am terribly ill and do not think I will live much longer. Therefore this is my last letter. June, do not delay in making your mother a grandmother. Bill, remember that integrity is the most important thing of all. Let that always be your aim. Mildred, remember that for 24 years you have made me very, very happy.

That was all. Kim, reading the message, was puzzled. Why did Dean say he was ill? Why not say he was about to be executed? Didn't Dean realize they could now kill him without being blamed?

"You dumb bastard!" said Dean, who explained, as to an idiot, that he'd written it not for Kim, but for his own family, and he wanted them to receive it. If he'd said he was about to be killed, obviously the letter would never be sent. Kim stomped out, after promising to see Dean in the morning at the torture chamber.

Dean now realized they intended to torture him until he was dead. Was this willingness to let prisoners die, or to kill them outright, part of a pattern? Unfortunately it was. Up to this point, the enemy, realizing the value of an important POW as a possible bargaining chip, had made an effort to keep their high-ranking prisoner alive. For other POWs, however, there were no such compunctions, either then or later.

By the time truce talks began, for example, the South Koreans carried over 88,000 men missing in action and the United States more than 11,500. The Communists, however, who had earlier claimed via news releases and radio broadcasts to have taken more than 65,000 prisoners, said they held only 7,142 South Koreans and 3,198 Americans. Obviously the vast majority of those captured died while in enemy hands.

As Dean was being threatened with torture and death, it would only have added to his pain had he known what was taking place only a few miles away, where eighty-seven civilian noncombatants were being herded into line and told to start walking.

Had Dean known of them, he would have protested strongly on their behalf, though it would have done little good. The little band included a Salvation Army official, many Roman Catholic nuns and priests, and six Methodist missionaries, both men and women. Presently they fell in behind a long line of about 700 haggard American POWs, many of whom, with bleeding feet, were near collapse. It was the beginning of a ghastly journey of death, one which would rival in cruelty the infamous Bataan Death March of World War II.

After stumbling along for hours through bitter cold, they were lined up in front of a North Korean major. The major—they thought of him as the Tiger—told them they would have to march in military column to a city a hundred miles away. They must first abandon all their belongings, even the walking sticks used by some of the elderly.

Was the major insane? One of the nuns, Mother Thérèse, was being carried in an improvised stretcher. Eighty-two-year-old Father Villemot and seventy-six-year-old Mother Beatrix could walk only with help. Then there was blind Sister Marie-Madeleine, whom Sister Bernadette had to lead by the hand.

Commissioner Herbert Lord of the Salvation Army tried to protest: "They will die if they have to march!"

"Then let them march till they die. That is a military order!"

On they went. That night, sleeping in an open field, they huddled together for warmth. Next day, in the snow, they started out again, and before long people were collapsing by the wayside, too exhausted to continue. The major stopped the column and screamed: "I order you not to allow anyone to drop out. If you do, I will punish you with the extreme penalty of military discipline. Even the dead must be carried!"

The march resumed, but before long, people again began to fall out. "Who is responsible for my orders not being obeyed?" asked the major. Irrationally, he now threatened to shoot them all.

During their captivity, the Tiger's victims would see many splendid examples of self-sacrifice, some of which are long forgotten. However, the magnificent act of moral courage that now took place was one they would always remember.

From the column, a young officer, Lieutenant Cordus Thornton, stepped forward and said that if anyone was responsible, he was.

"Why did you let those five men drop out?"

"Because they were dying, sir."

"Why didn't you obey my orders?" Because, said Thornton, to force anyone to carry the dead would have meant condemning those people to die as well.

Very well, if Thornton was accepting responsibility for all, the major would act accordingly. One of the guards, taking a small towel, bandaged Thornton's eyes. Then the major stepped behind the young lieutenant, pulled up the flap of Thornton's pile cap, cocked his pistol, and pulled the trigger.

Those nearby felt they had witnessed the death of a martyr. Two of the soldiers then carried Thornton's body to the side. An American sergeant, using a stick, started to dig a grave. "Won't anyone help me?" he asked.

Other volunteers, joining in, began scratching at the ground with sticks or even with their bare hands. Eventually they clawed out a shallow grave, and in it they laid the heroic lieutenant's body.

The march continued, but the horrors had not yet ended. Mother Beatrix, too tired to go on, collapsed by the roadside. Mother Eugénie pleaded with the guards for compassion, saying Beatrix, seventy-six years old, had for fifty years been caring for Korea's poor and orphans.

It was no use. "Go on, my sister, go," said Beatrix. The guards pushed Eugénie down the road. She heard a shot, and looking back, saw a tiny body being shoved down a steep slope, rolling over and over, and finally coming to rest at the bottom of a ravine.

Before the long trek was over, the prisoners would plod a hundred miles over rugged terrain, and nearly a hundred bodies would be left behind in the snow and cold.

Bill Dean, like the heroic Lieutenant Thornton, was faced with a decision. The easier choice, cooperating with the enemy, he dismissed at once. Up to now, he had given them nothing of value. Under torture, however, while he might very well die, he might also reveal something they could use. He was, for example, intimately familiar with the defense plans for Japan.

He could not take the chance of revealing valuable information, and as he saw it, there was only one way to choose the "harder right": He must take his own life. If possible, of course, he wanted to go down fighting. If he could seize a weapon, perhaps he could take someone with him, preferably the sadistic Colonel Kim. In any case, he'd save the last bullet for himself.

In Dean's room was a Western-style padded chair, which Dean himself was forbidden to use. Although a light was always on, the ever-present guard would sometimes slump into that chair and doze off. Previously, there also had been a cot in the room, but on Kim's orders, it had been taken away and was now next door, in the room where the guards stayed.

This had to be the night. Peeking through a crack into the guards' room, Dean saw a submachine gun leaning against the wall. Perhaps, when the guard in his room fell asleep, and the men next door went to eat, he could slip in and grab that weapon. He would then point it out the window and fire a burst toward the building where Kim slept. Kim would come running out, and Dean, after shooting Kim, would then stick the barrel in his own mouth and pull the trigger.

Soon after dark, just as he'd hoped, his guard eased into the chair and closed his eyes. A bit later, the men next door all left to eat. It was now or never. Slowly, Bill Dean began to crawl along the floor, out of his room and into the next one. He found the weapon, lifted it, and pulled back on the bolt. It wouldn't budge. Again and again, he tried forcing it, and in doing so he must have made a noise.

The room wasn't empty. Someone was sleeping on the cot—it was Colonel Hong. Hong, a brave man, rushed at Dean, right in the face of the submachine gun. Hong grabbed Dean, who was still trying vainly to work the bolt. Meanwhile, his own guard, who had come awake, dashed in and jumped Dean from the rear. Soon there were Koreans all over him. It didn't take much to overpower the weakened American.

"You were trying to escape, weren't you?"

"No, in my condition I don't think I could have. I wanted to kill Colonel Kim, and then I was going to kill myself."

Next morning, Bill Dean was criticized for his actions. Nevertheless, something seemed to have changed. He never again saw the vicious Colonel Kim. Perhaps the suicide attempt had caused Kim to lose face. If so, thought Dean, that was more than fine by him. In any case, Colonel Choi gave orders that Dean be given new clothes, that his cot be returned, and that a doctor come and try to restore him to good health.

A few days later, Dean was again moved to a new location. The last person who talked to him was Lee, an interpreter who'd been present at all the interrogations. Lee whispered: "Good-bye, General. Don't give up hope or try to kill yourself. You must live, and everything will be fine again, and you will see your family once more."

Lee was right. Many more months were to pass, none of them pleasant, but General Bill Dean, through courage and fortitude, did manage to survive and to come home with head held high.

Dean never felt he himself had done anything special; he was truly surprised when a grateful nation rewarded him with the Congressional Medal of Honor. If he'd had his way, he'd probably have given his medal to someone else, perhaps to someone such as Lieutenant Stanley Tabor, who had refused to leave his companion and go on alone, or to Lieutenant Cordus Thornton, a man Dean never met, but who he knew had given his life so that others on the terrible journey of death might live.

Unfortunately neither Tabor nor Thornton managed to survive America's "forgotten war" in Korea. Both men, however, along with the indomitable General Bill Dean, the highest-ranking American POW of the twentieth century, surely deserve to be remembered and appreciated by a grateful nation.

CHAPTER 13

# Decision at the Pentagon

T hroughout his career, Maxwell
Davenport Taylor was known not only as a fine soldier but also as a
skilled linguist and a gifted scholar. He had graduated near the top of
his West Point class and had taught both French and Spanish at the
Academy. Later, while stationed in Japan, and after becoming profi-
cient in both written and spoken Japanese, he had observed Japanese
soldiers in the field, studied their manuals, and come to know the
Japanese army as well as any other American. His study of Japanese
military doctrine even became the standard U.S. Army text on the
subject, remaining so well into the Pacific war.

During World War II, following the Sicily campaign, Taylor assumed the role of secret agent as he slipped into Rome on a crucial diplomatic mission while Italy was still under enemy control. Of that mission, Dwight D. Eisenhower would write: "The risks he ran were greater than I asked any other agent or emissary to undertake during the war—he carried weighty responsibilities and discharged them with unerring judgment, and every minute was in imminent danger of discovery and death."

In June 1944, leading the paratroopers of the 101st Airborne Division, Maxwell Taylor jumped into Normandy on D-Day and went on to command the famed "Screaming Eagles" with distinction for the remainder of the war. Then, in June 1945, while still in Europe, Taylor learned he had been chosen to become superintendent of the U.S. Military Academy at West Point. He would be the fortieth man in history to hold that position; his predecessors included such notables as Robert E. Lee and Douglas MacArthur. At forty-four, Taylor would also be the second-youngest superintendent ever; only MacArthur had been younger. Moreover, just as MacArthur had made significant changes at West Point after World War I, Superintendent Taylor, assuming the position following another great war, would have a similar opportunity—to pass on lessons he'd learned in combat and to influence future leaders with his core beliefs.

Major General Taylor had been superintendent for only nine days when he received a letter from General George Patton, one of his wartime bosses, urging drastic changes in the West Point curriculum. Patton, who loved to shock, said the Department of Tactics, responsible for military training, should determine 50 percent of a cadet's class standing. "Nothing I learned in electricity or hydraulics or higher mathematics or in drawing in any way contributed to my military career," Patton wrote. "Therefore, I would markedly reduce or wholly jettison the above subjects."

Taylor's views were not that extreme, nor could they be. After all, a West Point degree had always represented a high level of academic achievement, and needed to keep doing so. Still, he agreed with Patton on the Academy's primary role. In a speech at Britain's Sandhurst, Taylor would say: "West Point is essentially a school for leaders. What it teaches its graduates from books is important, but is not everything. . . . We err if we measure West Point only by the yardstick of curriculum. West Point succeeds or fails in the future to the degree in which it continues to produce broad men of character, capable of leading other men to victory in battle."

To help him in this new assignment, Taylor brought to the Academy several officers who had served with him in the 101st Airborne Division. One of these, Brigadier General Gerald Higgins, his former Chief of Staff, was made Commandant of Cadets. As head of the Department of Tactics, Higgins would be responsible for all military training. During the war, Taylor and Higgins, discussing the Academy, had noted the paradox that West Point, whose mission was to develop leaders, had no formal course in leadership. Early on, with Taylor's concurrence, Higgins went about developing such a course, one to have the same standing as any academic subject.

Commandant Higgins soon learned he had opposition. The powerful department heads who made up the Academic Board unanimously rejected his proposal; among other things, no department was about to surrender any of its allotted classroom hours. Higgins later wrote that he could not recall "a meeting of responsible individuals where rancor so filled the air" as it did when his formal recommendation went before the board. In turn, each professor spoke out against the new leadership course; when the matter was put to a vote, only Higgins supported it.

"That settles it!" said the department head who had led the opposition. Superintendent Taylor, although present for the meeting, had abstained from the voting. At this point Taylor proceeded to change the smiles to startled gasps. He thanked those present for their comments, then calmly announced that the course would be instituted at the beginning of the next academic year.

Higgins described what happened next:

> It would be hard to describe the tension and looks of disbelief that arose! The Dean got up and in a very formal tone *informed* the Superintendent that the Academic Department was responsible for all educational courses and that they had decided that the course should not go forward. [Taylor] smiled, rose, and very politely informed those present that he appreciated their *advice*, but that the Superintendent made the decisions—and that he had decided to go forward with the course on leadership.

Never in history had a superintendent gone against the Academic Board on such a matter. Clearly the new "supe," despite his gracious, almost courtly manner, was a man to be reckoned with.

Installing the new course, "Military Psychology and Leadership," was but one of several measures taken to modernize the Academy. During Taylor's tenure, three new languages, Russian, German, and Portuguese, were added to the curriculum. The Department of Military Art and Engineering reduced the number of engineering hours and devoted more time to the practical study of military history and the military art. Fencing and horsemanship were dropped, and some of the hours saved were used to add amphibious training in close coordination with the Naval Academy. By the time Max Taylor left West Point, he had made a lasting contribution.

Taylor had begun his superintendency shortly after the entry of the class of '49. He would have liked to have been on hand for their graduation, but it was not to be. In the spring of 1949, he was ordered back to Europe to become U.S. commander in Berlin. In the new job, he would report to Army general Thomas Handy in Heidelberg on military matters and to John J. McCloy, the U.S. high commissioner in Frankfurt, on political questions.

In Berlin, although the blockade had recently been lifted, the Communists were still causing problems, as when East Germany announced that on Whitsunday, May 28, 1950, some 100,000 members of the Communist-inspired Free German Youth would hold a rally, followed by a mass invasion of the Western sectors. The small number of West German police could never control such a crowd, and if armed troops had to be called out, the Communists would have an obvious opportunity to provoke an ugly incident.

Taylor, rising to the occasion, launched a crash program on crowd control. Troops were given extensive briefings on problems that might be encountered and on the disciplined behavior that would be demanded of them. Training emphasized maximum restraint coupled with the use of nonlethal measures such as tear gas or water cannons. The preparations did not go unnoticed; when the rally was held, the participants confined themselves to the Soviet sector.

When the crisis was over, Taylor held a press briefing in which he "apologized" to reporters for "a rather dull weekend" and gave his analysis of why the threat had failed: "The West Germans and their Western Allies showed by word and deed that they would not give an inch to the communist threat, and were prepared to defend their rights in this city. It is a formula that has always worked in the past, and one which recommends itself for wide application in the future." Whether his opponents were a group of senior professors or an unruly mob, Maxwell Taylor was not a man to be bullied.

Soon Taylor was called to another assignment, this time to Washington as a deputy to Army Chief of Staff J. Lawton Collins. One of the unpleasant tasks coming his way was serving as Collins's representative in a highly embarrassing matter involving West Point. Some ninety cadets, most of them football players, had been found guilty of cheating on exams. A board had recommended unanimously that all ninety be discharged, and Taylor concurred. For one thing, he felt that the Corps of Cadets, to whom the honor system was sacred, would never be willing to accept any of the ninety back into the corps. In a letter written in connection with this painful affair, Taylor expressed the opinion that those involved, "while openly admitting their violation of the Cadet Code of Honor, are not fundamentally men of bad morals or character. They have, however, fallen into evil ways; they have not, in the words of the Cadet Prayer, preferred the 'harder right instead of the easier wrong,' and in their failure have brought sorrow upon themselves and upon the Military Academy."

Most of Taylor's concerns during this period, however, were with the war in Korea, where ill-prepared American forces, under United Nations auspices, had been heavily engaged since the summer of 1950. After disheartening early reversals, the U.S. Eighth Army, along with the allies, had gained the upper hand. Then Red China had entered the war; the initiative had been lost and, after more bitter fighting, the Korean conflict had devolved into a costly, bloody stalemate. Although continued fighting didn't seem to be proving anything, many young men, including several junior officers who had been cadets under Taylor, were still becoming casualties. Understandably, the country was becoming less supportive of what seemed a no-win situation.

Truce talks had been under way since June 1951, and as 1953 began, General James A. Van Fleet, the Eighth Army commander, had become increasingly frustrated by policies requiring a defensive, inconclusive strategy. In February 1953, Maxwell Taylor replaced Van Fleet as Eighth Army commander, even though, as he later said, "the defensive strategy to which the Eighth Army was condemned was no more appealing to me than it had been to Van Fleet." Taylor, however, was a realist, and he recognized that by this time the United States had neither the national will nor the resources to resume the offensive. The following summer, after much haggling over issues such as the repatriation of Communist POWs, a truce agreement was finally reached. Soon afterward, Taylor was named to head all army forces in the Far East.

As 1955 began, the guns in Korea had been silent for over a year. World War II was nearly a decade in the past. Dwight Eisenhower, a heroic and trusted military figure, was living in the White House. Despite these signs of peaceful prosperity, however, a great many Americans felt insecure and apprehensive. By this time the United States no longer held a monopoly on nuclear weapons; at home, at school, in the workplace, people knew they lived with a very real, constant threat of atomic war.

Secretary of State John Foster Dulles, writing a position paper with help from his CIA brother, Allen, had said: "There is one solution and only one: that is for the free world to develop the will and organize the means to retaliate *instantly* against open aggression by the Red armies, so that, if it occurred anywhere, we could and would strike back where it hurts, by means of our own choosing."

This implied, of course, a willingness to use atomic weapons and to risk the consequences. At the State Department, it was believed that smaller nations should be ready to defend themselves on the ground, with the United States perhaps providing air and sea support in special situations. If the threat became major, and vital U.S. interests were threatened, then the Bomb would be used. This had become known as a doctrine of "massive retaliation," of getting "a bigger bang for a buck," of averting war by a willingness to go "to the brink."

Dwight Eisenhower's management style was one of delegation, so despite his military expertise, he relied on the experts at State and Defense to set the tone of national security. In many circles, the Dulles doctrine of "massive retaliation" was popular both politically and economically, implying as it did that limited future wars could be fought on the cheap, without U.S. ground troops and without significant U.S. casualties.

Some strategists, of course, were not so sure. To them, it seemed unrealistic to threaten the use of hydrogen bombs if anyone tried to upset the balance of global power. It sounded, in fact, like a smoke screen to conceal the fact that the U.S. armed forces were in a dangerously thin condition. As evidence, critics noted that Secretary of the Treasury George Humphrey had already cut the defense budget drastically. Of the three services, the Army had the smallest portion of that budget, and the Army's strength was now less than half what it had been during the Korean War. Clearly the United States was in no position to fight a "brushfire" war in Korea, Indochina, or elsewhere. It would have to be the big blaze or nothing.

Following the signing of the Korean armistice, Max Taylor wrote an after-action paper questioning the wisdom of relying on nuclear weapons. In his report, he noted that Korea truly had been an "infantryman's war." By its very nature, it had largely nullified the Air Force's bombers, the Navy's capital ships, even the Army's tanks. Significantly, the United States had chosen not to employ nuclear weapons, even when it still had a monopoly. Obviously future wars might see both sides tacitly agreeing to cancel out atomic weapons, making the United States, he said, "rely again on conventional means" of achieving its objectives.

Despite the misgivings of Taylor, his army colleagues, or anyone else, "massive retaliation" seemed to have taken hold as U.S. policy. Officers who valued their careers did well not to question it.

In late 1954, Taylor moved from Korea to Tokyo, Japan, where he was joined by his wife, Lydia, known to everyone as Diddy. It was not the first time the Taylors had lived in Tokyo. Back in the mid-1930s, however, the situation had been far different. Max, serving as a military attaché, had been a junior captain. Now, thanks to his recent promotion, he was wearing four stars and they were living in far better style. Nevertheless, they both had fond memories of those earlier days.

In Japan, Taylor's direct superior was General John E. "Ed" Hull, head of the Far East Command. According to Max's wartime boss Matthew Ridgway, now the Army Chief of Staff, Hull was thinking of retiring, in which case Taylor would probably be named to replace him.

Suddenly, in February of 1955, Taylor was called to Washington for a series of meetings, the nature of which was a bit of a mystery. As Max began packing for the trip, which promised to be a short one, he told Diddy they might have something to do with his next assignment. Perhaps, he said, Ridgway just wanted to discuss the timing of Hull's retirement and of his assuming Hull's job. On the other hand, something more significant might be in the works. Scuttlebutt had it that Ridgway wasn't getting on too well with Charles Erwin Wilson, the present secretary of defense. Wilson, a former General Motors chairman, would be best remembered for saying that what was good for GM was good for America. Known as "Engine Charley" to distinguish him from "Electric Charley" (Charles Edward) Wilson of GE, he had, according to Ridgway, come to Washington "with an extensive ignorance of the military establishment and a well-established dislike for the Army." From the start, he had clashed with the outspoken Ridgway, who was clearly critical of America's reliance on "massive retaliation."

Diddy Taylor, like her husband, wondered what was meant by the urgent summons to Washington. If it meant a new posting, that would affect both of them, and she didn't much like being kept in the dark all the time he was away. Max, the dutiful husband, came up with an idea. Maybe, as soon as he learned what was coming, he could get word to her through some sort of code. By this time the whole Taylor family knew the famous "Code Word Innocuous" story from Max's Italian adventure during World War II (see Chapter 9). Twelve years later, in far different circumstances, a code word might still be useful. This time, though, the code would be for Diddy's benefit rather than Eisenhower's.

Max and Diddy agreed: If they talked to him about replacing General Ed Hull, he'd cable her that Lucille Hull sent her regards. If it turned out to be the chief of staff job, he'd send her regards from Penny Ridgway. With that, he was on his way.

In Washington, Taylor's first stop was at the Pentagon, where he called on his longtime friend Ridgway. Because of Pentagon politics, which often kept him out of the loop, Ridgway had not been made privy to the discussions about his own successor. Consequently the two ex-paratroopers and wartime comrades mainly discussed the overall situation in the Far East, General Ed Hull's pending retirement, and Taylor's presumed assumption of Hull's command. Diddy Taylor, who had but recently gotten settled in Tokyo and didn't relish another quick move, was pleased with the cable she got. It ended: "Lucille Hull sends her regards."

Taylor's next Pentagon visit was with Secretary of Defense Wilson, "Engine Charlie." The first part of the conversation was rather one-sided: Wilson went into a long rambling discussion of the situation in the Far East. Then the meeting took an unexpected turn.

Wilson asked how Taylor felt about taking orders. The answer was obvious. For Maxwell Taylor, as for any career soldier, obeying one's lawful superiors was as natural as breathing.

Wilson persisted: "But how do you feel about obeying orders with which you disagree?"

Taylor, not caring for this line of questioning, framed his reply carefully, pointing out an officer's duty to express his opinion, even his disagreement, but always with the intent of following orders once a decision was made.

Evidently the reply was satisfactory, for Wilson next said that Taylor was being considered to replace Ridgway as Army Chief of Staff. The following day, Taylor was called to the White House to meet with the President. Eisenhower greeted him warmly and for a few moments the two reminisced about shared experiences. The eve of D-Day, when Eisenhower had visited the paratroopers of Taylor's 101st Airborne as they prepared for their jump into Normandy, didn't seem that far in the past. Then it was back to business, and Eisenhower, rewarding Taylor with one of the now-famous "Ike smiles," confirmed what Wilson had said, that Taylor was being considered for Army Chief of Staff.

Eisenhower's next comments, however, began to resemble those of Wilson. Once again Taylor was asked how he felt about carrying out policies with which he might disagree, and once again he chose his words carefully. Evidently the President was satisfied with his response. He said he'd nominate Taylor as Chief of Staff after he'd served briefly as Far East commander, and the meeting ended on a warm note. It was the last time Taylor and Eisenhower ever met by themselves.

Taylor sent another wire to his wife, this one containing the phrase "Penny Ridgway sends her regards." It managed to confuse Diddy completely.

In late May, the Taylors said their farewells and returned to Washington by way of Europe. In his briefcase, Taylor had a series of "think pieces" he'd been developing—his thoughts about the Army's future and its role in the overall scheme of national defense, together with his personal evaluation of Wilson's "New Look" and its accompanying strategy of massive retaliation.

Clearly there was much to be done; not the least of Taylor's goals was somehow to remove the chill that affected the President's attitude toward his old service, and to work out some way of seeing him regularly.

On June 30, 1955, Max Taylor was sworn in as the U.S. Army's twentieth Chief of Staff. He explained his new job to Diddy as one in which he'd be wearing two hats. First, he'd be working for the secretary of the Army, Wilbur Brucker, helping him with recommendations and assisting him in his dealings with the secretary of defense and the Congress. He wouldn't have any command authority, of course; any Army-wide instructions would be issued only in the name of the Secretary. Second, he'd be the Army representative on the Joint Chiefs of Staff, working with the other service chiefs and with the JCS chairman, Admiral Arthur W. Radford.

Theoretically, Taylor knew, the service chiefs reasoned together to develop a consensus, one giving due weight to each man's input. Ironically, it was the Chairman himself who did most to bring disharmony to the discussions. Soon it became clear, to Taylor and the others, that Radford's opinions were the only ones that counted. Radford, for example, a supporter of the administration's "bigger bang for a buck" strategy, was the only JCS member to meet directly with the President.

It was a frustrating situation. Taylor's skepticism about reliance on massive retaliation was keeping him constantly out of step. The "think pieces" he'd prepared when first called to the job took little cognizance of Washington politics; looking over them now, he saw they were remarkably naïve.

The New Look's goal was to maintain military expenditures at a fixed level; if costs could be stabilized, it was felt an efficient defense effort could be combined with a healthy national economy.

All this sounded good, especially politically, but Taylor soon realized it simply didn't work out in practice. First, the inevitable inflation meant that a fixed military budget was really a declining one. Moreover, a massive-retaliation strategy relied on missiles, bombers, and submarines, high-tech weapons with whose costs no one had any experience. Every innovation seemed to produce a cost overrun. With the administration's insistence on a balanced budget, something had to give, and obviously it was military manpower, with the Army taking most of the cuts.

Despite Taylor's and Brucker's best efforts, the Army continued to decline, from eighteen divisions to sixteen, from over a million men to 870,000. Meanwhile, there was little money to replace or modernize Army equipment, most of which still dated from World War II.

Try as they might, Taylor and Brucker were stymied whenever they attempted to make the case for limited war, even though none of the most serious international situations during the Eisenhower administration—the Suez crisis, the Hungarian revolution, the intervention in Lebanon—were susceptible to solution by atomic weapons.

The Air Force continued to call for more and more strategic bombers, and the Navy liked its nuclear submarines. Gradually, however, military planners, with the possible exception of some in the Air Force, began to accept the fact that nuclear weapons had produced a state of mutual deterrence. Future conflicts were likely to be of a limited nature, with an emphasis on ground-force capability. Taylor believed this with all his heart, and it was maddening, when he said so, to be accused of parochialism.

Among civilian strategists, meanwhile, Taylor's views were gaining acceptance and would hardly have been called either radical or parochial. The respected George Kennan, for example, writing in 1954, had concluded that "the day of total war has passed. . . . From now on, limited military operations are the only ones which could conceivably serve any coherent purpose." When Taylor said such things, however, he was suspected by many in the Eisenhower administration of not being enough of a "team player."

Four years later, reflecting on these experiences, he couldn't say he hadn't been warned. When he first arrived, the outgoing Chief of Naval Operations, Admiral Bob Carney, had told him: "You're one of the Good New Chiefs now, but you'll be surprised how soon you will become one of the Bad Old Chiefs!" By the end of 1955 he had achieved the changeover, and he'd been considered a "Bad Chief" ever since.

In 1959 his term as Army Chief of Staff was coming to a close. There wasn't much chance he'd ever be appointed JCS Chairman, even though normal rotation would have made it the Army's turn. In many ways he was disappointed. On the other hand, he didn't think the Chairman *should* be someone who disagreed with administration policies. Perhaps, now that he'd been in uniform for more than forty years, it was time to call it quits. Neil McElroy, who had replaced Wilson as secretary of defense, suggested that Taylor might be kept on for a second tour as Army Chief of Staff, but Taylor declined. Then an even better opportunity came his way.

The message was delivered by General Andrew Goodpaster, a brilliant engineer from the West Point class of 1939 who was currently Eisenhower's staff secretary, and who was in many ways the de facto Army liaison to the White House.

Knowing Taylor's dislike of small talk, Goodpaster got to the point. President Eisenhower, according to Goodpaster, knew that Taylor was completing his term as Army Chief of Staff and also knew that Taylor had told Secretary McElroy he wasn't interested in an extension.

Taylor said that was correct. In his opinion, a new man, perhaps one more in step with the administration, would be better for the Army. By "administration," of course, Taylor meant Eisenhower himself. In later years, Taylor wrote: "While I never particularly minded the conflicts with my Pentagon peers, I felt keenly the increasing coolness of my relations with the President."

Goodpaster, a longtime admirer of Taylor's, felt strongly that Taylor's planned retirement would be a great loss, both to the Army and to the nation. Consequently, he had taken the liberty of approaching President Eisenhower directly on what was obviously a delicate matter. Goodpaster knew, of course, that the President wasn't likely to nominate Taylor to succeed Air Force general Nate Twining for the JCS chairmanship. After all, even though it was the Army's turn, it wouldn't be logical for Eisenhower, much as he might admire Taylor, to appoint someone who disagreed with him on overall defense policies.

Taylor said he understood that and respected it. At this point, Goodpaster came up with a surprising possibility. The President, he said, had asked him to sound Taylor out about becoming the Supreme Allied Commander for NATO.

Taylor was frankly surprised, and more than a little flattered. Despite their differences over policy, Eisenhower was making a generous offer. The NATO position, whose first incumbent had been Eisenhower himself, was every bit as important as the JCS chairmanship.

It was a tempting possibility. Despite Taylor's best efforts, he had seen the Army decline in share of the budget, in manpower, and, what was worse, in combat capability. Although many of his associates assured him he had restored the Army's prestige at a time when it was held in open contempt by Eisenhower's top appointees, Taylor felt, for the first time in his life, that he had failed.

It was not a happy thought, to be taking off the uniform on a down note. The NATO position, on the other hand, would allow him not only to continue serving but to conclude his active military career with all flags flying and at the very pinnacle of his profession.

Despite all that, Taylor asked Goodpaster to thank the President for his consideration, but to say he wouldn't be interested in the NATO assignment.

Maxwell Taylor was choosing the "harder right." He told a sympathetic Goodpaster that he was convinced America's national-defense

strategy was wrong. Moreover, unless something changed, he feared
the country might end up blundering into a nuclear war, just because
we were not capable of fighting any other kind. He had decided that,
for the good of the country, he had to leave the service and as an
unfettered civilian take his case to the American public.

For Max Taylor, this 1959 retirement, after forty-one years in uniform, was accompanied by an overwhelming feeling of frustration,
even a sense of defeat. His Army colleagues, however, from senior
generals to those who had been cadets during his West Point superintendency, saw him as their champion, who had fought the good fight
on their behalf. "You need have no regrets," Douglas MacArthur
wrote him. "Your record as Chief of Staff was outstanding and has
earned you the admiration of all Army men."

Taylor's retirement did not go unnoticed. John Taylor, in a fine
biography of his father published in 1989, wrote:

> Eisenhower was about to leave the presidency with his per-
> sonal popularity intact but his policies, foreign and domestic,
> under heavy fire. The U-2 affair, in which the Soviets had
> exposed administration attempts to cover up the loss of a spy
> plane over the Soviet Union, was only the most recent embar-
> rassment. In part because of the country's continued affection
> for Ike as a person, dissenters such as Taylor, who opposed
> administration policies but who did not deal in personalities,
> were much in demand by the media.

Within two weeks of his retirement, Taylor was appearing on *Meet
the Press*, being asked why he had stepped down. "As you can imagine," he replied, "there are a variety of reasons, some of them personal, some of them official. I would say that in the four years I was
Chief of Staff I pressed as hard as I could to obtain a thorough reap-
praisal of our national military strategy. I was only partially successful. I feel that in four years I have done all I can as part of the defense
team. . . . I now go out and perhaps I can contribute from the outside."

For some time, Taylor had been considering how best to sway public opinion. Back in 1956, he had written an article for *Foreign Affairs*
arguing against too much reliance on massive retaliation. In thoughtful, well-reasoned terms, he urged a U.S. capability for flexible
response. However, his article never saw the light of day; censors at
State and Defense forbade publication, calling it "more the kind of

material to be discussed among military personnel on a confidential basis than used for public purposes" and saying "the strong thread that runs through the entire 13 pages—that the policy of deterrence is in grave question—should be watered down and made much more speculative."

Taylor, of course, felt that the American public was entitled to know these things. Now out of uniform, he was free to speak his mind and free to publish. Almost immediately, he began writing *The Uncertain Trumpet*, explaining the pitfalls of massive retaliation and citing the lack of a coherent overall defense strategy. He took his title from I Corinthians: "For if the trumpet gives an uncertain sound, who shall prepare himself for battle?"

"I have undertaken to write this book," he said in the foreword, "because of my conviction that the defense of the United States is presently controlled largely by nonmilitary factors or by military factors which have become outmoded. While there are strong arguments for a cooling period after leaving the post of Chief of Staff before committing my views to writing, I have the deep feeling that there is no time to waste."

The book, written thoughtfully rather than as an exposé, was hardly a page-turner. It dealt with issues rather than personalities and it avoided sensationalism; even Admiral Radford was treated with respect. Reviewers, however, gave it top billing and hailed it as a significant work. George Fielding Eliot, writing in the *New York Herald Tribune*, called it "frightening and timely." In *The New York Times*, Jack Raymond described it as "an important, rewarding, sometimes exciting book."

Army officers around the world read Taylor's book, savored its contents, and cheered its "incorrectness." When an informal poll at the Fort Leavenworth Command and General Staff College asked student officers to name their favorite book, *The Uncertain Trumpet* was a clear winner.

In the long run, the book's greatest impact came from the impression it made on a single reader: president-elect John F. Kennedy. Seldom has one person's act of moral courage had such a far-reaching effect. Kennedy sensed that in Taylor he had found a man of outstanding intellect and integrity. Early in his presidency, soon after the Bay of Pigs debacle, Kennedy asked Taylor to return to Washington and head a team that would examine what went wrong at the Bay of Pigs and would make recommendations to prevent similar tragedies in the future.

Soon Taylor became a full-fledged member of Kennedy's New Frontier. He was first named personal military advisor to the President and was later selected by Kennedy to return to active duty as Chairman of the Joint Chiefs of Staff, a post in which he could correct some of the flaws he had earlier perceived. In October 1962, as the country's senior military man, he was to play a key role during the Cuban Missile Crisis, and for the remainder of his life he was to figure prominently on the national scene.

Like other men of stature, Taylor had his share of critics, particularly during the Vietnam years. Even critics, however, recognized that Maxwell Taylor, through a sense of duty, was always working tirelessly, unselfishly, and patriotically in what he believed to be the national interest.

In the words of his son, John:

> Maxwell Taylor deserves to be remembered, and to be remembered for more than being a valiant soldier and a valued presidential counselor. For his was a voice that held— when such views seemed hopelessly out of fashion—that the United States is more than a collection of interest groups; that it has enduring security requirements that it must deal with rationally; and that citizenship in twentieth-century America carries with it obligations as well as privileges.

Upon General Taylor's death in 1987, Jacqueline Kennedy Onassis, writing to the Taylor family, composed a beautiful and moving tribute: "I have always felt so lucky to have known him. . . . His intelligence, the optimism and gaiety of his charm—this soldier, scholar, statesman, linguist, author—one found all these qualities in one man in the early days of this country, not in the twentieth century."

CHAPTER 14

# Decision at the NSC

A s far back as he could remember, Alexander Haig had dreamed of becoming a soldier. Perhaps it had something to do with those uniforms in his grandparents' attic, mementos of his father's service during World War I. There was a helmet, gas mask, canteen, cartridge belt—all wondrous things for a boy given to fantasizing. One by one, he managed to sneak the items back to his own home near Philadelphia. His father, an aloof, reserved lawyer, never commented on his son's pilferage, but secretly he must have been pleased. In later days, Al Haig, who was barely nine when his father died, wrote wistfully that somehow he could recall "that uniform I never saw him wear" better than he could picture the actual person.

Whatever the reason, Alexander Haig developed a boyhood goal: to attend West Point and to have a military career. Success didn't come without a struggle. After high school, he obtained a third alternate appointment to the Military Academy, but, as he himself put it: "This meant that I was good enough to be noticed but not good enough to be singled out. I was not selected."

A disappointed Haig, temporarily putting aside thoughts of a military career, entered Notre Dame, thinking he might become a lawyer like his father. In 1944, however, during his sophomore year at South Bend, another West Point appointment came through, and this time he was accepted. As a cadet, he was something of a maverick, amassing huge numbers of demerits for various carefree infractions, spending many an hour "walking the area," and finishing below the middle (215 out of 310) of a class whose wartime curriculum had been shortened to three years. Nevertheless, in June 1947, as a graduating second lieutenant, he had reached the first step of that boyhood goal. He was now a soldier.

At that point, however, even his best friends could never have guessed that Haig would one day wear four stars, become Supreme Allied Commander of NATO, and in Washington would serve one president as Chief of Staff and another as Secretary of State. Similarly, such lofty thoughts were far from Al Haig's mind on June 25, 1950, when as a junior first lieutenant just back from his honeymoon, he took his turn as duty officer in Douglas MacArthur's Tokyo headquarters on what promised to be an uneventful Sunday.

The telephone rang. Over a line crackling with static, twenty-five-year-old Lieutenant Haig heard the voice of John J. Muccio, the U.S. ambassador to South Korea. Muccio, calling from Seoul, reported that large numbers of North Korean troops had crossed the 38th Parallel early that morning. A full-scale invasion was under way.

Muccio stressed the seriousness of the report. "Lieutenant," he said emphatically, "this is not a false alarm." Haig relayed the message to MacArthur's Chief of Staff, General Ned Almond, who would in turn inform MacArthur. Before doing so, however, Almond wanted to make sure of the facts. Many past warnings of "imminent" attack had turned out to be just cries of wolf.

Haig repeated Muccio's message, saying that the ambassador had used the word "invasion" and had emphasized that this was "no false alarm." The lieutenant's report was clear and unambiguous. From his first day as a cadet, he'd learned that straight, honest messages were important.

Word of the unprincipled invasion was flashed to the world, and at the United Nations a measure was passed authorizing the use of force to repel the attack. Within days, U.S. troops were committed.

In later years, Haig wrote that "the fundamental task of diplomacy is to strip policy of its ambiguity." In June 1950, however, few people realized just how greatly ambiguity had contributed to the present Korean crisis. Both the Soviets and the Chinese, as it turned out, had been genuinely surprised by America's willingness to go to war over Korea. Had they known this in advance, the war might have been averted. Dean Rusk, for example, quoted in his memoirs a story of Soviet foreign minister Andrei Vyshinsky telling an American businessman why Soviet fears of America were justified. "Look at Korea," he said. "You did everything you could to tell us you were not interested in Korea, and when the North Koreans went in there, you put your troops in. We can't trust you Americans."

Vyshinsky had a point. In early 1950, not long after the United States had removed all its troops from Korea, Secretary of State Dean Acheson, speaking at the National Press Club, had seemed to exclude Korea and Taiwan from America's Pacific line of defense. Acheson referred to a perimeter that "runs along the Aleutians to Japan and then goes to the Ryukus . . . to the Philippines[;] . . . so far as the other areas of the Pacific are concerned, it must be clear that no person can guarantee these areas against military attack." Those who later fought and died in Korea's "forgotten war" were to pay a high price for this ambiguity.

In the coming months, Al Haig would spend much time in Korea, initially as an aide to General Ned Almond, then briefly as a member of a combat unit. To his regret, however, his combat tour ended abruptly when he contracted hepatitis and had to be evacuated. Working under the demanding, no-nonsense Almond and being privy to high-level discussions, Haig had seen firsthand the need for plain talk, for "telling it like it is" regardless of the consequences. And as a witness to the conference preceding the Inchon landing, he had also seen a dramatic demonstration of moral courage. At that meeting, Douglas MacArthur had stuck to his guns despite the opposition of such notables as Omar Bradley, Chairman of the Joint Chiefs of Staff, and J. Lawton Collins, Army Chief of Staff. According to Haig, MacArthur told the group: "Gentlemen, we will land at Inchon on

September 15 or you will have a new Supreme Commander in the Far East." The opposition was silenced, and the subsequent landing was a stunning triumph.

Referring to that meeting, Haig later wrote: "Even as it was happening, I realized that I had witnessed something that would go down in history, a Cincinnatian act of moral courage. Some years passed before I fully understood the lesson it contained: That when you are in a position of trust and a course you know to be right is questioned for political reasons, you must act on your own convictions based on your own experience, because that is your duty to the American people."

In the years that followed, Haig learned with regret that not all leaders possessed that kind of courage. During his first tour in the Pentagon, for example, he saw that many in Washington considered ambiguity something of a virtue. A case in point arose in 1961, when Haig was in Iran as junior member of a team evaluating future aid to the shah. General Hamilton Twitchell, heading the team, was a Washington realist who recognized that the shah had fallen out of favor with the Kennedy administration. Consequently the team's final report on Iran's military requirements, while accurate as far as it went, attached little importance to the shah's personal opinions and recommendations.

Haig and Dick Kenedy, another junior member of the team, had been impressed by the shah's shrewd evaluation of the Iranian situation. They wanted to present his viewpoint, to tell the whole unvarnished truth as they saw it. It was not to be. In Twitchell's considered opinion, the whole report might have been rejected had they done so.

Haig felt disillusioned. The final report had omitted some important facts in the name of bureaucratic discretion, and fell short, as he said, "of the ideal of reporting the whole truth that had been instilled in me at West Point." He hoped that, when it was up to him, he could do better.

As a lieutenant, Al Haig had received the phone call from Ambassador Muccio that triggered U.S. participation in the Korean conflict. Fourteen years later, in August 1964, Haig as a Pentagon staff officer was among the first to learn of the incident which became the cause, or at least the pretext, for America's major commitment to the tragic Vietnam War. This was the apparent attack on U.S. warships off the Gulf of Tonkin, following which President

Lyndon Johnson ordered the immediate launching of retaliatory attacks by U.S. carrier-based aircraft.

Strikes were made against a North Vietnamese oil refinery at Vinh and five patrol-boat bases. What Haig remembered most vividly, however, was the aftermath of concurrent secret bombing attacks against potential North Vietnamese infiltration routes.

A flash message came in: An American plane had been shot down and the pilot had parachuted into the jungle. Fortunately the man was alive and had turned on a radio homing beacon to guide rescue helicopters to his location. However, the rescue attempt was being delayed, possibly because those on the scene didn't want to risk betraying the secrecy of the mission. Whatever the reason, no one wanted to take responsibility for landing a helicopter, an act which might be interpreted as a violation of North Vietnamese territory. A request to make the rescue was passed through channels, all the way across the Pacific and eventually to the nation's capital.

In Washington, Secretary of Defense Robert McNamara had gone to bed for the night. At the Pentagon, as the lonely, faraway beacon continued to send out its signals, civilians left in charge debated what to do. Bureaucratically, they seemed to feel that the major problem was maintaining the secrecy of the operation. To Al Haig, as to DeWitt Smith, another officer on duty that night, the main consideration was rescuing the pilot. At one point, as the debate dragged on, Haig lost his temper and began to shout.

His exact words, as he later recalled (and as confirmed by one who was present) were: "The U.S. Navy had just bombed the shit out of an oil refinery and five other targets in North Vietnam, and it's no secret to the enemy that this pilot dropped bombs on them, too. He's where he is because he loves and trusts his country. It's too late now to worry about international incidents or cover stories. We sent that young man in there and we've got to get him out." Smith and others supported his position, but the debate continued.

Time passed. Helicopters orbited over the jungle, listening to the beeps and waiting for permission to effect the rescue. Obviously there was a danger that the North Vietnamese were also hearing the signals and trying to home in on them. More conversations took place as senior officials hemmed and hawed.

Inevitably, time ran out. There was a final ominous message: "The pilot's beacon has stopped transmitting." At the Pentagon, the office where Haig and his brother officers had gathered grew deathly still. Their emotions ran the gamut: shame, anger, impotence. Dawn was breaking as Haig headed for home, feeling that someone's lack of moral courage had caused a brave American to be betrayed.

Ironically, when all the facts were known, it became clear, although it was never made public, that the Gulf of Tonkin reports had been premature. No enemy vessels had actually been seen, and nervous sonar men on American destroyers seemed to have interpreted the wake from their own ships as the sound of enemy torpedoes. No real attack had ever taken place. Meanwhile, however, Congress had passed the Gulf of Tonkin Resolution authorizing U.S. armed intervention, and the die had been cast.

Alexander Haig's career continued to progress. He attended the Army War College, following which he received orders for Germany. In his mind, however, a career army officer belonged wherever his nation was at war. After many pleas, and with help from his former boss, Army secretary Cyrus Vance, he managed to have his orders changed from Germany to Southeast Asia.

In Vietnam, Haig served initially as a division operations officer, or G-3. His closest call during this period came as he tried to capture an enemy guerrilla for interrogation purposes. The Vietcong exploded a grenade, killing himself and severely wounding Haig, who began bleeding profusely. Blood streamed down his face and neck, and even after he tried wiping it away, he was unable to see. A small wire from the homemade grenade had passed through the lid and underside of Haig's right eyeball. Had he been blinded? Soon he was on an operating table in Saigon, where he heard a surgeon say, "It's a miracle. It missed the optic nerve. It missed everything."

A week later, Haig was back on duty. He went on to command a battalion and later moved up to lead a brigade. In both assignments, he performed successfully, but even so, he came to realize that too many factors other than battle were involved, and that American efforts, despite costly sacrifices and noble intentions, might never be enough.

In November of 1968, after Richard Nixon defeated Hubert Humphrey in a close presidential election, events were set in motion that were to affect Alexander Haig for the rest of his career. A key player in these events was a brilliant Harvard professor named Henry Kissinger.

Kissinger had been born in Germany, son of a respected, gentle Jewish schoolteacher whose position was abolished by the Nazis in

1933. In August 1938, only three months before the infamous *Kristallnacht*, when Nazi thugs rampaged against Jewish property and Jewish lives all over Germany, the Kissinger family managed to emigrate to America. Had they not, they might well have ended up victims of the Holocaust like many of their relatives.

By 1968, Henry Kissinger, having long before overcome any handicap caused by his immigrant status, had served in the army, had won academic distinction, and as a Harvard professor had established himself as an expert on foreign affairs. He had written five books and dozens of scholarly articles, had served as a consultant to senior government figures of both parties, and during the run-up to the recent campaign, had acted as an advisor to would-be candidate Nelson Rockefeller.

On Friday, November 22, 1968, following the election, Kissinger had flown from Cambridge to New York for his standing lunch date with Rockefeller. As they chatted, their discussion doubtless concerned the growing speculation that Rockefeller would be offered a key position in the Nixon cabinet.

During the lunch, there was a telephone message. Surprisingly, it wasn't for Rockefeller; it was for Kissinger. Could he meet with Nixon the following Tuesday in New York at the Hotel Pierre? He could. (Rockefeller, as it turned out, was not offered a cabinet position.)

Kissinger, who had opposed Nixon during the primaries, presumed the president-elect merely wanted to discuss foreign affairs. But to his surprise, Richard Nixon offered him a prestigious position: head of the National Security Council. And yes, he could take a week to think it over.

Kissinger discussed the offer with several of his friends. He knew in advance, of course, that members of the Eastern establishment would see his crossing over to Nixon as something of a defection. A key voice, however, was that of Kissinger's World War II friend and mentor, the eminent Dr. Fritz Kraemer, who summarized what lay ahead, particularly with reference to Vietnam.

"As your friend," Kraemer said, "I can only say this will be an ordeal. The 'right' will call you the Jew who lost Southeast Asia; the 'left' will call you a traitor to the cause. But as a citizen, of course, you have to take it because no one is better qualified and your personal happiness is of no importance." Kissinger accepted the position.

Al Haig that month, back from Vietnam and now a full colonel, was stationed at West Point, serving on the faculty as deputy commandant of cadets. He was midway through a three-year tour of duty, and already he was wondering about his next assignment. Perhaps he'd be returning to Vietnam to command a brigade—at least, that would be his personal preference.

Then came a surprise call from General Andrew Goodpaster, an officer who had known Richard Nixon during the Eisenhower administration and who was now helping the president-elect to assemble a greatly restructured National Security Council. According to Goodpaster, Henry Kissinger, newly appointed to head the NSC, was looking for someone to serve as his military assistant. Haig's name had been thrown into the hat by Joseph Califano and Fritz Kraemer, both of whom had known him in the Pentagon. Could Colonel Haig come to New York and meet with Dr. Kissinger at the Hotel Pierre?

Haig learned that he was but one of several officers who'd been nominated for the military-assistant position. The others were all senior to him, so it didn't seem there was much chance he'd be selected. In fact he wasn't even sure he would want the job. Nevertheless, as he arrived at the Pierre, a grand hotel of the old-fashioned, luxurious style, he felt rather insecure, wondering if he was out of his depth.

Kissinger, looking owlish and slightly rumpled, was a pleasant surprise. Haig knew of his reputation for brilliance, had even read most of his books and heard him lecture a couple of times. In person, he turned out to be easy to talk to, extremely likable, and possessed of a self-deprecating, disarming sense of humor.

"Tell me, are you a military intellectual?" was Kissinger's first question.

"Not at all," Haig said, going on to describe himself as a career soldier who preferred troop duty but who, through circumstances, had several times been diverted to staff jobs.

Kissinger asked Haig his opinion about several matters, including the ongoing war in Vietnam; the conversation lasted much longer than Haig had anticipated, becoming so informal that Haig was convinced he wasn't under serious consideration. Nevertheless, Kissinger went on to describe the job. As a start, each morning the assistant would monitor the many streams of foreign intelligence flowing into the White House, then would brief Kissinger and/or the President on the state of the world. Realistically, of course, it'd be Kissinger who did most of the talking to the President, but the assistant himself would have a hand in deciding what was most significant, and when military considerations were involved, his input would be important.

"What would you think of a job like that?" Kissinger asked.

"It seems, to put it mildly, like the sort of position one dreams about."

"Very well," said Kissinger, "report for duty immediately." Haig, hoping his jaw didn't drop, could only nod his assent.

Several weeks later, Al Haig, following his new routine, was driving to work at 5:30 in the morning along dark, nearly deserted Washington streets. The winter day was starting out cold and dreary, but since he hardly ever saw the outdoors in this new job, he guessed it didn't make that much difference.

At the White House entrance gate, he showed his identification badge to the security guard, then headed for his office. As usual, the workday would begin at six and probably last some fourteen or fifteen hours. His life had surely changed drastically these past few weeks, and in a way he was still wondering, "Why me?"

Since that first meeting with Kissinger, Haig had moved his family to Washington, found himself a desk in the Old Executive Office Building next to the White House, and tried to learn the ways of a new culture and a demanding new boss. Now, sitting at his desk in the early-morning quiet, he started his daily routine, sifting through the secret dispatches and estimates that had arrived during the night and selecting items for the summary that would go to the President.

Haig, ignoring the pressure, worked swiftly and competently, in a way that over the coming months would win the trust and respect of Henry Kissinger, no easy thing.

"It is said," a reporter once commented to Kissinger, "that you are a reasonably demanding taskmaster."

Kissinger corrected him. "No, I'm *extremely* demanding. But first of all, I don't demand anything of my associates that I don't do myself."

Haig was no stranger to pressured assignments. His best preparation for serving under Kissinger, in fact, may have been his time in Korea as aide-de-camp to the difficult and often unreasonable corps commander Ned Almond. In any event, as the months went by, Haig would probably have agreed with Winston Lord, a fellow member of the NSC staff, who said: "You do things for Henry you didn't think you were capable of. . . . I think of Henry as a Vince Lombardi in search of excellence."

As he began to recognize Haig's ability, Kissinger assigned him increasingly important tasks and began moving him up in the White

House hierarchy. He also moved him physically, from the Executive Office Building and into the White House itself, although the new office was admittedly only a tiny basement cubbyhole.

Kissinger often grumbled about one thing or another, such as Haig's overly formal, rather military writing style, but on the whole, Haig was learning the ropes and fitting in. Of course he had little background in the diplomatic field, but to tell the truth, he didn't know if that was all bad.

During his cadet days, Haig had been taught that messages should be expressed clearly, honestly, and without quibbling. In Washington, though, too often that wasn't the case. He felt, for example, that accounts of the 1962 Cuban Missile Crisis had never told the full story. As a Pentagon mid-level action officer, then-Major Haig had been on a team trying to put together a paper accurately describing what had happened, but also using the administration's version of events and reflecting the public's perception of the outcome. At the time, he knew that after the crisis some fifteen U.S. Jupiter missiles were removed secretly from Turkey. More Jupiters had also come out of Italy. It looked to him as though a deal had been arranged—Soviet missiles out of Cuba in exchange for U.S. missiles out of Turkey and Italy. That, of course, was not the way the affair had been presented, which was troubling. Just as in that 1961 report from Iran, people seemed willing to equivocate, telling the boss what the boss wanted to hear.

Maybe that was the way things worked, but young Colonel Haig wasn't at all sure it was the best way. Well, at least he was learning that Henry Kissinger, while he was a difficult taskmaster, was also an honest and ethical person, one who might be guilty of diplomatic quibbles, but who abhorred outright lying. In his autobiography, Israeli foreign minister Abba Eban described Kissinger's methods by saying: "I felt that if he wanted to sell us a car with a wheel missing, he would achieve his purpose by an eloquent and cogent eulogy of the three wheels that remained!"

While some might accuse Kissinger of dissembling, the press corps by this time was also learning to see him as an excellent news source. For example, before any of Richard Nixon's major speeches on foreign policy (and the White House billed every Nixon speech as "major") Kissinger met with reporters beforehand in a "backgrounder" to make sure they understood the main points the President was trying to communicate.

Reporters also understood that it was often impossible for Kissinger to be completely open. When a reporter told Kissinger he'd like to have an extremely candid answer, Kissinger wisecracked, even before the question was asked, "What do you want me to do, make history?"

From the very start, of course, the press corps, like Haig, had recognized Kissinger's intelligence. Richard Valeriani was only being honest when he wrote that, in a rare admission, the White House and State Department reporters acknowledged that Kissinger was actually smarter than they were.

Some also saw, of course, the difficult, demanding side of Henry Kissinger. Fortunately Al Haig, like his boss, could be a workaholic. Months went by, and for the rest of 1969, then into 1970, Haig was on hand, a key staff assistant and an interested observer, as the Vietnam War wound down and new crises arose, in Cambodia, Jordan, Syria, and elsewhere.

In September 1970, a U-2 reconnaissance plane, flying its routine, once-a-month pattern over Cuba, and only 240 miles south of Miami, snapped a picture of a soccer field on a tiny island in Cienfuegos Bay on the southern coast of Cuba. Nearby were military barracks, some new, some still under construction. CIA photo interpreters sensed the significance; Cubans played baseball, not soccer. The field was probably for recreational use by Soviet seamen.

U-2 flights were stepped up. Barracks construction, which had been under way for about three weeks, was nearly finished. In the harbor was an *Ugra*-class submarine tender. Nearby were two barges of the type normally used to store radioactive wastes from nuclear-powered submarines. Farther down the coast, another base was equipped with a new dock, fuel-storage tanks, and a powerful communications facility guarded by radar and anti-aircraft missiles. Moreover, a sizable Soviet naval force was steaming in that direction.

In the words of Kissinger biographer Walter Isaacson: "What the Soviets were doing, with clever ambiguity, was testing the fuzzy margins that had been established after the 1962 Cuban missile crisis." At Cienfuegos, the Soviets clearly were establishing a base suitable for submarine operations in the Atlantic and the Caribbean. Once the base was operational, submarines from there, presumably equipped with nuclear missiles, would be in a position to strike every major area in the United States.

To the Americans, Cienfuegos was a blatant violation of the 1962 agreement between Kennedy and Khrushchev. Under that accord, the Soviets, while able to assist defensively, had promised to never again build offensive installations in Cuba. Now, in view of the powerful new intermediate-range ballistic missiles that had been developed in recent years, they were posing a far greater threat to U.S. security than that which had faced President John F. Kennedy in 1962.

At the Pentagon, the Joint Chiefs recommended calling up the reserves to show how seriously the United States viewed the threat, then doing whatever it took to eliminate the Cienfuegos base. The State Department, somewhat predictably, recommended taking no action at the present time. In State's analysis, the Soviet move was mostly symbolic. Secretary of State William Rogers would be meeting with Soviet foreign minister Andrei Gromyko at the U.N. in about a month; he could take the matter up at that time. Above all, nothing should be done that might alarm the American people, at least not until after the November elections.

Haig and others at the National Security Council felt that this wasn't good enough. Henry Kissinger, who believed in "secret diplomacy, secretly negotiated," hoped to make the Soviets withdraw, but without having to make them back down publicly. Richard Nixon agreed. Both men knew how much the Soviets resented the public's perception that Khrushchev had been forced to give way in the face of Kennedy's firmness; many felt this had contributed greatly to Khrushchev's downfall.

Kissinger, meeting with Soviet ambassador Anatoly Dobrynin privately in the White House Map Room, said the United States considered what it saw at Cienfuegos a violation of the 1962 agreement and a matter of "utmost gravity." Dobrynin, expressing concern, said he would communicate this to Moscow.

As a result of this rather mild rebuke, reconnaissance flights showed that construction at Cienfuegos, while still under way, began to slow down.

At the NSC, crisis piled upon crisis. In the Middle East, Syria was threatening to invade Jordan. If that happened, the United States might encourage Israel to intervene, despite the fear of Russia's possible reaction. In Paris, Vietnam peace talks had just been resumed. In Chile, there were rumors of a coup to overthrow President Salvador Allende. Kissinger, as he tried keeping several balls in the air at once, grew ever more demanding and difficult.

About this time, an interview with U.S. Attorney General John Mitchell appeared in *Women's Wear Daily*. In it, Mitchell called Henry Kissinger, among other things, an "egocentric maniac." Kissinger shrugged off the matter, saying, "At Harvard, it took me ten years to achieve an environment of total hostility. Here I've done it in twenty months."

Through someone's leak, perhaps inadvertent, perhaps deliberate, word of the Cienfuegos construction got out. C. L. Sulzberger's column in *The New York Times*, which broke the story, was headed "Ugly Clouds in the South." A Pentagon spokesman confirmed what Sulzberger had written. An AP wire story followed, saying: "The Pentagon said today it has firm indications the Soviet Union may be establishing a permanent submarine base in Cuba." Overall, however, the press was minimizing the story's importance, as were many of the Democrats on Capitol Hill. Perhaps neither wanted to give Richard Nixon a chance to act macho in the weeks preceding the midterm elections. Haig, however, like others in the know, realized the situation had become critical.

On September 27, Nixon, Kissinger, Secretary of State William Rogers, and Defense Secretary Melvin Laird all left on a long-planned diplomatic trip to Europe. Meanwhile, the U-2 photos showed that Cienfuegos construction was still going forward.

Kissinger phoned Haig from Air Force One. "Haig, I want you to call on Ambassador Dobrynin and deliver the message again."

"In the same terms as before?"

"No, take a stronger line."

What exactly did that mean? Haig, after all, was only a colonel, with no authority in his own right. If he spoke *too* strongly, and upset the diplomatic applecart, he might be left alone, twisting in the wind because of a career-ending blunder. In the past, he'd known of military men—paratroop generals Matthew Ridgway and James Gavin came to mind—who had spoken out forthrightly and courageously. They, however, had already established themselves as World War II combat leaders. Few such men existed today, and many of those getting ahead seemed to be those with political savvy, ones who practiced "Go along to get along." No doubt about it, the safest course would be to deliver what Kissinger called a stronger line while adhering to diplomatic niceties. But would that get the true, unambiguous message across?

Haig called the Soviet embassy and set up an appointment with Ambassador Dobrynin, saying he had a message from the President for the Soviet government. As he hung up the phone he could feel himself growing tense. How strong a message was he authorized to convey? After all, Dobrynin had served in Washington for twenty-four years and was dean of the diplomatic corps. He knew all the buttons to push, and was well capable of ruining the career of a rather junior army officer.

Ironically, in the years ahead, as Al Haig moved into ever higher positions on the national scene, he became adept at what the press called Haigspeak, the ability to answer a question at length while saying little and while going through what he called a mental card file to decide just how much he was able to reveal. In private, however, he was always able to make his point plainly and decisively.

In this instance, knowing what was at stake, Haig felt strongly about the proper approach. For encouragement, he may have remembered how much he'd resented the ambiguous talk by Dean Acheson that had preceded the Korean War. In any case, he was determined to talk straight.

At the embassy, Anatoly Dobrynin met with Haig in a darkened office where shades and steel shutters covered the windows to prevent eavesdropping. Dobrynin, the soul of graciousness, greeted his visitor with a warm smile and a firm handshake. He was living up to his reputation as a man who knew all the diplomatic courtesies and who, when he wanted, could be a real charmer.

Haig did not return the smile. Instead, in a steady voice, he said: "Mr. Ambassador, I am instructed to say the following. You are putting offensive weapons into Cuba. This is an intolerable violation of the 1962 understanding between our two countries. *Either you take those weapons out and dismantle the base or we will do it for you.*"

In an instant, Dobrynin's charm vanished and his smile was replaced by an angry glare. His face became flushed, and in a loud, menacing voice, he said: "You are threatening the Soviet Union. *That* is what is intolerable!" Dobrynin was saying, and in no uncertain terms, that if the Americans wanted trouble, the Soviets would be happy to oblige.

Calmly, Haig answered: "Mr. Ambassador, I have delivered my message. Now I will leave."

Once back at the White House, Haig sent a message to Kissinger, reporting his words with Dobrynin. Soon after, he received a priority call from Kissinger on Air Force One. It soon became apparent that Anatoly Dobrynin's anger had been nothing compared to that of Henry Kissinger.

"I'm furious! The President is furious!" By this time Kissinger was shouting. "You can't talk to the Russians that way! You may have started a war!"

Haig, who didn't agree, didn't try to argue. He waited, wondering what would come next. To his great relief, and as he'd hoped, new reconnaissance photos soon showed the Soviets to be dismantling the base. On the day Nixon returned to Washington, Dobrynin urgently asked to see Kissinger. At the meeting, Dobrynin delivered a note insisting that the Soviets had never done anything to violate the 1962 agreement. That included Cienfuegos. Moreover, they would never do anything like that in the future. As Nixon had hoped, the Soviets were withdrawing privately and gracefully, all the while maintaining the fiction that the Cienfuegos base had never existed.

"For what it's worth," Haig later wrote, "after this incident my own relations with Dobrynin took on a new cordiality that lasted through the many years of diplomatic contact that remained ahead."

CHAPTER 15

# Decision in the Gulf

In the spring of 1991, at the conclusion of Operation Desert Storm, America had its first battlefield hero in decades. He was General H. Norman Schwarzkopf, Jr., whom reporters sometimes referred to as Stormin' Norman, which he didn't much care for. His men, on the other hand, knew him as the Bear, a name affectionately given him in Vietnam, and which somehow seemed to fit. By any label, he was surely man of the hour, a burly, four-star, larger-than-life figure in desert camouflage who had arrived prominently on the international scene.

Saddam Hussein, threatening U.S. president George Bush, had promised "the mother of all battles": "Thousands of Americans you have pushed into this dark tunnel will go home shrouded in sad coffins." When it came to pass, however, the actual war had been made to appear almost too easy. Schwarzkopf had led an Allied force to one of the most complete, one-sided victories in history, a victory that might have been compared to Hannibal's at Cannae or Napoleon's at Jena. He had overwhelmed a numerically superior force, had wrought massive destruction, and had achieved it with but a minimum number of friendly casualties.

Looking back over the past six months, however, or for that matter reviewing his entire life, Schwarzkopf knew it had *not* been easy. Along the way, he had faced many tests and hurdles. Often the path had been strewn with rocks and the future clouded in uncertainty.

Shortly after his twelfth birthday, Norman Schwarzkopf left home to join his father, head of the U.S. military mission in Iran. Herbert Schwarzkopf, West Point class of 1917, had left the service in 1921 to head the New Jersey State Police and had gained national prominence in the early 1930s as chief investigator of the Lindbergh kidnapping case. He'd returned to active duty during World War II, had been promoted to general, and had spent much of the war overseas. By 1946, the elder Schwarzkopf decided not only that he missed his only son, but that living in a foreign country would be a great experience for the boy.

Young Norman idolized his dad; arriving in Iran, he was determined to emulate his father and to live up to his high standards. He'd later say: "'Duty, Honor, Country,' the West Point motto, was his creed, and it became mine." However, to follow the creed often took a bit of doing. For example, there was the time they visited the camp of a Baluchi chieftain.

After the preliminaries, dinner was served in a main tent whose floor was covered by thick, multicolored rugs with geometric patterns. Norman sat next to his father amid a circle of fierce-looking tribesmen. Soon servants brought in sheep which had been roasted whole on spits.

To the Baluchis, it seemed, a sheep's eyeball was a great delicacy. Accordingly, an eye was plucked out and offered ceremoniously to General Schwarzkopf, who picked it up along with a handful of rice, put it in his mouth, and solemnly chewed.

To the boy's horror, the chieftain then announced they must also honor the general's son with an eyeball. "I'm not going to eat that," the youngster whispered to his dad.

"You *will* eat it!" was the reply, and somehow Norman managed to do so. Later, after explaining that refusal would have been considered an insult, his father said: "But instead you ate it, and by doing that you made a contribution to American-Iranian relations. I'm proud of you." It was a compliment he'd always cherish.

After attending various schools, many of them overseas, the general's son, H. Norman Junior, went on to West Point, from which he graduated in 1956. Then came a series of junior officer assignments with troop units in the States and in Germany, followed by still more schooling, both civil and military. In 1964 he received a master's degree in engineering from USC, which led to a teaching assignment at the Military Academy.

Meanwhile, of course, Schwarzkopf was well aware of the brewing troubles in Southeast Asia. In 1961, for example, with the war going poorly for the South Vietnamese, he'd read of President John F. Kennedy directing a major expansion of the U.S. military advisory effort, and had watched with interest as the number of advisors increased dramatically, from about 900 in January of 1961 to 17,000 by the end of 1963. In his Vietnam memoir, Army general Bruce Palmer called these advisors "unsung heroes," working "unrecognized and unappreciated" at jobs which were "thankless, dangerous, and difficult."

In 1965, then-Captain Schwarzkopf decided, with his country at war, that he as a professional soldier should be doing his part. Despite friends who said advisory duty would do nothing for his career, he volunteered to cut short his instructor tour at West Point so as to serve in Vietnam. His decision to volunteer, he would write, "had nothing to do with careerism. It had to do with ideals."

Arriving in Vietnam, thirty-year-old Captain Schwarzkopf was assigned as one of the advisors to the Vietnamese Airborne Brigade. During an early operation, he and the unit to which he was attached made a long trek into the jungle, after which they camped for several days while a South Vietnamese engineer unit repaired a bridge damaged by the Vietcong. When the job had been completed, the engineers invited the airborne officers and their advisor to a bridge-blessing ceremony. They watched as a pig was slaughtered, after which each man was given a half-glass of Scotch. Their glasses were then filled the rest of the way with blood from the pig.

Schwarzkopf, no doubt recalling his boyish discomfort at the Baluchi feast in Iran, knew what was expected. While the American advisor with the engineers refused to touch his drink, Schwarzkopf, toasting the bridge, drained his glass with a mighty gulp. Later, his Vietnamese counterpart told him that the engineer commander had hoped to embarrass the Americans who were present, and that by his action he had brought great credit to the airborne. Schwarzkopf had passed a test, thereby doing much to cement relations with his Vietnamese comrades.

Before long, another test would arise—one not only more difficult, but with career-threatening implications.

Captain Schwarzkopf studied the order that had just come down from higher headquarters. It looked good—even impressive. When he'd first arrived in Vietnam, things had seemed rather ragged. Now, however, as he read the message and admired the staff work that apparently had gone into it, he nodded his appreciation.

The order called for a mission in support of Major General Vinh Loc, commander of the Vietnamese II Corps. Someone at Vinh Loc's headquarters, no doubt with the help of an American advisor, had spelled everything out precisely in a directive that would have received a high grade at Fort Benning or any of the other U.S. service schools.

A task force under Major Nghi (pronounced "knee"), with Schwarzkopf as advisor, would attack to drive the Vietcong away from the South Vietnamese special forces camp at Duc Co, near the Cambodian border. The camp, set up to prevent infiltrators from slipping into Vietnam from Cambodia, had for weeks been under attack by Vietcong guerrillas, and was more or less under siege.

According to the order, in forty-eight hours Nghi and his men would make a massive helicopter assault, using a landing zone (LZ) seven miles from Duc Co after a preparatory twenty-minute air strike. That was good: No one wanted a "hot" LZ (one under enemy fire), since helicopters, swift in normal flight, could be sitting ducks when they slowed, hovered, and touched down. The air strike should take care very nicely of keeping the LZ clear of any Vietcong.

Once on the ground, the order said, the task force would be supported by "all available" artillery. Moving on foot to the Cambodian border, and under cover of a fighter-bomber "air cap," they would then swing in a wide arc around Duc Co. This should allow them to pinch off the guerrillas, whose strength was an estimated two battalions, about 700 men. Nghi's force should be adequate for the job, but as an added precaution, a South Vietnamese ranger battalion would be standing by to help if needed.

Major Nghi was something of a question mark. Some said he was weak, that he owed his job to political connections through his brother, a famous war hero. Others said he had never been the same after a painful training accident in which an incendiary grenade, mistaken for a smoke grenade, had gone off in his hand and left him horribly scarred. In any case, Schwarzkopf, as his designated advisor, was determined to give Nghi the fullest possible support.

Together, Schwarzkopf and the major went over the operations order, planning how they would implement it. Which unit would be assigned to which helicopters? Who would take the lead once they were on the ground? Where would Nghi and Schwarzkopf position themselves during the operation? How would they call for supporting fire? After working through much of the night, they decided they had a solid and workable tactical plan.

Next morning, with less than twenty-four hours remaining before the scheduled assault, Nghi began to brief his commanders. While he was doing this, Schwarzkopf decided to double-check various elements of the plan. He began by getting with the helicopter flight leader.

First step was flying to Duc Co to check out the landing zone. Taking out his map, Schwarzkopf showed the pilot the clearing they'd be using. Soon they were in the air and skimming over the jungle, flying low to keep from attracting any ground fire. High-flying choppers, audible from a distance, often gave the Vietcong time to start shooting. A low-flying helicopter, on the other hand, normally had time to come and go before anyone could react. Schwarzkopf kept peering down, trying to detect any ground activity. The lush triple-canopy jungle, however, formed an impenetrable screen. All he could see was solid vegetation. The Vietcong were down there, that was for sure, but only when he was on the ground himself would he learn, and perhaps unpleasantly, just where that was.

They came over the spot designated as the landing zone. Looking down, Schwarzkopf saw only trees where the clearing should have been. He rechecked his map. There must be a mistake; the clear area designated as an LZ was nowhere to be seen. Evidently some staff officer, without checking, had taken a map and marked a spot that looked open, not realizing that in the jungle a clearing could soon become a forest. Schwarzkopf asked the pilot to keep circling until they found a suitable LZ. Finally they found an alternate site, about fifteen miles the other side of Duc Co. The change in LZ site meant the timing of the whole operation would also have to change.

Back on the ground, Schwarzkopf went to the air section at General Vinh Loc's headquarters to coordinate the air strike. The man at the desk, giving him a blank look, said: "We don't know anything about an operation at Duc Co."

Schwarzkopf took out the operations order and pointed out the paragraph indicating a twenty-minute preparation. Yes, it was there all right, but the man insisted they'd never received any such request. "And by the way," the man added, "if you're going tomorrow, you won't have any air, because we need forty-eight hours to line up the planes."

Schwarzkopf began getting a sinking feeling in his stomach. What was happening here? Well, if there was no air, he'd better get busy and line up lots of artillery support. He hurried to the office of the fire support coordinator, showed the operations order to the two men on duty and explained how crucial fire support would be.

"What artillery is in that area?" he asked.

The men began to laugh. One of them said: "Do you know what 'available' artillery is? There's one mortar tube within the special forces camp!"

The second man, grinning, chimed in: "And they have only twenty rounds of ammo left!"

Their humor was lost on Schwarzkopf, who stormed out, fuming. Back at Pleiku, he went into the snack bar to cool off, and there received what appeared to be the first bit of good luck. At a nearby table was Captain Paul Leckinger, a friend from Fort Benning days, and currently an advisor to the South Vietnamese ranger battalion.

Schwarzkopf told Leckinger about the mixed-up operations order and the lack of artillery and air support. It made him appreciate the availability of the Vietnamese rangers. "At least you'll be there if we need you," he said.

Leckinger had the same blank look as the people at the air section. "What are you talking about? My battalion has just come back from three weeks in the field. We sent them all home to their villages for a break. We couldn't get them back together in less than three or four days."

That hollowness in the stomach was turning more and more into a feeling of panic. This thing was shaping up as a real disaster. Schwarzkopf went looking for the task force commander.

Major Nghi, a somewhat reluctant warrior at best, became visibly shaken when Schwarzkopf told what he'd found: no landing zone where it was supposed to be, no support from either air or artillery,

no ranger battalion standing by. It was now about seven P.M., and
they were supposed to start the attack the next morning.

"What do you advise, Captain?"

"Sir, I advise that we not go! We need a forty-eight-hour delay to
sort some of this out." The major quickly agreed.

Nghi first notified his parent unit, the airborne headquarters back
in Saigon. Then he placed a call to General Vinh Loc, the man in
whose corps zone they'd be operating, and the one whose headquarters had issued the order.

Schwarzkopf sat down; he was beginning to feel a little better.
Watching Nghi, however, it soon became clear the conversation was
not going well. Even from across the room, he could hear Vinh Loc
screaming at the hapless Nghi.

Nghi hung up the phone. In a subdued voice, he said they wanted
to see Nghi and Schwarzkopf in person. They were to be at General
Vinh Loc's house at ten for a special meeting. Vinh Loc, according to
Nghi, was a Vietnamese prince, a very powerful person who was used
to having people do exactly as he said. And at the moment he was
very, very angry.

At the appointed time, Schwarzkopf and Nghi arrived at Vinh
Loc's place, an imposing colonial mansion in downtown Pleiku. An
aide motioned them to follow, and they were ushered into a large
marble-floored hall. At the far end was a dais, behind which sat a row
of officers, looking very much like a military tribunal. General Vinh
Loc sat in the center, in the place of honor. Next to him was his
American advisor, a full colonel. On either side were several
Vietnamese generals and colonels, with *their* American advisors. Two
straight chairs had been placed facing the dais. To Schwarzkopf, this
looked like an arrangement more suited for prisoners in the docket
than for a military conference.

General Vinh Loc, speaking in Vietnamese, got right to the point.
Looking menacingly at Major Nghi, and mincing no words, he shout-
ed: "How *dare* you say you are not going to attack tomorrow?"
Who, he wanted to know, was responsible for this outrage?

Major Nghi, squirming, said that he was willing to attack but had
requested a postponement on the advice of his American advisor,
Captain Schwarzkopf.

Vinh Loc turned to his own advisor, the American colonel, with a
look which seemed to imply that now he understood: This foul-up
was all the fault of the Americans!

The colonel, clearly embarrassed, and not wanting to lose face before the Vietnamese, glared at Schwarzkopf. "Captain, how *dare* you tell them not to attack?"

Schwarzkopf, trying to sound calm, explained that despite what it said in the operations order, they had neither air nor artillery support, nor did they have a reserve. Moreover, they'd had to switch to a new landing zone, which meant they didn't even have a proper ground tactical plan.

Schwarzkopf had been in Vietnam only a month and a half, and this was his first time in combat. Obviously the colonel thought he had no right to question any orders from a higher headquarters.

"For crying out loud," said the colonel, "it's just a couple of VC battalions! And what do you mean, you don't have any air support? If you get in trouble, we'll divert airplanes from someplace else. That's the way we operate."

Schwarzkopf knew all eyes were focused on him, and not very friendly eyes at that. He was determined not to be intimidated. "Sir, I just don't consider that adequate air support."

The colonel, red-faced, was becoming more and more irritated. In a sarcastic voice, he asked: "And just what *would* you consider to be proper air support?"

For the first time, Schwarzkopf let his own anger show. "Sir, when it's my ass out there on the ground, about a hundred B-52's circling overhead would be just barely adequate. Now, I'm willing to settle for something less, but I'm not willing to settle for nothing."

That did it. The colonel was livid. He went into a tirade, lashing out at Schwarzkopf and his impertinence, at one point telling him he was an embarrassment to the American army. Now what did he have to say for himself?

Schwarzkopf said he still felt the attack should be postponed, at which the colonel replied that Schwarzkopf was obviously unsuited for the job, and he therefore should consider himself relieved of his duties.

Norman Schwarzkopf had grown up in a military family, had been further ingrained at West Point and elsewhere with a respect for those in authority. Moreover, he knew that an officer who was relieved from a job, particularly during combat, could kiss his career good-bye. Nevertheless, he felt sure he was right, and despite the bullying, he stood his ground and told the colonel that was an improper order. The only one who could relieve him was his senior airborne advisor, Colonel Francis Naughton.

"Get him on the phone!"

It was now nearly midnight, but somehow they managed to track down Colonel Naughton back in Saigon. Naughton listened to the colonel, who spared no words as he told of his own outrage as well as that of General Vinh Loc. Then Naughton asked to speak to Schwarzkopf, who explained his own side of the story.

There was a dramatic pause. Then Naughton's voice came over the phone. He reminded everyone that this was a Vietnamese airborne unit under the operational control of Saigon. Next he said: "I support Captain Schwarzkopf and my Vietnamese counterpart here supports Major Nghi. All we ask is a forty-eight-hour delay."

With that, Schwarzkopf had become the most unpopular man in Pleiku. Next morning, Colonel Naughton arrived at Vinh Loc's headquarters to help sort things out. Meanwhile, the staff officers on hand, both American and Vietnamese, kept telling Schwarzkopf he was being overly concerned about "only a couple of measly VC battalions." Clearly they considered him to be a troublemaker, one they'd remember.

Naughton looked over the plans, asked questions, and then announced that Schwarzkopf was right. The operation was postponed for seventy-two hours, much to the relief of Major Nghi and his under-the-gun advisor.

Before leaving, Naughton announced he had one more piece of business. In a stern voice, he called Schwarzkopf forward and had him stand at attention. Nearby staff officers stopped work and grew quiet. Were they about to witness a royal chewing-out?

Colonel Naughton's serious expression turned into a broad smile. Beaming, he reached in his pocket and took out a gold leaf, which he then proceeded to pin on Schwarzkopf's collar. Orders promoting Schwarzkopf to major had just come through, and Naughton had decided this was a highly appropriate time and place to hold the ceremony.

The new major, grinning from ear to ear, thanked his boss profusely. Not only did he appreciate the support and the promotion, he also thought Naughton showed real class by announcing the promotion at that particular moment, and before a group that considered H. Norman Schwarzkopf to be, in Schwarzkopf's words, "the world's biggest pain in the ass." The promotion was great, of course, but even more important was the fact they'd managed to forestall a potential military debacle.

By the time Schwarzkopf had completed his tour in Vietnam, he recognized the difficulty of ever winning an all-out military victory. And, like other advisors, though he was fully committed to the struggle he had also come to resent the overly optimistic reports emanating from higher headquarters.

Schwarzkopf returned to the States to complete his West Point instructor assignment and to attend the Army's Command and General Staff College at Fort Leavenworth. He then volunteered to go back to Vietnam for a second tour. In 1970, at the end of that tour, he wrote: "The Army had not only reached its nadir but also lost the confidence of the American people. I agonized over the question of whether to stay in—and decided I would, in the hope of someday getting to help fix what I thought was wrong."

Schwarzkopf's ability to "fix what was wrong" of course depended in large part on attaining some degree of seniority. Over the next eighteen years he worked hard, distinguished himself in a series of important assignments, and was rewarded by continued promotion. Finally, in the summer of 1988, he learned he was in line to receive his fourth star. Even so, things did not come easily.

Schwarzkopf had requested an assignment as head of Central Command, or Centcom, the military organization with responsibility for the Middle East. In the past, the job had alternated between the Marines and the Army, so when Schwarzkopf was nominated to replace the current incumbent, Marine general George Crist, it seemed likely the posting would go to him. However, while the Army and the Air Force supported Schwarzkopf's nomination, the Navy and the Marines supported a Navy admiral for the job. The Chairman of the Joint Chiefs, Admiral William Crowe, although submitting both names to Secretary of Defense Frank Carlucci for consideration, had sent along a note of personal support for the admiral. It didn't look good for Schwarzkopf. However, after a successful interview with Carlucci, Schwarzkopf was given the assignment. In November 1988, he received his fourth star and took over as head of Central Command, with headquarters at MacDill Air Force Base near Tampa.

Over the next few months, as he visited with foreign leaders, both civil and military, Schwarzkopf began to appreciate even more the importance of America's role in the Middle East. Then, after studying the Centcom mission, he concluded that current contingency plans were outdated and began drafting new ones. His predecessor, General Crist, had had similar ideas. Crist had told *The New York Times* in an interview that preparing mainly for a Soviet thrust into Iran was an outmoded strategy. What the United States needed, Crist had said, was the flexibility to deal with other potential threats in the region. Schwarzkopf definitely agreed with this, and when revised plans were drawn up, he discussed them with top civilian strategists in the Pentagon. Happily, his ideas were also concurred in by his four-star colleague, General Colin Powell, who many felt would be the next Chairman of the Joint Chiefs of Staff.

Meanwhile, however, the present Chairman, Admiral Crowe, was preparing his own recommendations on military strategy for delivery to the Congress. His first draft, when circulated to the Joint Chiefs for comment, made no provision whatever for the Middle East. The premise, apparently, was that American resources should be reserved only for the continental United States, NATO, and the Pacific.

Schwarzkopf naturally was dismayed by the omission and by what he considered its shortsightedness. He argued and tried to make his point with fellow military people, but got nowhere. The Chairman himself had approved the plan, and Schwarzkopf wasn't even able to arrange a face-to-face meeting with Admiral Crowe to voice his concerns.

Fortunately, when the plan reached the secretary of defense—now Dick Cheney—for comment, those same civilian strategists Schwarzkopf had consulted earlier called him and asked if the general agreed with it.

"Of course not!" growled Schwarzkopf, who made it clear he'd been stonewalled. The problem was then presented to Secretary Cheney, who immediately ordered the Middle East to be written in.

In late July 1989, Centcom began a "command post exercise," code-named Internal Look, to test the new plan. A mock headquarters was set up and dummy messages were dispatched, with a scenario based on a hypothetical attack by an aggressor nation against other Arab states, with consequent danger to Mideast oil fields. Participants had no trouble identifying the unnamed aggressor as Iraq, which had by this time become one of the world's strongest and most belligerent military powers.

Incredibly, as Internal Look was taking place, parallel events were occurring in real life. Saddam Hussein was complaining that Kuwait was infringing on the Iraqi portion of the Rumaila oil field that straddled the two countries. Iraqi divisions were massing on the Kuwaiti border, and invasion seemed imminent. Many, of course, still viewed all this as a bluff; most Arab nations, as well as the U.S. State Department, found it inconceivable that Iraq would consider attacking fellow Arabs.

Then, on August 2, less than a week after the conclusion of Internal Look, Saddam Hussein did what the exercise had anticipated. Iraqi forces stormed into Kuwait. Colin Powell, by this time Chairman of the Joint Chiefs, called Schwarzkopf and said: "Well, you were right. They've crossed the border."

Schwarzkopf ordered contingency plans to be set in motion, then flew to Washington to assist in briefing President Bush. Diplomatic wheels were turning. At the United Nations, the invasion was condemned and a resolution was passed demanding immediate Iraqi withdrawal.

American President George Bush said Iraq's aggression would not be allowed to stand: "Nobody is willing to accept anything less than total withdrawal of the Iraqi forces and no puppet regime." Saudi Arabia, still shocked by the invasion, and now fearing for its own safety, agreed to have United Nations forces stationed on Saudi territory.

The operation to defend Saudi Arabia, by this time named Desert Shield, was under way. Schwarzkopf was designated overall commander-in-chief. The first unit to arrive in the Gulf was a brigade of the 82nd Airborne Division. While planes and troops went by air, heavier equipment was being loaded concurrently for travel by sea. As days went by, and the buildup continued, Schwarzkopf began to relax a little—Saddam had missed his chance to score an easy, unopposed victory. By mid-September, Centcom forces were in position to defend Saudi Arabia and the immediate threat of further invasion had lessened. Centcom, however, was a long way from being able to take the offensive. In fact, during a meeting at Camp David right after the Iraqui invasion, Schwarzkopf had explained that his plans were designed initially only for the defense of Saudi Arabia. At the same meeting, he had shocked his listeners by telling them that to go on the offensive would take a lot more troops and a lot more time, probably eight to ten months.

A few days after that, and only a week into Desert Shield, Chairman Colin Powell had startled Schwarzkopf by asking him how he'd go about it if he had to kick the Iraqis out of Kuwait "right now."

"I couldn't!" said Schwarzkopf. "I've made it clear to everyone that we aren't sending enough forces to do that."

"Suppose you were ordered to."

Hastily, Schwarzkopf sketched out a rough outline of how he'd attack, again stressing that his planners had told him it couldn't be done successfully with the force on hand. An attack would be a calamity.

Even so, Powell kept the sketch, and later told Schwarzkopf: "I've shown your plan to the President."

Schwarzkopf was dumbfounded. "Wait a minute," he said, "that's not my recommendation!" He remembered Vietnam all too vividly, and the way commanders had frequently misled their leaders and the American people by their confident assertions.

"Don't worry, Norm," Powell said. "I just used it as an illustration." Fortunately the two had a solid, trusting relationship, one in which Schwarzkopf had a free hand in the field while Powell, the link to the President and the secretary of defense, handled things in Washington.

Before leaving the States for his headquarters in Riyadh, Schwarzkopf had met again with Powell on a Saturday morning in the nearly deserted Pentagon. He had sketched out a plan for a possible air campaign against Iraqi forces, but had again stressed that launching the existing ground forces into Kuwait seemed no less foolish than it had before. He had also talked with General Denny Reimer, the Army operations deputy, and said he needed to be sure some people in Washington were willing to stand up and be counted—to say how dumb it would be to let ourselves be pushed into something we weren't ready for or capable of doing.

Through the rest of the summer, and into the fall of 1990, the Gulf buildup continued. Meanwhile, Saddam Hussein had announced Iraq's "annexation" of Kuwait. A day later, the United Nations passed a resolution, the first of many, denouncing Iraqi aggression and rejecting the idea of annexation.

By this time, big C-5 Galaxy transports and smaller C-141 StarLifters were landing in Saudi Arabia every ten minutes at the Dhahran air base. Ships were also starting to arrive at the port of Dammam. Norman Schwarzkopf was now working eighteen-hour days, making decisions about troop deployments, about the logistic buildup, about commitments from his U.N. allies, about ensuring that Americans exposed to a foreign culture did nothing to offend their Saudi hosts. He was hard on himself, and hard on his staff, to the point that many in the headquarters, while respecting his results, came to resent his rough, impatient manner and his perfectionist demands. In the field, however, his concern for the troops and attention to detail paid off handsomely in efficiency, morale, and personal popularity.

Now that there was a solid defensive capability, while Saddam Hussein continued to resist all calls for withdrawal, Schwarzkopf knew there was a real possibility they'd be called on to attack. He invited planners from the States to help him develop an offensive plan. So far Desert Shield had been concerned with defense. To keep this new offensive contingency separated in everyone's mind, they decided to give it a new name. When the United States and its allies went on the attack, Desert Shield would become Desert Storm.

The Stateside team, from the School of Advanced Military Studies, came up with a plan similar to that Schwarzkopf had sketched out earlier. It assumed a preliminary air campaign followed by a ground offensive, and involved an attack straight into Kuwait to seize the critical highway junction north of the capital. The plan had the allies going right into the teeth of Iraqi defenses and would doubtless involve heavy casualties. The SAMS team predicted (too optimistically, in Schwarzkopf's opinion) some 8,000 wounded and 2,000 dead for the U.S. forces, and that didn't even consider the potential mass casualties if Iraq used its chemical weapons. Schwarzkopf now liked the plan even less than when he'd envisioned it himself.

Although he was constantly busy with a million pressing details, he never forgot the most important thing of all: safeguarding the lives of the men under his command. "Every waking and sleeping moment," he told a group of journalists, "my nightmare is the fact that I will give an order that will cause countless numbers of human beings to lose their lives. I don't want my troops to die. I don't want my troops to be maimed. It's an intensely personal, emotional thing for me. Any decision that you have to make that involves the loss of human life is nothing you do lightly. I agonize over it."

A few people worried about that particular interview, fearing the public might be concerned about a commander who suffered mental anguish. Even Schwarzkopf's friend Colin Powell suggested he might try to avoid so much candor when discussing personal matters. However, the American people were apparently undisturbed, even seeming to appreciate a general who felt as Schwarzkopf did.

The troop buildup continued. However, it was still far from complete when a call came from General Powell asking Centcom to send a team to brief Secretary of Defense Cheney, the Joint Chiefs, and possibly the President on the plans for Desert Storm.

"I gotta tell you," said Schwarzkopf, "as far as a ground offensive is concerned, we've still got nothing."

"Well, your air offensive plan is so good that I want these people to hear it. But you can't just brief the air plan. You have to brief the ground plan too."

Schwarzkopf, describing his feelings at that moment, later wrote: "I got a sinking feeling in my stomach. . . . I suspected Washington was finally about to confront the question of what came next. My old fear returned that we'd be ordered to do something foolish."

Schwarzkopf asked if he could conduct the briefing himself, but was told his return to Washington might start too many rumors. He thought that was a mistake; other commanders, from Eisenhower to Westmoreland, had been called back for meetings, and now he was under orders to send in a plan he "believed could result in a blood-bath."

This was a crucial moment. The easiest course, one that could never be faulted either personally or professionally, would be to outline his capabilities, both strengths and weaknesses. Then, if he were ordered to launch an attack with present force levels, it would be someone else's responsibility, not his. It was obvious that many of the key people back home would welcome a bit of self-confident bravado on Schwarzkopf's part. In fact, if he sounded *too* cautious, there was always a chance he might be replaced by someone who said what people wanted to hear. However, he was damned if he'd repeat the mistakes of Vietnam. He still remembered all those rosy predictions by people who "saw the light at the end of the tunnel."

Unhesitatingly, Schwarzkopf chose a course he knew to be right. When he met with those who were to return and present the briefings, he set down firm guidelines. They were to explain Centcom capabilities, but they were *not* to tell the President anything beyond that. There'd be no speculating or giving of personal opinions, no showboat "can do" attitude. If anyone exceeded those instructions, Schwarzkopf assured them they'd be relieved of their duties and sent home.

The briefing was given exactly as ordered. As the final step, and on specific instructions from Schwarzkopf, three summary slides were shown:

## CINC'S ASSESSMENT

- Offensive ground plan not solid. We do not have the capability to attack on ground at this time.

- Need additional heavy corps to guarantee successful out-come.

- Defensive plan solid—as promised the president during the first week in August, United States Military Forces are now capable of defending Saudi Arabia and executing a wide range of retaliatory attacks against Iraq.

In general, the briefing went well. General Robert B. Johnston, the key briefer, told Schwarzkopf that by the time of the final summary, most of the key points had already been covered and understood. Nevertheless, when the final slide was shown, one of the President's key advisors was heard to say, "My God, he's already got all the force he needs. Why won't he attack?"

When he heard that, Schwarzkopf phoned Colin Powell to ask if that had really been said. "That's right," Powell told him. "Somebody even said, 'Schwarzkopf is just another McClellan.'" The reference was to George McClellan, a Civil War general who was notorious for having "the slows" and for being overly cautious. The hawkish civilian who made the remark evidently had been watching Ken Burns's excellent Civil War series on public television and now considered himself something of a military expert. Powell, however, assured Schwarzkopf of not only his own full support but also that of the President. Schwarzkopf would get what he needed to "do it right."

Despite all the diplomatic maneuvers and the sanctions, Iraq remained defiant. On January 17, 1991, the last U.N. deadline for withdrawal had come and gone. It was time to force Saddam Hussein out of Kuwait. Meanwhile, thanks to the providing of additional forces, Centcom had developed a new and far better tactical plan.

In the headquarters war room, Schwarzkopf read his message to the troops: "Our cause is just. Now you must be the thunder and lightning of Desert Storm. May God be with you, your loved ones at home, and our country."

A tape was played of Lee Greenwood singing "God Bless the U.S.A.," which had become something of an unofficial anthem. Then Schwarzkopf said brusquely: "Okay, gentlemen, let's go to work."

Desert Storm began with a devastating and highly successful air campaign. Five weeks later, over 100,000 sorties had been flown, cutting Iraqi communications and isolating the front lines. Stubbornly, Saddam Hussein rejected one last call for withdrawal and surrender, and Schwarzkopf was authorized to launch the ground phase of Desert Storm. Coalition forces moved across the borders of both Kuwait and Iraq in what proved to be the shortest and most successful campaign in U.S. military history. The new tactical plan involved a dual approach. While one force moved straight ahead against the weakened Iraqis along the Kuwaiti border, the main effort, with a preponderance of power, was made far to the west, in a brilliantly conceived wide envelopment. Less than three days later, Iraq informed the United Nations that it had accepted the Security Council resolutions.

Norman Schwarzkopf had risked a great deal by holding out for more troops and resisting a premature, "straight-ahead" offensive. He had been called "another McClellan"; with different leaders, he might even have ended up like McClellan, relieved of his command. However, he had stuck to his principles, and with the support of those who believed in him, he had achieved a brilliant tactical and strategic success with but a handful of friendly casualties. His decision had not only been proven correct, it had also been the right thing to do.

# Bibliography

CHAPTER 1: Decision at Cowpens

Army War College Historical Section. *The Battle of Kings Mountain and the Battle of Cowpens*. Washington, D.C.: Government Printing Office, 1928.

Callahan, North. *Daniel Morgan, Ranger of the Revolution*. New York: Holt, Rinehart and Winston, 1961.

Dupuy, R. Ernest, and Trevor N. Dupuy. *Military Heritage of America*. New York: McGraw-Hill, 1956.

Higginbotham, Don. *Daniel Morgan, Revolutionary Rifleman*. Chapel Hill, N.C.: University of North Carolina Press, 1961.

Roberts, Kenneth. *The Battle of Cowpens*. New York: Doubleday, 1958.

Ward, Christopher L. *The Delaware Continentals 1776–1783*. Wilmington: The Historical Society of Delaware, 1941.

CHAPTER 2: Decision in Panama

Church, William C. *Ulysses S. Grant*. Garden City, N.Y.: Garden City Publishing Company, 1926.

Grant, Ulysses S. *Personal Memoirs* (2 vols). Vol. 1. New York: Charles L. Webster and Company, 1886.

*Three Centuries Under Three Flags: The Story of Governors Island from 1637*. Headquarters First Army: Governors Island, N.Y., 1951.

Lewis, Lloyd. *Captain Sam Grant*. Boston: Little, Brown and Company, 1950.

Mack, Gerstle. *The Land Divided: A History of the Panama Canal and Other Isthmian Canal Projects*. New York: Knopf, 1944.

Maihafer, Harry J. "Grant in Panama," *America's Civil War*, vol. 1, no. 2, July 1988.

———. "Lieutenant Sam and the Sisters," *Liguorian*, vol. 76, no. 9, September 1988.

Simon, John Y., ed. *The Papers of Ulysses S. Grant*. Vol. 1: 1837–1861. Carbondale, Ill.: Southern Illinois University Press, 1967.

Tripler, Charles. *Report of the Regimental Surgeon, Fourth Infantry, U.S.A.* San Francisco, 1852.

Woodward, William E. *Meet General Grant*. New York: The Literary Guild of America, 1928.

## CHAPTER 3: Decision at Arlington

Bowen, Catherine Drinker. *Miracle at Philadelphia: The Story of the Constitutional Convention*. Boston: Little, Brown and Company, 1966.

Dowdey, Clifford. *Lee*. New York: Bonanza Books, 1965.

Fleming, Thomas J. *West Point: The Men and Times of the United States Military Academy*. New York: William Morrow and Company, 1969.

Freeman, Douglas Southall. *Robert E. Lee* (4 vols.). New York: Scribners, 1934–1935.

Smith, Gene. *Lee and Grant*. New York: McGraw-Hill, 1984.

## CHAPTER 4: Decision on the Mississippi

*Chicago Tribune*, February 8 and 14, 1862.

Eads, James B. "Recollections of Foote and the Gun Boats." In *Battles and Leaders of the Civil War*. Buel, Clarence C. and Robert U. Johnson, ed: (4 vols.) vol. 1: *From Sumter to Shiloh*. New York: Castle Books, 1956.

Foote, Shelby. *The Civil War: A Narrative*. (3 vols.) vol. 1: *From Sumter to Perrryville*. New York: Random House, 1958.

Maihafer, Harry J. "The Partnership—Grant and Foote." *U.S. Naval Institute Proceedings*, vol. 93, no. 5, May 1967.

———. "U.S. Grant and the Northern Press." Unpublished master's thesis, University of Missouri, 1966.

McFeely, William S. *Grant: A Biography*. New York: W. W. Norton, 1981.

Nevins, Allan. *The War for the Union*. Vol. 1: *The Improvised War, 1861–1862*. New York: Scribners, 1959.

*New York Herald*, January 24, 1862.

Walke, Rear Admiral Henry. "The Gunboats at Belmont and Fort Henry" and "The Western Flotilla at Fort Donelson, Island Number Ten, Fort Pillow, and Memphis." In *Battles and Leaders of the Civil War*. Buel, Clarence C. and Robert U. Johnson, ed.: (4 vols.) vol. 1: *From Sumter to Shiloh*. New York: Castle Books, 1956.


## CHAPTER 5: Decision at Chancellorsville

Douglas, Henry Kyd. *I Rode with Stonewall*. Chapel Hill, N.C.: University of North Carolina Press, 1940.

Farwell, Byron. *Stonewall: A Biography of General Thomas J. Jackson*. New York: W. W. Norton, 1992.

Foote, Shelby. *The Civil War: A Narrative*. (3 vols.) vol. 2: *Fredericksburg to Meridian*. New York: Random House, 1963.

Vandiver, Frank E. *Mighty Stonewall*. College Station, Texas: Texas A&M University Press, 1957.


## CHAPTER 6: Decision at Round Top

Catton, Bruce. *Glory Road*. New York: Doubleday, 1963.

Crary, Catherine S. *Dear Belle: Letters from a Cadet and Officer to His Sweetheart 1858–1865*. Middletown, Conn.: Wesleyan University Press, 1965.

Dyer, Frederick H. *A Compendium of the War of the Rebellion* (3 vols.). New York and London: Thos. Yoseloff, 1909.

Farley, Col. Joseph P. *West Point in the Early Sixties*. Troy, N.Y.: Pafraets Book Company, 1902.

Freeman, Douglas S. *Lee's Lieutenants* (3 vols.). New York: Scribners, 1942.

Haydon, Frederick S. *Aeronautics in the Union and Confederate Armies*. London: Oxford University Press, 1941.

Johnson, Rossiter. *The Fight for the Republic*. New York and London: The Knickerbocker Press, 1917.

Montgomery, James S. *The Shaping of a Battle: Gettysburg*. Philadelphia and New York: Chilton Company, 1959.

New York Battle Monuments Commission. *Final Report of the Battle of Gettysburg*. Albany, N.Y.: J.B. Lyon Company, 1900.

*Register of Graduates and Former Cadets of the United States Military Academy*. West Point: USMA Association of Graduates, 1990.

Schaff, Morris. *The Spirit of Old West Point*. Boston and New York, 1897.

Steele, Matthew F. *American Campaigns*. Harrisburg: The Telegraph Press, 1947.

Tucker, Glenn. *High Tide at Gettysburg*. New York: Bobbs-Merrill, 1958.

## CHAPTER 7: Decision at Abbeville

Goldhurst, Richard. *Pipe Clay and Drill*. New York: Crowell, 1977.

Pershing, John J. *Final Report of Gen. John J . Pershing, A.E.F.* Washington, D.C.: Government Printing Office, 1920.

Smythe, Donald. *Guerrilla Warrior: The Early Life of John J. Pershing*. New York: Scribners, 1973.

———. *Pershing: General of the Armies*. Bloomington: Indiana University Press, 1986.

Vandiver, Frank E. *Illustrious Americans: John J. Pershing*. Morristown, N.J.: Silver Burdett, 1967.

Wukovits, John F. "Best Case Scenario Exceeded." *Military History*, vol. 9, no. 5, December 1992.

## CHAPTER 8: Decision in Texas

Davis, Burke. *The Billy Mitchell Affair*. New York: Random House, 1967.

Gauvreau, Emile, and Lester Cohen. *Billy Mitchell: Founder of Our Air Force and Prophet Without Honor*. New York: Dutton, 1942.

Hurley, Alfred F. *Billy Mitchell, Crusader for Air Power*. New York: Franklin Watts, 1964.

## CHAPTER 9: Decision in Sicily

Blair, Clay. *Ridgway's Paratroopers: The American Airborne in World War II*. New York: Doubleday, 1985.

Eisenhower, Dwight D. *Crusade in Europe*. New York: Doubleday, 1948.

Ridgway, Matthew B. *Soldier: The Memoirs of Matthew B. Ridgway*. New York: Harper and Brothers, 1956.

Taylor, John M. *General Maxwell Taylor*. New York: Doubleday, 1989.

## CHAPTER 10: Decision at Atsugi

Hunt, Frazier. *The Untold Story of Douglas MacArthur*. New York: Signet Books, 1954.

MacArthur, Douglas. *Reminiscences*. New York: McGraw-Hill, 1964.

Manchester, William. *American Caesar: Douglas MacArthur*. Boston: Little, Brown and Company, 1978.

Ramsey, Edwin P., and Stephen J. Rivele. *Lieutenant Ramsey's War*. New York: Knightsbridge Publishing Company, 1990.

Sulzberger, C. L. *The American Heritage Picture History of World War II*. New York: Crown, 1966.

## CHAPTER 11: Decision in Berlin

Clay, General Lucius D. *Decison in Germany*. New York: Doubleday, 1950.

Smith, Jean Edward. *Lucius D. Clay: An American Life*. New York: Holt, 1990.

Tusa, Ann, and John Tusa. *The Berlin Airlift*. New York: Athenaeum, 1988.

## CHAPTER 12: Decision in Korea

Appleman, Roy E. *South to the Naktong, North to the Yalu: The U.S. Army in the Korean War*. Washington, D.C.: Office of the Chief of Military History, Department of the Army, 1961.

Blair, Clay. *The Forgotten War: America in Korea, 1950–53*. New York: Times Books, 1987.

Detzer, David. *Thunder of the Captains: The Short Summer in 1950*. New York: Crowell, 1977.

Toland, John. *In Mortal Combat: Korea 1950–1953*. New York: William Morrow, 1991.

Worden, William L. *General Dean's Story*. New York: Viking Press, 1954.

## CHAPTER 13: Decision in the Pentagon

Ambrose, Stephen E. *Duty, Honor, Country: A History of West Point*. Baltimore: The Johns Hopkins University Press, 1966.

Eisenhower, Dwight D. *Crusade in Europe*. New York: Doubleday, 1948.

Fleming, Thomas J. *West Point: The Men and Times of the United States Military Academy*. New York: William Morrow, 1969.

Kinnard, Douglas. *The Certain Trumpet: Maxwell Taylor and the American Experience in Vietnam*. McLean, Va.: Brassey's, 1991.

Mosley, Leonard. *Dulles*. New York: Dial Press, 1978.

Ridgway, Matthew B. *Soldier: The Memoirs of Matthew B. Ridgway*. New York: Harper and Brothers, 1956.

Taylor, John M. *General Maxwell Taylor: The Sword and the Pen*. New York: Doubleday, 1989.

Taylor, Maxwell D. *Swords and Ploughshares*. New York: W. W. Norton, 1972.

———. *The Uncertain Trumpet*. New York: Harper & Brothers, 1959.

## CHAPTER 14: Decision at the NSC

Haig, Alexander, Jr., with Charles McCarry. *Inner Circles: How America Changed the World*. New York: Warner Books, 1992.

Isaacson, Walter. *Kissinger: A Biography*. New York: Simon and Schuster, 1992.

Kalb, Marvin, and Bernard Kalb. *Kissinger*. Boston: Little, Brown and Company, 1974.

Kissinger, Henry. *White House Years*. Boston: Little, Brown and Company, 1979.

Rusk, Dean. *As I Saw It*. New York: W. W. Norton, 1990.

Valeriani, Richard. *Travels with Henry*. Boston: Houghton Mifflin, 1979.

## CHAPTER 15: Decision in the Gulf

Atkinson, Rick. *Crusade: The Untold Story of the Persian Gulf War*. Boston and New York: Houghton Mifflin, 1993.

Blair, Arthur H. *At War in the Gulf: A Chronology*. College Station, Texas: Texas A&M University Press, 1992.

Krepinevich, Andrew F., Jr. *The Army and Vietnam*. Baltimore: The Johns Hopkins University Press, 1986.

Palmer, General Bruce, Jr. *The 25-Year War*. Lexington, Ky.: The University Press of Kentucky, 1984.

*Register of Graduates and Former Cadets of the United States Military Academy*. West Point, USMA Association of Graduates, 1991.

Schwarzkopf, General H. Norman. *It Doesn't Take a Hero*. New York: Bantam Doubleday Dell, 1992.

# Index

# About the Author

COLONEL HARRY J. MAIHAFER is a 1949 graduate of the U.S. Military Academy and holds a master's degree in journalism from the University of Missouri. A former infantry officer, he is the author of *From the Hudson to the Yalu: West Point '49 in the Korean War*. His articles have appeared in *The Wall Street Journal, Military History, U.S. Naval Institute Proceedings, Military Review,* and other publications. He and his wife live in Nashville, Tennessee.